D0898475

Recovering Our Ancestors' Gardens

*Indigenous Recipes
and Guide to
Diet and Fitness*

REVISED EDITION

Devon A. Mihesuah

University of Nebraska Press
LINCOLN

Library of Congress Cataloging-in-Publication Data
Names: Mihesuah, Devon A., 1957– author.
Title: Recovering our ancestors' gardens: indigenous
recipes and guide to diet and fitness / Devon A.
Mihesuah.
Other titles: Indigenous recipes and guide to diet and
fitness
Description: Revised edition. | Lincoln: University
of Nebraska Press, [2020] | Series: At table | Includes
bibliographical references and index.
Identifiers: LCCN 2020005369
ISBN 9780803245259 (paperback)
ISBN 9781496223876 (epub)
ISBN 9781496223883 (mobi)
ISBN 9781496223890 (pdf)
Subjects: LCSH: Indian cooking. | Indians of North
America—Food. | LCGFT: Cookbooks.
Classification: LCC TX715 .M6364 2020 |
DDC 641.59/297—dc23
LC record available at
https://lccn.loc.gov/2020005369

Set in New Baskerville ITC by Mikala R. Kolander.

To my beautiful daughter
Ariana Taryn,
cook, gardener, athlete, and
enchantress extraordinaire

Contents

List of Illustrations   xi

List of Tables   xii

Preface to the Revised Edition   xiii

Acknowledgments   xvii

Introduction   1

1. Traditional Diets and Activities   11

    Case Study 1: *The Five Tribes*   34

2. The State of Indigenous Health   42

    Case Study 2: *Changing Diets*
    and Health in Indian Territory   53

3. Challenges to Recovering Health   72

    Case Study 3: *Frybread*   90

4. What Are You Ingesting?   113

5. Calories, Exercise, and Recovering Fitness   125

6. Changing What We Eat   138

7. Importance of Backyard Gardens   155

    Curriculum Guide   169

    Recipes   213

    APPETIZERS   216

      Guacamole Dip   216

      Lima Bean Hummus   217

      Summer Salsa   218

SALADS, SOUPS, AND STEWS 221

Dandelion Salad 221

Poke Salat 221

Vegetable, Turkey, and Game Stocks 222

Butternut Squash Soup 224

Dakota *Waskuya* (Dakota Dried
Sweet Corn Soup) 226

Gazpacho 227

Elk Stew 228

Choctaw Stew 229

Osage Strip Meat Soup (*Ta-ni'*) 230

Posole 230

MAIN DISHES 232

Meat and Vegetable Kabobs 232

Venison Steaks 233

Good for Your Heart Fried Moose Meat 234

Venison Burgers 235

Salmon 236

Venison Meatloaf 237

Osage Pounded Meat (*Ta'-pshe*) 237

Corn Crust Pizza 238

Enchiladas 239

VEGETABLES AND SIDE DISHES 240

Pumpkins 240

Tepary Bean–Prickly Pear Casserole 242

Comanche *Ata-Kwasa* 243

Baked New Potatoes 244

Vegetable Sauté 245

Sweet Potatoes	246
Mamaw Helton's Creamed Corn	246
Osage *Yonkopin* (*Tse'-wa-the*), Water Chinkapin Roots and Seeds	248
Chahta Tanfula	248
Pashofa	250
Pinto Beans	251
Avocados	252
Prickly Pear Paddles	254
Grilled Corn on the Cob	255
Luiseño *Weewish*	256
Wild Onions	259
Zucchini Canoes	259
Stuffed Bell Peppers	260
Poblano Peppers Stuffed with Wild Rice, Cranberries, or Vegetables	262
Mashed Potatoes with Corn Gravy	263
Grits	264
Spaghetti Squash	266
BREADS	267
Banaha	267
Osage Persimmon Cakes (*Wah-zha'-zhe wa-dsiu'-e çta-in'-ge*)	268
Corn, Bean, and Turkey Bread	269
Blue Corn Pancakes	269
DRINKS AND DESSERTS	271
Abuske	271
Pawpaw Sorbet	272
Grape Dumplings	274

No Wheat, Butter, Eggs, or Sugar Cookies 275

Mamaw Helton's Stewed Fruit 277

Wojapi 278

Cranberry Pie with Cornmeal Crust 279

PRESERVING FOOD 281

Roasted Pumpkin Seeds 281

Pemmican 282

Appendix A: Precontact Foods of the
Western Hemisphere 287

Appendix B: Diet Chart for One Week 293

Notes 301

Index 341

Illustrations

Following page 154

1. Devon Abbott and Thomas Abbott in front of his Muscogee garden, 1960
2. Hopi woman grinding corn, 1919
3. A Hopi runner, 1920
4. Hopi men plant a cornfield by using planting sticks, 1970
5. Creek man pounding corn to make sofky, 1890–1916

6. Pecans, walnuts, pumpkin seeds, blueberries, and dried cranberries   215
7. Lima bean hummus   217
8. Summer salsa and baked tortilla chips   219
9. Dandelion salad   220
10. Butternut squash soup   225
11. Elk stew   228
12. Posole   231
13. Venison steaks   233
14. Enchiladas   239
15. Roasted and stuffed pumpkins   241
16. Vegetable sauté and quinoa   245
17. Pinto beans   251
18. Avocado halves   253
19. Prickly pear paddles   254
20. Stuffed bell peppers   261
21. Mashed potatoes with corn gravy   264

22. Choctaw *banaha*   267

23. Blue corn pancakes   270

24. Pawpaw half   273

25. Pawpaw sorbet   273

26. Grape dumplings   274

27. Cookies   276

28. Cranberry pie with corn meal crust   280

29. Roasted pumpkin seeds   281

Tables

1. Sample diet for one day   114

Preface to the Revised Edition

In 2003 my editorial "Decolonizing Our Diets by Recovering Our Ancestors' Gardens" was published in the *American Indian Quarterly*. After reading that, a colleague embarked on a personal diet makeover and lost 125 pounds. That response was gratifying enough for me to continue with the themes in that editorial and to expand it into the book *Recovering Our Ancestors' Gardens*. It seems like a lifetime ago.

Around that time Loretta Oden's PBS series *Seasoned with Spirit: A Native Chef's Journey* was released, and Lois Ellen Frank's *Foods of the Southwest Indian Nations* won the James Beard Award. A few years later what I refer to as the "Indigenous foodie" movement (a term that elicits snickers among my foodie friends), today more commonly known as the "Indigenous food sovereignty" (IFS) movement, took off like a rocket. Until 2005 some 230 articles had appeared about "Native American food." By 2019 that number increased to 503. There were, however, at least twelve thousand publications about "American Indian diabetes" up to 2005, and that tally almost doubled in the next fifteen years. Many variables are of course involved in statistics like these, including different terminology, such as "Native American," "Indigenous," sustainability, specific diseases, and so on. But the point is that until recently, much more has been written about the health problems Natives face than about solutions to those maladies. Also of note is that although "food sovereignty" is a concept that has been around for decades, that is not the same as "Indigenous food sovereignty." Another look at Google scholar shows that only three publications used the latter term until 2005, but from 2005 to today, that has increased to more than five hundred.

To be sure, many of us have always eaten our traditional foods, and we have cultivated gardens, foraged, hunted, fished, and attempted to educate others. But it has only been in the past decade that Indigenous food initiatives, usually organized from the grassroots level by interested individuals, have been created in significant numbers. In the last few years I have met many people who have just discovered the IFS movement. These enthusiastic Natives—young and old—are aware of some of their food traditions, but initially most had not given much thought to the connections between poor health of Natives, the loss of precontact ways of eating, and the diminishment of the natural world. Now they know. They talk excitedly about becoming a farmer, a writer, a teacher and a tribal politician. They want to protest environmental destruction, learn to save seeds, start a farm, forage wild plants, and make traditional tools, baskets, and fishing gear. They plan to speak about food and health issues, attend food summits, and write books and policies. And as if all that were not enough, they also want to attend culinary school, open an Indigenous-themed restaurant, and teach Natives around the country how to cook their precontact foods.

Indeed, tribal food summits are now scheduled throughout the year. Indigenous food websites and Facebook pages offer recipes and links to resources. National food alliances provide grants and fellowships. Courses and programs are offered from K–12 levels through universities. Community, tribal, and school gardens have proliferated. Dozens of young Indigenous men and women have followed the leads of the first Indigenous chefs—Loretta Barrett Owen, Lois Ellen Frank, Walter Whitewater, Nephi Craig (founder of the Native American Culinary Association), and Eddie Bitsui. They organize food pop-ups and give culinary lessons. Seed saver initiatives collect and distribute heirloom seeds. Perhaps one reason for this explosion of activity is that many tribespeople may have been suspicious of outsiders telling them what to eat and how to exercise. But now, much of the information comes from other Natives. We are more inclined to listen to them talk about healthy living and organizing food initiatives, especially if they actually live that lifestyle and we can see them as activists willing to put in the energy to make changes. *Recovering Our Ancestors' Gardens* focused on the personal choices we make about our lifestyles—provided that we have choices, that is. What was not addressed in the 2005 edition were the myriad other factors that contribute to food-related health problems.

The themes and goals of this revised and expanded volume remain the same as in the first version: to inspire, suggest ideas, and reinforce the reality that personal accountability plays a pivotal role in recovering and maintaining good health. Also included now are discussions about the other crucial elements that must fall in line so that Indigenous people have access to nutritious foods, clean water and air, and healthy environments.

When I asked readers what they wanted to see in a revision, most said that they want specifics about their particular tribe(s). There are 573 federally recognized tribes in the United States and hundreds of tribes in Canada; obviously I could not include discussion about all of them, even if I possessed the expertise. I teach a course on "Foodways of Latin America," and that also is too vast a topic to include here (although I do offer a section on Latin America in the Curriculum Guide). I focus much of my research and writing on eastern Indian Territory (now Oklahoma) because that is where my family settled after removal from the Southeast in the 1830s. I use those writings as case studies so that readers can use them as research models for finding foodways information about their own tribes.

New here are:

Corrections, updated statistics, and new sources.
Detailed case studies and appendixes to supplement the chapter themes.
An expanded recipe section.

A curriculum/resource guide for teachers, librarians, and
those wanting to know more about Indigenous foodways,
including objectives, resources, study questions for each
chapter, assignments, and activities.

I hope the IFS movement will continue to grow. The reality, however, is that most of us have limited time, money, and
energy to participate in many initiatives, especially if they are
held during the work week and across the country. Money is also
an issue for many desiring to purchase expensive game meats,
fresh organic produce, and chef's dishes. We need to prioritize
what we can realistically afford and undertake. However, one of
the foundational elements of the IFS movement is what we do
in our own homes and communities. Even if we are strapped
for funds and have little free time, we can accomplish much.

We need to continue to learn about healthy eating. We can
educate others if we have the expertise and can network with
others in our tribes who also are interested in tribal food sustainability and sovereignty. Activism, especially when one deals
with politics, can be exhausting, but we must persevere and
challenge the status quo and our tribal councils. It is not easy to
advocate consistently for political, social, and economic changes
that will allow everyone access to nutritious, sustainable, and,
whenever possible, culturally related foods. But as I have written previously, no one else will do it for us.

Acknowledgments

Thanks to Matthew Bokovoy, Wallace Coffey, Jeff Corntassel, Matt DeSpain, Mary Jo Tippeconnic Fox, Marcia Haag, Elizabeth Hoover, Andrea Hunter, Daniel Heath Justice, Jill Koelling, Susan Miller, Gary Nabhan, Pamela Jean Owens, Joely Proudfit, Richard Quartaroli, Robert Redsteer, Martin Reinhardt, Richard Stoekel, Barbara Valvo, Jess Vogelsang, Taryn Abbott Wilson, and Brad Young.

Portions of case studies 1 and 2 appeared in Devon Mihesuah, "Sustenance and Health among the Five Tribes in Indian Territory, Post-Removal to Statehood," *Ethnohistory* 62, no. 2 (April 2015): 263–84. Copyright 2015 by the American Society for Ethnohistory. All rights reserved. Reprinted by permission of the copyright holder and the present publisher, Duke University Press. www.dukeupress.edu.

Portions of case study 2 appeared in Devon Mihesuah, "Historical Research and Diabetes in Indian Territory: Revisiting Kelly M. West's Theory of 1940," *American Indian Culture and Research Journal* 40, no. 4 (2016): 1–21. Copyright 2016 by the Regents of the University of California. Reprinted by permission of the American Indian Studies Center, UCLA.

Portions of case study 3 appeared in Devon Mihesuah, "Indigenous Health Initiatives, Frybread, and the Marketing of Non-Traditional 'Traditional' American Indian Foods," *Native American and Indigenous Studies* 3, no. 2 (Fall 2016): 45–69. Reprinted by permission of the University of Minnesota Press.

Portions of chapters 3 and 4 appeared in Devon Mihesuah, "Searching for *Haknip Achukma* (Good Health): Challenges to Food Sovereignty Initiatives in Oklahoma," in special issue, *American Indian Culture and Research Journal* 41, no. 3 (2017): 9–30. Copyright 2017 by the Regents of the University of California. Reprinted by permission of the American Indian Studies Center, UCLA.

Recovering Our Ancestors' Gardens

Introduction

Poor health resulting from lifestyle choice is a serious problem for many Americans, including Indigenous peoples. Anyone who reads their tribal newspaper, women's and men's magazines (in every doctor's waiting room), any of the countless online fitness blogs, or who listens to the radio and watches television is exposed to information about the repercussions of a bad diet. Additionally, the dire consequences of global warming, widespread use of pesticides, unchecked deforestation, availability of cheap and unhealthy foods, and acceptance of obesity as the norm also contribute to our health problems.

In attempts to combat our health and environmental problems, many Indigenous activists are diligently working on a variety of initiatives. Some serve on their tribal councils or are on boards of national food alliances and seed saver networks. Others research and write about traditional foodways, have started farms, or teach people to prepare traditional dishes. However, despite the myriad food summits, school and tribal programs and gardens, and beautiful meals created by Indigenous chefs, the food and environmentally related health maladies Natives suffer have not improved. There have, of course, been some success stories, but our health statistics and the environmental crises are worsening. Some reasons might be that food summits can be costly, and not everyone can take time from work to attend. Nor does everyone have the land or resources to cultivate gardens. Many have inadequate health care and cannot afford ingredients needed to replicate dishes from cookbooks or on Indigenous food blogs and Facebook pages. Food deserts pervade tribal lands. Some tribal governments are more concerned about food security (which does not always entail nutritious foods) as opposed to creating systems that allow their nations to produce and control their own healthy food supply. While some Indigenous peoples have continued to farm, hunt, fish, and forage for food as their ancestors did, even more have not been educated about nutrition or their traditional foodways. Climate change has diminished food resources, and pollutants contaminate air and water.

Even if we manage to consume precontact foods every day, those nutritious foods do not help much if we also drink milkshakes and eat double cheeseburgers, fries, frybread, and sugary desserts. Fatty, greasy, salty and sugary foods pervade the marketplace, schools, and homes. Those who do have access to restaurants find that commercial enterprises serve portions of processed foods that are more than an adult should eat at one sitting. Deceptive and manipulative food industry commercials mislead consumers into thinking that processed foods are nutritious. As a result we buy unhealthy products and are now facing the consequences. Television and video games have replaced sports and other outdoor activities. Indeed, political, economic, social, religious, and environmental factors all pose great challenges to the long-term success of many Indigenous food sovereignty initiatives and to personal goals.

All Americans face the potential for developing unhealthy lifestyle habits and struggle with the challenges of a diminished natural world, unhealthy food, or little food. It is particularly distressing to see that Natives across the Americas often have few choices when it comes to food and have lost touch with their healthy, traditional methods of cultivating, preparing, and preserving foods, besides losing the consistent activity that kept them physically and mentally fit.

Precontact tribes ate no processed foods and appeared to be physically fit, but they did have health issues. Some developed malnutrition from mono-diets, crop failures, and game animal scarcity, and some may have had type 1 diabetes. They also suffered broken bones, parasites, insect and animal bites, contact dermatitis, cracked teeth, and other injuries as well food poisoning. Even if we have access to our precontact foods today, often those nutritious foods are contaminated with pesticides, farm animal wastes, and genetically modified organisms. Still, prior to the introduction of sugar and wheat flour, Indigenous peoples appeared to have suffered fewer food-related maladies than they do today—maladies such as type 2 diabetes, obesity, high blood pressure, and celiac disease.

How can we become healthy? This book offers suggestions on how to get started. First, we must begin with how we used to live and trace developments through time to understand how we arrived at our present situations.

Chapter 1, "Traditional Diets and Activities," is an overview of the way we were: precontact diets and activities, including what some tribes ate, how they prepared their food, and how their lives revolved around hunting, gathering, cultivating, and preserving. Case study 1, "The Five Tribes," focuses on Cherokees, Choctaws, Chickasaws, Muscogees (Creeks), and Seminoles and their food resources where they lived in the Southeast prior to their forced removal to Indian Territory in the 1830s. Where does one obtain this information? I utilized eighteenth- and nineteenth-century diaries, journals, sketchbooks, and reports of travelers, Indian agents, ethnographers, and military personnel who made observations of flora, fauna, and terrain. The Oklahoma Natural Heritage Inventory links plants and animals to specific historical habitats. Tribal census records itemize tribal citizens' lands and resources, and surveys at the Oklahoma State Archives detail the tribal nations' topography, vegetation, bodies of water, and soil types. The Indian and Pioneer Papers are a collection of some eighty thousand interviews conducted in the 1930s and include testimonies from elderly Indians whose families were removed from the Southeast one hundred years earlier. The methods I used to compile this case study can be used by those who want to research their tribal foodways.

Chapter 2, "The State of Indigenous Health," is a discussion of the problems we face because of an abundance of fat, salt, grease, sugar (and too much of everything else bad for us). While initial contact with the colonizers benefited many Natives, notably through the addition to their diet of cattle, sheep, goats, chickens, peaches, and other flora and fauna, it was not long before we began to overeat and to prepare food with too much lard, salt, and sugar. Many of our resources disappeared, and more recently our air, water, and soils have become polluted—as have plants and animals. This chapter explores evidence that shows us our ancestors were physically strong, and while some did suffer from diseases, these diseases were not self-induced; that is, our forebears did not die from gluttony, arteriosclerosis, or other problems associated with over-indulgence. This chapter also discusses food-related maladies many Natives suffer as a result from adopting introduced foods: celiac disease from consuming gluten and the inability to digest lactose in dairy products. While tribes have used tobacco for ceremonial purposes, the use of commercial cigarettes has resulted in lung cancer. The chapter then traces what happened through the centuries to make Natives so sick and explores the main factors—both realities and excuses—that keep Natives from regaining their health.

Case study 2, "Changing Diets and Health in Indian Territory," explores how tribes in Indian Territory had access to a vast array of fruits, vegetables, and game meats, and until the Civil War their health problems appeared to be maladies such as wounds, parasites, contagious diseases, and illnesses associated with unsanitary conditions. Around the mid-1860s Natives' diets began changing in two ways: either they included an overabundance of wheat flour, sugar, salt, and lard that resulted in diet-related ailments such as diabetes, obesity, and tooth decay; or the amount of food was inadequate, and Natives suffered from malnutrition. This study refutes the theory of the late Kelly M. West (also known as the "father of diabetes epidemiology") that diabetes was extremely rare among Oklahoma Indians prior to 1940. To the contrary, my research of historical and ethnobotanical data clearly reveals that Indians in Indian Territory (made the state of Oklahoma in 1907) began suffering from food-related illnesses, including diabetes or pre-diabetes, before the Civil War. West's theory of 1940 is important because its flaws reinforce the importance of utilizing ethnohistorical data in medical studies dealing with Indigenous health as well as the need to understand the connection between the loss of traditional foodways and the modern health crisis.

Chapter 3, "Challenges to Recovering Health," outlines the challenges of addressing social, political, religious, economic, and environmental concerns. Achieving good health and sustainable resources is not just about planting gardens. We are faced with combating uneven food quality, environmental destruction, climate change, intra-tribal factionalism, racism, poor leadership, and the glaring dichotomy of affluence and extreme poverty. Most of the examples used are from Oklahoma, but readers may recognize these obstacles in their own communities. This chapter also considers the term "Indigenous food sovereignty" and whether it is possible to achieve this, or if it even matters if we do not, as long as we continue to try.

Case study 3, "Frybread," discusses how the disconnection some Natives have from their tribal foodways complicates the initiatives of the Indigenous food sovereignty movement. Frybread is especially controversial. Some people view frybread as a symbol of "Indianness," while others deem fried flour one of the negative results of colonialism. The frybread mythology tells us that Navajos survived the 1860s incarceration at the Bosque Redondo reservation because they created frybread from government-supplied flour and lard. Although there are no documents or oral testimonies to substantiate that claim, the frybread legend persists. This case study also considers how labeling frybread as "traditional" provides frybread advocates a justification for eating it (some consume it almost every day) and simultaneously allows them to reaffirm their Indigenous identity.

Chapter 4, "What Are You Ingesting?" serves as a wakeup call for those who have not paid attention to their diets. Using a sample diet chart as an example, readers can track their own diets for one week in order to assess how many nutrients they consume, see what they tend to overuse, and understand what they are lacking. Not all Indigenous people fall prey to the seductive ads of McDonald's playgrounds that lure in children—and therefore their parents. Many opt for the salads, parfaits, small hamburgers, and iced coffee without sugar and whipped cream. We exercise daily or as close to that as we can manage. If we falter in our quest to eat healthy, unprocessed foods, it is in small amounts and not very often. Although a Cherokee friend joked about this project, "As an Indian I do my duty and eat as much chocolate as I can," this is not exactly the kind of helpful advice we should emulate.

In chapter 5, "Calories, Exercise, and Recovering Fitness," is a calculator for figuring out how many calories are needed to function in comparison to how many one is taking in. The food we eat must be nutritious, not just "low calorie." And those who burn significant energy through physical labor and athletics must also consume nutritious foods. This chapter offers ideas for changing a sedentary lifestyle, ranging from a walking program to lifting weights to hiking and exploring the natural world around us.

Chapter 6, "Changing What We Eat," offers suggestions for adjusting our diets so that we consume nutritious foods only in the amounts we need. All the suggestions revolve around this ideology: unprocessed, fresh and organic foods are the foundation for a healthy body. It may not be possible to give up all the tasty, processed foods that surround us, but if we primarily eat foods rich in vitamins, minerals, and fiber, then a few processed treats now and then will not do as much damage as if we consume fatty, sweet, and salty foods and drinks every day.

Chapter 7, "Importance of Backyard Gardens," discusses how we can supplement our diets with produce we harvest ourselves.

Historically, tribes across Native North America had sophisticated agricultural systems that required cooperation from everyone in the tribe. Today, however, not every tribe is situated on a reservation, and in many cases the citizens are scattered and community farms and gardens are not feasible. This chapter begins with a short history of backyard gardens among southeastern tribes. Natives did indeed survive because of community efforts, but also in large part based on garden produce families cultivated and what they hunted and gathered in the nearby forests. Some tribespeople started growing corn, wheat, and other crops on a large scale for profit by the 1840s, but most families had small gardens—what nineteenth-century residents of Indian Territory referred to as "patches" or "roasting ear patches." The chapter offers the rationales for backyard gardens as well as instructions for planting a large garden either in our yard or as a neighborhood project. For those who have limited or poor land to garden, there also are suggestions for container gardens.

The curriculum guide is a resource of suggested lessons, readings, questions, and activities about Native foodways, food-related health problems, and Indigenous food sovereignty. All these topics are complex and multifaceted, and many of the issues can be contentious. That is not necessarily a bad thing; terminology such as "traditional," the dish frybread, and reasons for socio-economic differences within tribes can be important points of departure for discussion. There are a myriad books, articles, blogs, websites, and textualized testimonies about Indigenous histories and cultures as they pertain to foodways. Many are listed in this guide, but it is not possible to list them all. I assume readers have access to libraries and the internet.

The "Recipes" section is a compilation of dishes from my family and some colleagues, and I have tried to make these as simple as possible. As in the original book, I include Old World ingredients, and those are designated with an asterisk. Cooks can add and alter these recipes to their liking, of course. Beware, however, of recipes on the web for "traditional" Native foods, because there are numerous sites with hundreds of recipes featuring ingredients that are not indigenous to this hemisphere. An example is "traditional grape dumplings," which invariably include ingredients from the Old World (flour, sugar, shortening) and Concord grapes (a developed grape, not the possum grapes that were used traditionally).

All tribes face a similar dilemma: once our people were strong and physically healthy. Now we are facing a health crisis of epidemic proportions. The ailments discussed here should be incentive enough to spur us into action. Whatever way you choose to become involved, keep these things in mind:

Fresh, unprocessed foods are healthier than fried, processed ones.

Foods that are home grown can help develop pride and healthy bodies.

Natives gathered, hunted, and cultivated foods that kept them healthy. Foods eaten at fast food joints are the opposite.

Food we prepare in our kitchens gives us control over what we and our families eat. When we buy food at fast food restaurants, others are given control over what we consume.

Preparing food in our kitchens gives us pleasure and peace of mind. It can be relaxing and gives us time to think.

Cultivating and preparing our foods slows us down and puts us in a calm state. We can escape from the stress of our jobs and fast-paced life. Pulling weeds, fertilizing, picking fruit and vegetables, peeling potatoes, shucking and grinding corn, and making meals are among the best ways to relax and think. And when you're in the kitchen preparing meals, people tend not to bother you.

A little bit of exercise every day adds up in the long run.

No one can force us to smoke or to be sedentary.

Educate yourself about nutrition and fitness and you can change your life.

As Cherokee scholar Daniel Heath Justice commented to me: "I was amazed to discover how much better I felt when I started increasing the Indigenous content of my diet. It's been a slow process, but thoughtfully substituting turkey for beef, cornmeal for white flour, and adding more beans, squash, fresh corn, fruits, and nuts to my diet while cutting back on beef, chicken, wheat, sugar, and milk products has made me not only more energetic, it's made me more mindful about my body and its needs. It's a gradual process—moderation in all things—but I've been surprised at how well it's worked."

I am not a nutritionist, and neither are the recipe contributors. But consider that the majority of physicians we see about our various ailments and concerns also have no training in nutrition. Physicians attempt to fix physical problems, but usually they do not instruct patients on how to prevent them. If some Natives can step forward with healthy, personalized suggestions that have worked for them, then perhaps others can benefit. After decades of reading about nutrition and exercise I have a fairly good grasp of what my body needs to stay healthy. At sixty-two years of age and 132 pounds at five feet ten inches tall, plus no physical problems (except job-related stress headaches and old sports injuries) because of a lifetime of eating right and exercising, I and others who live the same lifestyle I do may be onto something good. My diet has always consisted of fruits, vegetables, lean meats, and whole grains. This strong nutritional foundation allows me to indulge in occasional non-nutritious additions (wintergreen Lifesavers, gum, tortilla chips, and wine at dinner are my "vices"). I have been interested in nutrition most of my life, beginning in junior high when I began to play competitive sports. I realized that paying closer attention to what I ate and drank would enhance my abilities in the sports I played. Today I continue to make it a point to know how many nutrients I and my family consume.

Working on one's diet and activity level is only part of what we should be doing. We also need to investigate what our tribes ate, how they cultivated crops, what and how they hunted and fished, and how they prepared foods and saved seeds for the future. How can we participate in the preservation of agricultural techniques? What are our tribes' ceremonies associated with food? What are the names of our foods and animals in our tribes' languages? Working to eradicate racism, stereotypes, and discrimination and to improve curriculums, social services, and the environment gives us strength and provides hope for others. Becoming aware of our tribes' history, learning our language, engaging our elders, and becoming politically active all contribute toward decolonizing, building pride, and shaping our identity as Indigenous people. Improving diets and lifestyles is all a part of the larger picture of empowering our tribes, our communities, our families, and ourselves.

We must take responsibility for our health and for the well-being of our children. In so doing, we pass on a legacy of self-respect and tribal strength to future generations.

1. Traditional Diets and Activities

Think of the American Thanksgiving dinner: appetizers of smoked salmon and peanuts; main course of turkey, cornbread stuffing, salad of red, green and yellow vegetables, green beans, squash, tomatoes, corn bread, corn bread stuffing, rice and cranberries, cranberry sauce, baked beans and maple syrup, and mashed potatoes; and desserts of peanut brittle, pecan, sweet potato and pumpkin pie. For this exercise, set aside the images of dishes such as white flour rolls and gravy, jello salad, roasted Brussels sprouts, candied yams or carrots, and bread pudding. What all the foods in the first sentence have in common is that they are indigenous to the Western Hemisphere. The "Americas," as we now call them, have provided the world with at least half the plant foods we know today. This "New World" was home to a plethora of flora and fauna, including those mentioned and tomatoes, an array of chile peppers that span the heat index, beans of many kinds, choke cherries, acorns, piñon nuts, black walnuts, hickory nuts, pecans, vanilla, avocado, peppers, manioc, raspberries, strawberries, blueberries, cactus, guava, papaya, passion fruit, pineapples, potatoes, Jerusalem artichoke, and cacao.[1] Corn played a major dietary role for many of the New World tribes. By 1492 Indigenous peoples were cultivating at least two hundred types of maize, some of which Columbus took with him back to Europe. From there maize was taken to the Mediterranean; the Venetians took it to the Near East, then to other places around the world.[2]

Some scholars argue that the basis of Natives' diet was "guts and grease." This is debatable, considering the sheer variety of plant foods available to some groups. While some tribes may have depended on animals for the majority of their diet (such as Arctic and Plains tribes), not all of them did.[3] Still, although during times of difficult hunting tribes would depend on vegetables, fruit, nuts, and seeds, Natives were not vegetarians, and many ate insects. Depending on where they lived, Natives consumed alligators, antelope, bears, beavers, bison, caribou, deer, moose, ducks, elk, rabbits, a variety of fish, geese, opossums, raccoons, squirrels, turtles, seals, shellfish, and whales, to name a few animals.

Tribes also included in their diets a variety of wild plants that are commonly referred to as "weeds": arrowroot, bearberry, black birch, black mustard, bulrush, buttercup, cattail, chickweed, chokecherry, coltsfoot, common plantain, dandelion, elderberry, evening primrose, great burdock, lamb's quarters, milkweed, mint, ostrich fern, stag sumac, stinging nettle, thistle, wild rose, wintergreen, wood sorrel, yellow clover, yellow waterlily. These plants were usually eaten raw, cooked, used to make a beverage, or mixed into soups and stews.[4]

Natives used a number of herbs for medicines, many of which are the basis for modern medicines. Earache, for example, was treated by Kickapoos with boiled and strained mescal beans poured into the ear; Sioux tribes used boiled white milkwort and Ho Chunks used boiled yarrow. Fevers were treated by Choctaws with bayberry tea, while Delawares and Alabamas boiled and drank dogwood bark. Pomos boiled the inner root bark of the western willow, the Natchez used red willow, and Pimas, Mohegans, and Penobscots also used willow for fevers and chills. Some tribes used dandelion leaves as poultices. Navajos used Fendler bladderpod tea, saltbrush, and crushed snakeweed to treat insect bites and stings. Dakotas and Ho Chunks placed crushed bulbs of garlic and onions on wounds.[5]

Foods of the Western Hemisphere Peoples

Native foods reflect regional differences. Plains tribes (Arikaras, Assiniboines, Blackfeet, Cheyennes, Comanches, Crees, Crows, Dakotas, Gros Ventres, Hidatsas, Ioways, Kiowas, Lakotas, Mandans, Missourias, Nakotas, Ojibwas, Omahas, Osages, Otoes, Pawnees, Poncas, Quapaws, Tonkawas, Wichitas) consumed plants such as beans (some taken from mice nests), buffalo berries, camas bulbs, chokecherries, currants, plums, and prairie turnips, and animals such as antelopes, beavers, buffalo, deer, ducks, elk, hackberries, muskrats, prairie dogs, rabbits, raccoons, porcupines, prairie chickens, and skunks. Bison supplied a variety of dishes: boiled meat, tripe soup perhaps thickened with brains, roasted intestines, and jerked or smoked meat; raw kidneys, liver, and tongue sprinkled with gall or bile were eaten immediately after a kill. One version of Plains tribes' long-lasting pemmican consists of thin strips of meat pounded together with marrow fat and chokecherries and dried.

Richard Irving Dodge, a career military officer who in the late 1870s penned his decidedly one-sided ideas about Natives in *The Plains of North America and Their Inhabitants*, also was a hunter with no apparent concern about environmental management. Dodge tells us about the animals he encountered on the Plains in his chapter about the plethora of creatures he killed in a two-week period in 1872: badgers, various birds (cranes, grouse, hawks, herons, meadowlarks, owls, robins, quail, turkeys), bison, deer, doves, ducks (teal, mallard, shoveler, widgeon, "butter duck," shelduck), elk, owls, raccoons, and rattlesnakes. He also observed bears (black bears and grizzlies) and cougars (known as pumas or panthers).[6]

Depending on where they lived, Natives of the vast area we now call Texas had numerous choices of plants, animals, and insects. Acorns, currants, opossum grapes, juniper berries, mulberries, pecans, persimmons, and plums grew in many locales. Atakapans and Karankawas along the coast ate bears, deer, alligators, clams, ducks, oysters, and turtles. Caddos in the lush eastern area grew beans, pumpkins, squash, and sunflowers in addition to hunting bears, deer, waterfowl, and occasionally bison. The Coahuiltecans of semi-arid South Texas and northern Mexico ate agave, prickly pear cactus, mesquite beans, and anything else edible in hard times, including maggots. Jumanos along the Rio Grande in West Texas grew beans, corn, and squash and gathered mesquite beans, screwbeans, and prickly pear. They consumed bison and cultivated crops after settling at the headwaters of the Brazos River, in addition to eating fish, clams, berries, pecans, and prickly pear cactus. The Wichita Confederacy tribes occupied north-central Texas and gardened corn, beans, and squash along the many waterways. The Karankawas were notable for being tall and strongly built. The Tonkawas of central Texas were described as wiry and short.

Tribes in the northeastern part of the continent had access to a different suite of plants and animals. Abenakis had a comparatively short growing season and did not depend on crops like their neighbors to the south. They fished for eels, shad, salmon, sturgeon, and smelt; hunted bear, caribou and deer; and gathered nuts, berries, and potatoes. Anishinaabe cultivated small gardens of the "Three Sisters"—corn, beans, and squash grown together symbiotically—fished, gathered wild rice, and collected maple sap to boil down into sugar. Mahicans depended on the same crops, in addition to gathering waterlily roots, mushrooms, berries, maple sap, deer, turkeys, and fish. Menominees also planted crops but to a lesser extent; instead, they gathered wild rice, fished, and hunted bison and deer. The Kaniengehawas, Oneidas, Potawatomies, Senecas, and Onondagas grew corn, squash, and beans in addition to hunting and gathering. The Hurons in the Georgian Bay of Lake Huron gathered artichokes and berries, fished, and hunted for bears, deer, and beaver, but they mainly depended on corn, a crop they cultivated in large amounts. Because of the very real chance of losing their crops each spring to frosts, Hurons planted enough for almost half a million bushels a year and stored most of it for times of famine. They also had access to flatfish, carp, pike, sturgeon, and whitefish in Lake Huron, and they hunted numerous animals: bears, beavers, elk, foxes, lynxes, martins, moose, mule and white-tailed deer, minks, otters, porcupines, sables, turkeys, weasels, and wood rats. Ho Chunks consumed a wide variety of foods, as did the Passamaquoddy, who ate a bit of everything, including cultivated crops, wild plants, game animals, fish, and marine mammals.

California tribes had a variety of foods available year-round, depending on their environment. Along the coasts of California and north into Canada the land and sea supplied a plethora of flora and fauna and supported hundreds of thousands of people. Even those inland had a variety of foods to utilize. The Cahuillas who lived south of the Bernardino Mountains ate antelope they boiled, roasted, or sun-dried; several types of acorns; cacti, deer, piñon nuts, rabbits, reptiles, screwbeans, and fish. The Chumash along the Pacific coast also ate fish, shellfish, and marine animals. Hupas in the Hoopa Valley consumed a variety of freshwater animals, such as eels, sturgeon, and trout, in addition to eating deer, elk, berries, nuts, roots, and acorns. Costanoans of the San Francisco area speared fish, gathered shellfish, and ate beached whales in addition to gathering acorns and a variety of fruits, insects, and honey. They practiced controlled burning, which allowed for more effective growth of plants and expanded the grazing area for animals. Although Kuroks in the middle area of the Klamath River valley had access to hundreds of plants and animals, they had taboos against eating bats, blue jays, caterpillars, coyotes, dogs, eagles, foxes, frogs, gophers, grasshoppers, hawks, lizards, meadowlarks, moles, owls, ravens, snakes, vultures, wildcats, and wolves. Shastas on the California-Oregon border used venison almost daily; fished for eels, salmon, and trout; and gathered acorns, berries, seeds, bulbs, and nuts.

Those living along the Northwest coast, such as the Bella Bellas, Bella Coolas, Chinooks, Coosans, Haidas, Kwakiutls, Makahs, Nootkans, Quileutes, Salish, Tillamooks, Tlingits, and Upper Umpquas, were supported by a vast amount of foods from the ocean and the lush land. Salmon was a major source of food, along with other fish including trout, halibut, and herring, followed by acorns, hundreds of different plants, marine mammals (whales, otters, seals), bears, beavers, lynx, deer, and small game like rabbits and hares.

Plateau tribes were the Cayuses, Coeur d'Alenes, Colvilles, Kalispels, Klikitats, Kootenais, Lillooets, Modocs, Nez Perces, Okanagons, Salish, Sanpoils, Sinkiuses, Spokans, Thompsons, Umatillas, and Yakimas. They ate salmon, trout, whitefish, mollusks, camas bulbs, wild waterlily seeds (used for flour), berries, deer, elk, antelope, moose, bears, and rabbits. Colville and Sinkiuse men fished for four types of salmon from May to October, while the women cleaned them. They normally acquired enough fish to dry and store for the winter.

The subarctic area that spans the continent provided tribes such as the Beavers, Carriers, Chilcotins, Chipewyans, Crees, Ingaliks, Kaskas, and Kutchins with bears, beavers, berries, camas bulbs, caribou, hares, moose, roots, salmon, trout, and whitefish; Tanainas around Cook Inlet ate salmon, catfish, beluga whales, seals, and otters as well as land animals and fowl. To the north, in the vast arctic region that stretches twelve thousand miles from the eastern Aleutian Islands to Greenland, Inuit peoples ate according to the environment: inland, mountain, or coastal. Widespread staples were salmon, berries, and caribou (and the greens in their stomachs). Coastal zones provided narwhal and beluga whales, seals and walruses, shellfish, cod and other arctic fish, polar bears, and guillemot eggs; inland were moose, squirrels, bears, wolverines, foxes, ptarmigans, owls, and other birds. Although some tribes ate mainly meats, historically those meats and fish were not polluted, and people did not of course mix sugar and processed foods into their diets.

In the Southwest, food was less abundant than in other parts of the Americas, but for those who knew how and where to look, the sometimes hard terrain supplied a variety of foods for tribes including the Cocopahs, Navajos, Apaches (Chiricahuas, Jicarillas, Lipans, Mescaleros, and White Mountain Apaches), Havasupais, Hualapais, Tohono O'odhams, Pimas, Mohaves,

Quecgans/Yumas, Yaquis, Hopis, Tiguas, and other Pueblo tribes of the Acoma, Cochiti, Isleta, Jemez, Laguna, Nambe, Picuris, Sandia, San Felipe, San Ildefonso, San Juan, Santa Clara, Taos, Tesuque, Zia, and Zuni pueblos.

Natives foraged for piñon nuts, cacti (saguaro, prickly pear, cholla), agaves or century plants, screwbeans, mesquite beans, insects, acorns, berries, and seeds and hunted turkeys, deer, rabbits, fish (saltwater varieties for those who lived by the Gulf of California) and antelope; some Apaches reportedly did not eat bears, turkeys, snakes, owls, coyotes, or fish. More sedentary tribes irrigated and cultivated the land for corn, cotton, pumpkins, sunflowers, and beans for themselves and to trade to other tribes for meats besides the game they hunted. The Apache tribes were more mobile and utilized an array of foods ranging from game animals to fruits, nuts, cactus, and rabbits, and they sometimes cultivated small crops. Some used corn to make *tiswin* or *tulupai*, a weak alcoholic drink. Cultivation of crops in the arid Southwest is nothing recent. Some two thousand years ago the Anasazi, Hohokam, and Mogollon peoples grew corn and squash. Physical evidence tells us that the Hohokam dug irrigation canals eight feet deep and thirty feet wide; some of the canals were twenty miles long.

Depending on where they lived, Great Basin tribes—Paiutes, Shoshones, Utes, and Washoes—consumed roots, bulbs, seeds, nuts (especially acorns and piñons), berries (chokecherries, service berries), grasses, cattails, ducks, rabbits, squirrels, antelope, beavers, deer, bison, elk, lizards, insects, grubs, the brine shrimp of ephemeral pools, and fish (salmon, sturgeon, perch, and trout in the Snake and Columbia Rivers and tributaries).

The first explorers in South America reported encountering a wide range of foods: animals as bears, deer, ducks, foxes, guanacos, guinea pigs, and llamas, and plants including avocados, beans, chile peppers, maize, manioc, peanuts, potatoes, squashes, and sweet potatoes. A variety of foods supplied Natives (most notably the Peruvians) with adequate nutrients: grains with twice the protein content of white rice or corn; potatoes with a naturally buttery taste; tubers that were pink, yellow and red striped; purple, white, and yellow roots tasting like celery, cabbage, and chestnuts. Incredibly, Natives of the Andes cultivated thousands of types of potatoes. Peruvians dried potatoes (creating *chunu*) by leaving the harvest in the cold air overnight then mashing out the moisture. Villagers repeated this process for up to five days until the potatoes had dried and were ready to be stored.[7]

Indigenous peoples in Mexico ate and still use the maguey slug or agave worm. Spaniards who landed on the shores of Cuba were introduced to cassava bread, a dish made with cassava root (also known as manioc or tapioca), which contains cyanide and is poisonous until the roots are either boiled and mashed or grated and mashed. Thus treated, the pulp was then shaped and baked and could be dried for later use. Reportedly the Spanish enjoyed this bread, and the French were even more enthusiastic, often using cassava bread instead of wheat bread. Cassava, although starchy and high in calories, is not particularly nutritious.[8]

Conquistadors reported their surprise at the neat and orderly city of Tenochtitlán, and not least among their surprises was the food offered. Meals consisted of tortillas made from boiled dried maize that had been rolled into a paste, formed into a thin cake and cooked, then served with tomato or pepper sauce and beans. Tortillas could be used as a wrap for tomatoes, fish, or meat then rolled in a corn husk and steamed. Another meal might consist of maize porridge and tamales, garnished with frogs, tadpoles, newts, white worms, or meat of iguanas, turkeys, or dogs.[9] Still, the conquistadors, in their religious and economic zeal, destroyed South American crops such as quinoa in favor of European wheat and barley. Fortunately, there is a resurgence of some of these foods, including quinoa, amaranth, cherimoya, tamarillo, and pepino dulce.[10]

Although tribes had hundreds of foods in their environments, all foods were not accessible at all times. The seasons, weather, drought, pestilence, and over-harvesting all had bearing on what was available. There were, of course, no grocery stores, and people had to rely on themselves and one another for sustenance. As discussed in the next section, tribal members expended a tremendous amount of calories just acquiring enough energy and nutrients to survive.

Religious Significance of Food

Many tribes' cosmology places food as a foundational element of Indigenous cultures. Numerous tribes in the Northeast and Southeast still observe the Green Corn ceremony each year as the corn matures. The ceremony is combination of thanksgiving and renewal because of the promise of corn for the year and also reserving seeds to plant the following spring. For Navajos, the word "mother," or "Changing Woman," represents the three major elements of Navajo subsistence: corn, earth, and sheep. This self-renewing entity symbolizes the growth, death, and rebirth of corn. Changing Woman is young in spring, is harvested in the summer, grows old and fades in the fall, dies in the winter, and then sprouts (is reborn) the next season.

Other tribes have similar stories about food. Old Salt Woman among the Cochitis provided the salt for Great Salt Lake and the people who use salt for the food. Cherokee women believe they came from Corn Mother or Selu. For the Tewa Pueblos, the first mothers were known as Blue Corn Woman and White Corn Maiden. Cheyennes believe their food is supplied by a female who takes the shape of an elder. Penobscots say First Mother renews herself each year with corn for her people. White Buffalo Woman of the Sioux ensured that her people would have bison to eat and use for clothing and tools, and the Sioux honored the bison by using very part of its body for food, shelter, and tools.

The Choctaws have several stories related to foods. The first: A long time ago there was a small Chahta boy named Achafa Chipota, who despite his stature ran faster and had better aim with his bow than any other child. One day Achafa Chipota accompanied his father and group of hunters on a trip to find game. He quickly proved himself to be tough and ready to work hard. He killed several rabbits and squirrels for the hunters to eat. One morning as he was hunting small game, he came across a large hog—a *shukhusi*—and he managed to kill her by shooting her through the eye with his small arrow. He then discovered that the *shukhusi* had a family of small piglets, which he took with him on the rest of the hunt and then back to his home. He cared for the piglets as they grew into hogs. Then they reproduced. One time a *minko* (district leader) came to his house for a meeting, and Achafa Chipota's parents did not have enough food. Achafa Chipota surprised them by killing one of his hogs to cook along with the acorns. Normally his mother would have served bear meat. The *minko* was delighted with what he called the sweet meat. The *minko* then renamed Achafa Chipota "*Pelichi Shukhusi*"—the tamer of pigs—and he was given the task of instructing Choctaw families how to raise hogs.

Another story: One time shortly after Achafa Chipota became Pelichi Shukhusi, two hunters got lost in the woods. They were cold and hungry with only one little rabbit to cook for dinner. As they watched the rabbit cook, they heard a woman crying. They rushed through the woods to find a young woman dressed in white, sobbing. They led her back to their fire and asked who she was and why she was out in the cold woods alone. She explained that she was the daughter of Hashtali (Sun Father) and Moon Mother, and while she was on an errand for them, she ran out of food and became too weak to continue. They gave her their small rabbit, but she took only one bite then told them they would be rewarded for their kindness. She told them to return the next morning to where they found her, and then she vanished. The surprised hunters ate the remainder of the rabbit and waited through the night to return to where they found her. Upon returning to the site, the two hunters found in the snow a green plant over six feet tall with a golden tassel at the top. The leaves were long, and within were long fruits.

The hunters took one of the fruits and peeled back the green covering to see what looked like small seeds set in neat rows. They took a bite and realized that the strange food would taste better cooked. They took the remaining five ears home and planted the kernels in the spring. In the fall they had a crop of the new food they called *tanchi*. Shortly afterward, Chahta families planted *tanchi* every spring, harvested in the fall, and learned to dry the kernels and to cook *tanchi* in a variety of ways. Chahtas liked it so much that *tanchi* and pork replaced their previous favorite dish of bear meat and acorns.

The story about the *shukhusi* must have arisen after contact with Europeans because pigs were brought to the Southeast by Hernando de Soto when he landed on the Atlantic Coast of Florida in 1539. But like with Apache groups who have stories saying horses were always part of those cultures, and Navajos who have similar stories about sheep, Chahtas have stories that imply pigs were always with them. These stories illustrate how quickly the animals and food sources became important to the tribes.

Many tribes had thirteen-month calendars that they say were based on the scutes of the carapaces of terrestrial turtles. Turtles have 13 large central and costal scutes, and 28 supracaudal scutes (that look like the edges of a skirt). Take a look at any photo of a box turtle, for example, and you can clearly see the 13/28 divisions. Traditionally Chahtas followed a thirteen-month calendar that reflected how they produced, gathered, and cultivated food. The old Choctaw thirteen-month calendar reflects their connection to the seasonal changes that impact their sustenance:

Hvsh mahli or *mahili* (month of the winds) saw warmer winds from the southeast, and patches of green began to show. Poke salat, sheepshank, sour dock, lamb's quarters, and wild onions were available for harvesting.

Hvsh bissa (month of the blackberry), *Hvsh bihi* (month of the mulberry), and *Hvsh takkon* (month of the each) tell us what fruits were picked during these times.

Hvsh watullak or *Hvsh watonlak* (month of the crane) is named after a white crane that lived in Mississippi; the squab (baby bird) was a favorite food, especially when mixed into a stew with corn and greens.

Late July and early August was *Hvsh luak mosholi* (month of the fires all out), when corn reached its roasting stage and the tribe danced the Green Corn dance. The Green Corn festival lasted several weeks and was a time for thanks. The tribe had become so dependent on *tanchi* that the Chahtas performed the Green Corn dance every year when *tanchi* reached the roasting stage. The Chahtas continued to perform the Green Corn dance well after they had been introduced to Christianity, and like many other Natives today, some Chahtas continue to dance every summer.

Hvsh tek ihvshi (month of the woman) was when young women were courted (although they were presumably courted during other times as well). This time was after the Green Corn dance, the weather was good, and heavy work for preparing for the year was not yet required.

Hvsh koinchush (month of the wildcat) and *Hvsh koichito* (month of the panther) are named after two large felines that were more populous than they are now. At this time of year the mother cats were easier to kill because their kittens had started to wander more and the mother was with them. Their meat was dried into jerky and reportedly lasted through the winter.

Hvsh hoponi (month of cooking) was when the gardens had to be harvested and the food stored in some way, either dried or cooked. Many foods were made into "breads" that included acorns, beans, berries, nuts, onions, peas, persimmons, squash, and sweet potatoes.

Hvsh kvf (month of sassafras) corresponds to our current December and early January, when tree sap is concentrated in the roots. Chahtas dug buckeye, sassafras, snakeroot, and witch hazel, which were used for medicines; dyes were made from the indigo plant native to the Western Hemisphere, and from maple, poke, puccoon, and walnut roots.

Hvsh chvfiskono (month of little famine) is our January and *Hvsh chvffo chito* (month of big famine) is February. As one might expect, by this time food supplies had dwindled and game animals were difficult to find.[11]

Indeed, among most tribes there was much ceremony associated with food production, cultivation, and distribution. Food was and still is a focal point of a society's survival and permeates daily activities, song, and celebration, as reflected in this Hopi song:

> Oh, for a heart as pure as pollen on corn blossoms,
> And for a life as sweet as honey gathered from the flowers,
> May I do good, as Corn has done good for my people
> Through all the days that were.
> Until my task is done and evening falls,
> Oh, Mighty Spirit, hear my grinding song.[12]

Traditional Activity

Until Indigenous people stopped cultivating crops, hunting, fishing and gathering food, building their homes, and generally performing life-sustaining chores, they possessed little body fat. Hunting, gardening, and domestic activities such as washing clothes, building structures, and finding firewood mainly used feet as transportation and thus burned thousands of calories.

And people looked fit. Many Euroamericans have commented on the Natives' healthy appearance. In the 1770s the intrepid explorer, navigator, and naturalist Bernard Romans described tribes of the Southeast as "well made, of a good stature, and neatly limbed," and said their "teeth are very good." Anyone who appeared "crooked, lame or otherwise deformed" was "accidental." He assessed the native men as generally "strong and active" and the women as "handsome, well-made . . . their strength is great, and they labour hard."[13] Eighteenth-century

English trader James Adair expressed admiration for Natives' endurance and ability to chase game or an enemy for hundreds of miles.[14]

Oglethorpe expedition member Edward Kimber said about the Natives in Florida in 1744: "As to their figure, 'tis generally of the largest size, well proportion'd, and robust, as you can imagine Persons nurs'd up in manly Exercises can be."[15] Vigorous outdoor living also made a person tough, as traveler Peter Kalm observed in 1750 when he made his way through Iroquois country:

> The natives are tremendously rugged. I saw them going about these days with only a shirt on and a weapon hanging over it, often without shoes though they had on their . . . stockings. The men wore no trousers, the women a short, thin skirt; neither of the sexes had anything on their heads. Thus they traveled at this time through the forests on their hunting trips, both in good and bad weather. They lay in this manner during cold and rainy nights in the damp and wet forests without having any other clothes to put under or on top of themselves at night than those they wore during the day.[16]

In 1846 Indian agent William Armstrong commented that the Choctaws prior to removal were "the most hearty, robust looking people I have ever seen."[17]

Numerous reports tell us about the physiques of historic Natives who ate unprocessed foods and who were consistently active. George Catlin observed tribes of the Upper Missouri and commented:

> They are undoubtedly the finest looking, best equipped, and most beautifully costumed of any on the Continent. They live in a country well-stocked with buffaloes and wild horses, which furnish them an excellent and easy living; their atmosphere is pure, which produces good health and long life; and they

are the most independent and the happiest races of Indians I have met with: they are all entirely in a state of primitive wildness, and consequently are picturesque and handsome, almost beyond description. . . . As far as my travels have yet led me into the Indian country, I have more than realized my former predictions that those Indians who could be found most entirely in a state of nature, with the least knowledge of civilized society, would be found to be the most cleanly in their persons, elegant in their dress and manners, and enjoying life to the greatest perfection.[18]

Europeans were surprised to see that the Indigenous people they encountered did not suffer from the same maladies they were accustomed to seeing in Europe. William Wood, a Puritan in Massachusetts, stated of the "Aberginians or Indians Northward" that they were

straight bodied, strongly composed, smooth-skinned, merry countenanced, of complexion something more swarthy than Spaniards, black haired, high foreheaded, black eyed, out-nosed, broad shouldered, brawny armed, long and slender handed, out breasted, small waisted, lank bellied, well thighed, flat kneed, handsome grown legs, and small feet. . . . It may puzzle belief to conceive how such lusty bodies should have their rise and daily supportment from so slender a fostering, their houses being mean, their lodging as homely, commons scant, their drink water, and nature their best clothing. In them the old proverb may well be verified: Natura paucis contenta, for though this be their daily portion, they still are healthful and lusty.[19]

Comments made by Europeans about the physical beauty of Indigenous peoples abound. Christopher Columbus remarked in his diary of October 12 and 13, 1492, about the peoples he encountered in Guanahani (San Salvador): "They are very well formed, with handsome bodies and good faces." The next day he wrote, "All alike have very straight legs and no belly but are very well formed."[20]

James Adair noted the "exquisitely fine proportioned limbs" of "Chikkasah" women in the Southeast.[21] Peter Kalm noted that the Hurons "are a tall, robust people, well shaped, and of a copper color."[22] The Shawnees were similarly endowed, according to Nicholas Cresswell: "They are tall, manly, well-shaped men," and "their persons are tall and remarkably straight."[23]

"The men are in general tall, active and well made, qualifications absolutely necessary for a race of hunters" is how Lieutenant James M. Hadden described men he encountered in Canada in 1776. Of course, women, who did the gathering and gardening and dressed the game would also have appeared fit, but true to the nature of the male writers of that day, women were for the most part misunderstood in the early narratives.[24] One hundred or so years later, white male writers were still describing Native women inaccurately, although we can see a kernel of truth every now and then. Sherry Smith's *A View from Officer's Row: Army Perceptions of Western Indians* (1990) is a compilation of observations by officers who encountered Native peoples. Although most of these men had derogatory things to say about Native women's physical appearance (usually because they were weathered from hard outdoor work), a few admired their capabilities and vitality, noting two Comanche women who reportedly "lassoed several antelope,"[25] and a Yuma woman whose body "was truly magnificent, and would have been a glory to a young sculptor,"[26] and the Native mothers who after childbirth "gathered up their babies and healthily, vigorously went on their way."[27]

Observers were interested in how the Natives stayed fit. A French soldier wrote about unnamed tribes in the area of New York: "They claim that the lack of hair results from the abundance of their blood, which is purer because of their simple diet, and which produces fewer excess substances." He concurs with the powers of a "simple diet," stating: "There is little doubt that their simple diet makes the savages swift runners."[28] Another traveler, Patrick M'Robert, made a similar observation in mid-1775 about tribes in that area: "These are a tall, nimble, well-made people; many of them about six feet high, with long black hair . . . their features good, especially the women. They live chiefly by hunting fishing, and upon fruits."[29]

Children worked and played without the same distractions we have today. No iPhones, television, video games, or Netflix to keep youngsters from staying consistently active. J. Carver, who wrote about his observations in the area in the 1760s, commented that upon seeing youngsters, "I ſaw about twenty naked young Indians, the moſt perfect in the ſhape, and by far the handsomeſt of any I had ever ſeen."[30]

Native people who foraged were not always assured of success and had to range long distances to search for food. And even if they were successful, the actual gathering and carrying the food all day was tiring. M. D. Eaton and colleagues researched modern gatherers in Africa and Paraguay and found that when women (the primary gatherers) leave for the day, they often are gone for up to twenty hours per week. These peoples usually find an average of fifteen different "staple" vegetables and perhaps up to sixty other foods, depending on the seasons.[31] It stands to reason that people in different parts of the world find more or less, depending on their environment. The amount of rainfall, type of soil, and nature of the terrain all figure into the relative abundance of foods available.

And as noted, even when food is available, it takes a huge effort to gather it. Using primarily a stick to dig, gatherers would often dig all day long to collect roots and bulbs. Anyone who gardens knows the feeling of fatigue and backache after just an hour of pulling weeds and bending over to inspect crops. Gatherers did much inspecting, pulling, and digging; they also put the food in their bags and packs and carried the heavy haul around—in addition to carrying their infants and small

children—often for miles and in all sorts of weather. It is estimated that the !Kung San women of South Africa walk up to
twelve miles in a day when foraging, and this does not include
their other daily activities.[32]

Hunters often have less success at finding food, but it still
takes much effort to try and obtain a deer, elk, moose, or bison.
And hunting could be precarious. Hooves, horns, teeth, claws
and massive body weight could easily injure or kill an unwary
hunter. Hunters today, equipped with thousands of dollars'
worth of rifles, special clothing, and all manner of technical
accessories know that even top-of-the-line equipment and endless patience are often not enough to garner you an animal.
Game animals catch on quickly when being stalked. Sometimes
an area is hunted out and game is hard to find. Poachers take
their toll. And despite being physically undemanding, sitting
quietly in a blind all day isn't easy for many. Historically hunters
used a variety of methods to kill animals: running buffalo and
horses over a cliff and butchering them at the bottom; driving
them into pits, marshes, or snow where they could be killed; or
throwing a spear or shooting arrows from a bow, either from
horseback or while on foot.

Eaton posits that modern hunters in Australia and Venezuela
spend twenty hours a week hunting (that is, stalking, waiting,
killing, butchering, and bringing the meat home), with two days
off, although game is now sparser than it was historically. Some,
like those in Paraguay, hunt every day.[33] Exhausted hunters who
have dragged even a medium-sized deer through rough terrain
know that killing, say, a buffalo far from one's truck presents
some special challenges in getting the meat home. Natives who
had no vehicles or horses had to bring the animal to camp
themselves, as described among the Delawares by the Rev. John
Heckewelder in 1788: "It is very common to see a hunter come
in with a whole deer on his back, fastened with a hoppis, a kind
of band with which they carry loads."[34]

Eaton and his colleagues measured young men's skinfold thickness (on the back of the upper arm) in several modern hunter-gatherer societies, and discovered that they had much less body fat (4.6 mm) compared to non-hunter-gatherers in Africa and Australia (10 mm—over twice as much).[35] He also found that diabetes, hypertension, obesity, and atherosclerosis were unknown among the modern Kenyan Kikuyus, Broaya pastoralists, and people of "pre-industrial" societies in Africa, Australia, and South America. He and his colleagues attribute this health to the reality that their diets consist of wild plants (and consequently large amounts of roughage) and of game that is high in protein and polyunsaturated fats. They eat little salt and saturated fat, drink only water, and consume honey as their only source of sugar.[36] If we were to combine their ways of eating and moving about with our advances in medicine, then we would be very healthy, indeed.

Games and Sports

Games, play, and sports were an integral part of Indigenous life. Men and women played a variety of active sports, such as stickball, horseracing, and numerous ball games. They competed at running (sprints and distance) and swimming. And they played snow snake, popular in the north where there is snow, and players slide or toss a pole called a "snake" along the frozen ground; and hoop and pole, in which a pole or spear is thrown at a rolling wheel or hoop with the goal of both landing close to each other or the hoop on top of the pole; as well as many sedentary games. Some games were played for religious reasons, not for profit. And there was a strong cultural connection between playing and a player's identity. A game might be played in hopes of healing the sick, ensuring a good harvest, to strengthen kinship ties, or out of respect for the Creator. Players might observe a strict diet for months before a game, in addition to specific praying and ceremonial rituals. Games also were team sports, not individual sports. When one gambled on a team or a person, the winnings were kept within the community, not going to the winner, as we see today. In addition, there were no superstars to admire since there was no commercialization (i.e., salaries and advertisements) associated with traditional Indigenous sports.[37]

The game today called lacrosse was known by various names among the tribes who played it, who were everywhere except in the Southwest. Many Natives claim that their tribe was the "inventor" of lacrosse; there is no debate over that in this book. Regardless of who did what first, it is generally agreed upon that many tribes played this type of game for enjoyment and in hopes that crops would be successful and the tribe would prosper.

The traditional game of *kapucha* (stickball) among Choctaws that is sometimes known as *ishtaboli* (although this can also mean "playing field") used to be played with extreme fervor and much ceremony; players and hundreds of spectators gathered at the field the day before in anticipation. George Catlin observed about Choctaws and their level of activity:

> These people seem, even in their troubles, to be happy; and have, like all the other remnants of tribes, preserved with great tenacity their different games, which it would seem they are everlastingly practicing for want of other occupations or amusements in life. Whilst I was staying at the Choctaw agency in the midst of their nation, it seemed to be a sort of season of amusements, a kind of holiday when the whole tribe almost, were assembled around the establishment, and from day to day we were entertained with some games or feats that were exceedingly amusing: horse-racing, dancing, wrestling, foot-racing, and ball-playing, were amongst the most exciting; and of all the catalogue, the most beautiful, was decidedly that of ball-playing.[38]

One field Catlin saw was reportedly around four hundred yards long and at each end of the field stood two poles set in the ground (the rules were apparently flexible as regards the size of the field, which varied from game to game). Historically, there often were hundreds of players on each side using *kabocca* (sticks) about three feet long with a pocket at one end, the pieces sewn together by sinew. The goal of each side was to hit or catch the leather ball, then throw it with their sticks until the ball touched the other team's poles at the other end of the field. The players stripped to the waist and wore paint on their chests, sometimes with a horse, raccoon, or big cat tail (perhaps a puma) and feathers on their heads, arms, and waists. After the men played, the women took the field and played just as aggressively. *Kapucha* was colorful and exciting, and bets were eagerly made. The game was also fast-paced and violent. Broken arms, legs, noses, and dislocated kneecaps were common, and the players wore their scars the rest of their lives. Some players even died from injuries sustained during the game.

Tribe members continued to play in significant numbers until the early twentieth century, by which time baseball and football had become popular. Today Chahtas in Mississippi and Oklahoma still play, usually at annual tribal celebrations but also in tournaments such as the "World Series of Stickball" held each year at the annual Choctaw Indian Fair in Mississippi. Players use hand-carved hickory sticks (in some games players are allowed to use two sticks) that have at one end a thong pocket made of leather or deer hide. The *towa* (ball) is made from cloth tightly wrapped around a small stone or piece of wood, with a leather thong wound over the cloth. But as with other sports that are played periodically, such as week-end touch football and seasonal softball, if one plays stickball only on special occasions, then the chances of injury are high. Running and practicing specific *kapucha* skills on a regular basis can keep one fit.

Hundreds of Natives continue to play lacrosse today and not just to stay physically fit; the psychological rewards are also great. Cherokee scholar Jeff Corntassel, for example, regularly plays *a-ne-jo-di* (the name Cherokees or Tsalagi have for the game).

He describes what *a-ne-jo-di* means to him: "Stickball for Tsalagi is more of a ceremony than a game. Originally called the 'little brother to war,' it was sometimes used to resolve territorial disputes with the Creeks, but also promoted unity amongst our people. Stickball is still played before stompdances and during the Green Corn Ceremony to remind us of our obligations to community as Ani-geel-aghi or 'keepers of the fire.' I play a contemporary version of stickball (lacrosse) to honor our ancestors and to ready myself as a warrior."[39]

Running has always been a part of traditional Indigenous lifestyles, originally out of necessity. Prior to acquiring horses, people obviously had to rely on their feet to get them from place to place; but on occasion they had to get somewhere fast. In 1680 Pueblo messengers in today's New Mexico ran at least three hundred miles from pueblo to pueblo to advise them of the uprising against the abusive Spanish. Runners had to chase game and carry messages. Natives had what Peter Nabakov calls "runner-systems" crisscrossing North and South America, the longest one being 2,500 miles from Ecuador to Chile.[40] The people who traversed these trails used only their feet. Runners often ran barefoot, with minimal food.

Importance of Precontact Foods to the World

The addition of Indigenous flora and fauna to the world's diets and medicine chests fantastically altered the human population. Because of the loss of their food resources, the Indigenous population of the Western Hemisphere plummeted dramatically while the population of the world doubled between 1650 and 1850, then doubled again in the next one hundred years. In the area we know as the United States, from 1492 to 1750, the non-Native population grew to 2 million; by 1900 that had grown to 83 million. In Europe the population in 1492 was approximately 70 to 88 million, then by 1900 it had exploded to 435 million. Much of this can be attributed to food, most notably because of corn that is now grown around the world; peanuts that became popular in Africa and China; sweet potatoes that were grown in Africa, Southeast Asia, and China; and manioc, a tropical shrub root that tolerates harsh environments. Of course, vaccinations, better health care and sanitary conditions also contributed to population increase. The Indigenous peoples were not so fortunate. In the Western Hemisphere their numbers decreased from an estimated 72 million in 1492 to 4.5 million in 1700. In the United States their numbers dropped from an estimated 5 million to 600,000 by 1800 and plunged to fewer than 125,000 in 1900 from disease, removal and relocation, loss of natural resources, fertility decline, poor food, depression, and other factors.[41] And as we shall see in case study 2, food and environmentally related maladies appeared shortly after contact.

Oklahoma became a state in 1907. Prior to that time it was called Indian Territory. The Indian Removal Act of 1830, signed by President Andrew Jackson, was a cruel and devastating policy that forced thousands of Indians to move to Indian Territory in order to make way for white settlement in the Southeast and elsewhere.[1] Sixty-seven tribes were moved to Indian Territory, but eventually some were allowed to return to their homelands or were moved to other states. Today there are thirty-eight tribal nations in Oklahoma. For Oklahoma tribes wishing to follow their foodway traditions, there is no one-size-fits-all model. Some tribes have an agricultural legacy but also depended on wild game and plants. Plains tribes, which arrived in the 1870s, hunted bison and other animals, but they expanded their resource base by gathering wild plant foods and trading with other tribes and non-Indians. Some, such as the Comanches ("Lords of the Plains"), had no agricultural tradition but were successful hunters, gatherers, and raiders

Among the Native peoples who came to Indian Territory, under great duress and with devastating loss of life, were the "Five Tribes" (Cherokees, Chickasaws, Choctaws, Muscogees [Creeks], and Seminoles). They found that much of their new land in the eastern parts of Indian Territory resembled their southeastern homelands. Game was plentiful in the forests and grasslands, and fertile soils allowed them to farm. They had ample water and a variety of nut trees and wild fruits.

Much of the Indian Territory environment was similar to parts of the Five Tribes' homelands in Georgia, North Carolina, Mississippi, Louisiana, Alabama, and Florida.[2] The Cherokees settled in northeastern Indian Territory in the grassy valleys and prairies between the Illinois, Grand, and Verdigris Rivers and farmed in the deep black soil between Vinita and Sapulpa.[3] Creek lands to the west of the Cherokees were "rich and productive" but not as lush as their neighbors' lands.[4] Choctaws were moved south of the Cherokees and north of Texas to the watersheds of the Arkansas, Canadian, Kiamichi, and Red Rivers.[5] The rich sandy hills area around Skullyville allowed for the "finest fruits and vegetables for a radius of twenty miles."[6]

The vicinity of Nvnih Chufvk (Sugar Loaf Mountain) in the Choctaw Nation was deemed a haven of springs, wild fruits, and game.[7] George Catlin, an American painter and writer, commented after traveling through the Cherokee and Choctaw territories in the 1840s that their beautiful land "affords one of the richest and most desirable countries in the world for agricultural pursuits."[8] Seminoles established themselves north of the Creeks, between the Arkansas and the Deep Fork of the Canadian River. Chickasaws settled on Boggy and Blue Creeks within the Choctaw Nation, lands deemed "at least as fertile as the ones they left."[9] Indeed, many residents of the tribal nations lauded their lands as affording them a "superabundance" of productive soil, crossed by streams with clear water and dotted with edible plants—a veritable Eden of food possibilities.[10]

Much of the eastern part of Indian Territory had timber cover, including blackjack oak, post oak, red oak, chinkapin, hickory, hackberry, walnut, persimmon, crabapple, sweet gum, cottonwood, elm, pecan, and sycamore, supplying nuts, fruits, and wood for shelter and tools. Soup, broth, mush, and "acorn pudding" could be made from shellbark hickory nuts (*Carya laciniosa*), and acorn flour served as a soup thickener. A Choctaw dish, *okshash*, is water oak acorns boiled and pounded into mush.[11] More than the other tribes, Choctaw families raised hogs (introduced by the Spanish in the 1500s) and allowed the animals to forage most of the year on calorie-dense acorns, hickory nuts, and walnuts. Tribespeople brought apple, peach, and pear tree seeds over the removal trail and in a few years shared seeds with neighbors. As the Territory population grew, representatives of tree nurseries distributed illustrated tree catalogues that served as orchard care advice and reading entertainment.[12] After the Civil War many members of the Five Tribes developed substantial orchards, and one Cherokee maintained a grove of more than two thousand fruit trees.[13]

The natural environment also supplied a variety of familiar vine and bush fruits, herbs, and vegetables. In early spring tribes gathered poke weed, sheep shank, sour dock, lamb's quarters, and wild onions. By February turnips had sprouted "little tender greens." Sunflowers, blackberries, dewberries, raspberries, grapes, huckleberries, plums, strawberries, and persimmons grew in abundance. Yellow apples that had escaped gardens grew in thickets.[14] Catlin commented in 1844 about his trek through Choctaw and Creek lands: "Scarcely a day has passed, in which we have not crossed oak ridges . . . with a sandy soil . . . where the ground was almost literally covered with vines, producing the greatest profusion of delicious grapes, of five-eighths of an inch in diameter, and hanging in such endless clusters."[15]

Some families created that "veritable Eden" on their property by growing corn, potatoes, pumpkins, beans, peanuts, sweet potatoes, and Old World black-eyed peas and cotton, along with groves of apple, peach, plum, pear, and cherry trees as well as berry bushes and grape vines. Seminoles cultivated beans to a greater extent than other tribes. Molasses was made from homegrown sugar cane. White residents commented that Choctaws were "crazy about" cornbread, turkey, coffee, and venison and added beans and peas to almost every dish. The Creeks produced enough beans, pumpkins, melons, potatoes, squash, and corn to sell to Fort Gibson. Many raised hogs, horses, chickens, turkeys, and small herds of cattle. Some families had favorite "bee trees," and a few kept apiaries.[16]

Indian agents in the 1840s stated in their annual reports that game had decreased steadily since the tribes' arrival. One agent even wrote that there was no game within 150 to 200 miles of the Cherokee Nation boundaries, so the natives had turned to increasing their agriculture.[17] Those who lived in Indian Territory, or those who in 1937 recalled stories from their parents and grandparents, however, said the opposite. In fact, hunting seemed to be a way of life for hundreds of residents at least until the end of the nineteenth century. This discrepancy between the agents' reports and the residents' stories might mean that the former were unaware of how the residents were living, or that officials were attempting to appease the federal government, which remained intent on making all Natives "civilized" farmers; or perhaps the agent was referring to enough wild game for the skin trade, and the residents were referring to subsistence level.

One resident stated that there was no pressure when one went out to kill an animal, because it was a given that you could do so. Wolves, foxes, coyotes, bobcats, beavers, and minks were used for the fur trade. Deer and turkeys congregated "in droves" in spring, and one could see them at other times in herds and flocks of hundreds.[18] John Benson relayed that all the Indians had to do was "kill what they wanted. . . . An Indian just had to get his gun on his shoulder and go out and he could kill a deer or a turkey in a little while."[19] Deer lay down in front yards, and turkeys roosted in shade trees by the houses. Some residents stockpiled wild turkeys, geese, and ducks in the home larder.[20] Prairie chickens were so prolific that one man put his family in their wagon and was able to kill an entire "raft" of the birds without disembarking.[21] Hunters crisscrossed tribal lands, leaving on trees and rocks emblems signifying the availability of game, and signs were left warning of snakes and bears.[22]

Bears lived in the forests of eastern Indian Territory, and they were hard to locate, especially in winter when they retreated to their dens. Cubs were born in February, but some Choctaw hunters used "poodle dogs" to coerce bears out of their dens before spring. They also had one technique in which two women stood apart, yelling alternately to get the bear's attention. The bear would ramble from voice to voice until the hunter killed it. While many residents ate bear meat, others reported that they thought it too fatty. There were also plenty of small game animals, including muskrats, opossums, rabbits, and raccoons.[23] One traveler who regularly went through Doaksville and Eagletown into Arkansas in the late 1800s did not have to carry much, since he killed fat squirrels three times a day: "fried for breakfast, stewed with dumplings for dinner and supper." One resident was partial to polecat (skunk) meat, which she prepared like squirrel, claiming you could not tell the difference.[24] Choctaw hunters used dogs to find turtles. Some roasted the hapless turtle alive or dropped it on its back to kill it first. The terrapins could be rolled in wet clay, then roasted alive on hot coals. Meat was accessed by removing the shell and scooping out the contents.[25]

Catfish, scalefish, bass, perch, crappie, buffalo, carp, and suckerfish filled streams and rivers.[26] Natives poisoned them using the long, slender roots of white snakeroot (*Ageratina altissima*), also known as the devil's shoestring, by beating the roots in the water or by dragging a bag of the mashed plant through the water. The dazed larger fish could easily be shot with arrows, but the poison often killed smaller ones.[27]

Families stored dried fruit and meats for the cold months. Some residents grew acres of watermelon and saved them through winter by melting paraffin over the fruits, then storing the waxed melons inside a straw stack.[28] Sassafras helped keep bugs and worms out of the dried fruit bags. Potatoes were thinly sliced and dried over a hickory fire. Roots or mud potatoes, known among Choctaws as *lokohok* (or *lokchok*) *ahi*, were considered by some to be better than Irish potatoes.[29]

String beans were strung up and stored in a dark place. When cured, the beans appeared black and musty, but after being immersed in warm water with a "preparation known only to housewives," the beans returned to their natural color, and supposedly no one could tell the difference.[30] Most farmers prepared garden vegetables for winter use by either sun drying or, for corn, shelling it and then storing it in flour sacks to keep it dry.[31] Residents jerked meat by cutting it into strips, then drying it on top of the house. The result was a hard, difficult-to-chew, saltless product.[32]

Few residents grew corn for their animals because of abundant grass.[33] As discussed in more detail in chapter 7, almost all families gardened, and corn was a prominent crop. Most gardens were small, grown around the house, and were referred to as "patches" or "roasting ear patches,"[34] although by the 1840s some tribespeople started growing corn on a large scale for profit.[35] There is no evidence that they grew corn, squash, and beans together in the "Three Sisters" fashion of the Northeast; that is, pole beans grow up around the cornstalks, and the large squash leaves provide shade that helps retain soil moisture.[36] Native gardeners grew five types of corn: dent corn for shuck bread (although some made shuck bread with burnt bean or pea hulls; the latter account for the greenish color); flint corn for sour bread; softer "Indian" or flour corn for most uses, including bread; sweet corn for early season use; and popcorn.

All the tribes made dishes from corn—what Cherokees call *kanahena*; Choctaws and Chickasaws call *tanchi*; and Creeks and Seminoles call *uche*. They processed corn in basically the same lengthy process that some explain as simply "beating into meal in a block of wood which had a bowl on the end of it" or "pounding it to make a cereal and mixed with water."[37] A log is cut off at around two or three feet, then hollowed out, leaving a thick floor as the bottom. The chips are fired, then the insides of the hollowed log are smoothed with glass. Corn is placed in the hole and pounded repeatedly with a pestle made from a smaller tree, about six inches in diameter. Hickory and beech are the woods mentioned most for the grinding process, although some argue that the block lasts longer if made from pecan or walnut.[38] Without machinery, grinding corn is indeed an arduous process (see figs. 1 and 2). One woman described beating the corn until "our arms felt like they would break."[39] The corn was then placed in a big sieve and thrown up into the wind, which carried off small particles. Meanwhile, green wood ashes were placed in a pan with small holes, and hot water was poured over the ashes; that water dripped into another pan underneath. Depending on the cook, varying amounts of the lye ash water was poured in with the corn, or the corn could be soaked overnight. Corn contains a variety of nutrients but is high in carbohydrates and deficient in vitamin B3. Because natives added wood lye ash to their preparation, they did not suffer from pellagra as did many people in Europe who used plain corn as a staple. Natives mixed corn with a variety of ingredients, including hickory nut kernels, pork, squirrel, pinto beans, sweet potato, red peppers, fruit, hickory oil, pecans, and so on, thus rendering the dishes nutritious and satisfying. Choctaws and Chickasaws refer to a bowl of corn mush with added ingredients as *tanfula* (and sometimes *tamfuller*). *Tash pishofa* (also seen as *pashofa, tash lubona,* or *tash hoshponi*) is unground, boiled corn and might contain hog meat. *Tan hlabo* can be made from green corn. The kernels are cut from the ear and boiled with lye and any kind of meat until the meat falls off the bone. *Walakshi* (also seen as *walusha*) are dumplings made from cornmeal, grape juice, and/or peaches and mixed with boiling water.[40] Hickory nuts were harvested in the summer and sometimes the oil was used to flavor dishes containing corn.

Corn dishes also include dumplings, corn roasted on the cob, dried corn as a traveling food to be reconstituted with water or milk, or corn crushed into mush to mix with fruits and meats.[41] Choctaw and Chickasaw *banaha,* Cherokee *ticanoolee,* and Creek *puyafekcuahke* are similar to tamales, generally made by mixing boiling water and cornmeal along with other ingredients such as beans, pork, and hickory or chestnut oil into dough that is shaped into rolls, then placed in corn shucks, tied with strips of shuck, and cooked under hot ashes or boiled. This "shuck bread" could be stored for months and recooked.[42] One woman claimed it kept indefinitely, "being as good a year after as the day it was cooked."[43] Another dish, Creek and Seminole *osafki,* or *sofky,* is a drink or soup made from flint corn ground like hominy and boiled with lye ash. Osafki still remains a social and ceremonial dish. Some versions are quite sour, and perhaps the distinctive taste is what caused W. P. Blake, who served as assistant engineer at the Seminole Emahaka Academy, to make this interesting claim: "I thought then [1894], and am sure now, that their early drinking of *osofke* as children created an appetite for whiskey."[44]

Cooks made persimmon bread, created by separating the seeds by kneading, then placing the pulp in a large bread pan and cooking it.[45] A few tribespeople brought peanut plants over the removal trail and cultivated these in their home gardens. Some made peanut bread by mixing parched corn and peanuts with sifted corn and a bit of salt. The peanuts held enough moisture to allow the mixture to be formed into long-lasting, uncooked "bread" balls.[46] Natives also made bread out of chestnuts, acorns, bamboo vine (*Smilex laurifolla*), also called "cane," and the root of the southeastern Indian Territory thorny greenbrier vine (*Smilax bona-nox*), which is peeled, after which the insides are crushed to make a paste, then fried in bear grease. Pounded acorns were placed in a cane sieve while water dripped over it to get rid of their bitterness, then formed into cakes and also fried in bear grease or molded around a stick to be roasted.[47] Seeds of the giant cane (*Arundinaria gigantean*) could also be ground into meal.[48] Much of the food was bland by modern standards, although some eaters liked the added seasonings of peppers, hickory oil, walnut oil, bear fat, and oil from blackjack oak acorns.[49] Possibly red autumn sassafras leaves were gathered, dried, ground into powder, and used as a soup flavoring. This ingredient, file gumbo, is used today in making gumbo.[50] In 1776 Romans stated that tribespeople did not normally use salt and only indulged after they had been without salt for a time. After removal, some residents continued to eschew salt except to preserve meats, but some began to sprinkle it liberally, as did white immigrants.[51]

Yet despite the assortment of foods that many Natives grew, gathered, and hunted, even before the Civil War, different foods were becoming available. Many Natives began suffering the consequences of altering their diets of vegetables, fruits, and game meats to rely instead on sugary, fatty, and starchy foods.

2. The State of Indigenous Health

In a 2000 commentary physicians Neal D. Barnard and Derek M. Brown stated that the federal government advocates a diet that is unlike'the traditional diets of Native peoples, saying: "For Native Americans, current federal dietary guidelines promoting a meaty, cheesy diet amounted to, perhaps inadvertently, the nutritional equivalent of smallpox-infected blankets."[1] Although the U.S. Dietary Guidelines now recommend lower intakes of sugar, sodium, and saturated fats, Native diets have not changed much in the last twenty years.[2] Indeed, many Natives continue to consume the absolute worst in food offered by the American food industry. Some may not have a choice and must rely on inadequate foods. Some tribal lands have few stores and many of those stores have little produce—and sometimes that produce is old, expensive, and not nutritious. Like many American consumers, Natives are not always educated about how those foods are processed and with what ingredients. Natives who purchase their own foods often fall prey to misleading ads that tell us that fried, salty, fatty, and sugary foods are good for us. In a sense, problems such as heart disease, stroke, diabetes, and cancers that develop from ingesting dangerous foods can be compared to death from smallpox. The signs and symptoms may differ, but the ultimate outcome is often the same.

An example of how out of step nutrition "experts" are with the needs of Natives is a gastroenterology study conducted in 1977 that revealed that 100 percent of Natives tested were lactose intolerant, which is a food intolerance to the lactose found in milk products. Those suffering from lactose intolerance are deficient in the enzyme lactase. If food has not started to be digested by lactase in the stomach, food then enters the colon, where it produces uncomfortable bloating, cramping, and diarrhea. Almost 50 million Americans have lactose intolerance, and it is estimated that 75 percent of American Indian adults have lactose intolerance. Yet, the Dietary Guidelines advise that everyone eat two or three daily servings of dairy foods, despite the reality that other foods such as green leafy vegetables and beans also supply calcium.[3]

Not everyone can tolerate foods containing wheat or gluten, either. A condition known as celiac disease disallows the consumption of foods made of wheat and containing gluten; barley and rye may likewise contain gluten, and even oats may have some, if processed in a facility also handling other grains. Those who eat these foods can suffer from bloating, diarrhea, headaches, and hives. If these problems are ignored, celiac disease can lead to dehydration, anemia, muscle spasms, bleeding, nerve damage, infertility, loss of appetite, fatigue, and impotence.[4] This is a tough problem for those who like foods containing gluten and wheat: bread, pasta, cookies, muffins, scones, pizza, pies, cobblers, Pop Tarts, hamburger buns, and—well, it is a long list. But these ingredients also show up in seemingly unlikely foods, like soups, rice products, fudge syrup, chocolate milk mixes, processed cereal products, laxatives, hydrolyzed vegetable protein, grain alcohol, and candy.

Lactose intolerance and celiac disease are not the only problems and ailments arising for Natives. Diabetes mellitus is the result of the pancreas slowing or stopping production of the hormone insulin that enables cells to utilize glucose for energy. Glucose is derived from the foods we consume, and insulin is needed for cellular absorption. If glucose is not used it is normally expelled into the bloodstream and into urine, but sustained, excessive glucose results in hyperglycemia and can eventually cause organ and tissue damage. Diabetics suffer from excessive urination, thirst, blurry vision, fatigue, and numbness, pain, or tingling in their hands and feet. Humans have suffered from type 1 diabetes at least since the mid-sixteenth century, but type 1—when the pancreas does not produce any insulin—is probably a hereditary disease. In contrast, obesity increases the chances of developing type 2. Those who suffer from diabetes have a higher chance of developing atherosclerosis and high blood pressure, which can lead to a stroke or heart attack. There is a chance of developing retinopathy, an eye disease that can lead to blindness, especially for those with type 2 diabetes. Nerve damage can also result, which can cause blindness and extremity amputations.

It is estimated that 30.3 million Americans, or 9.4 percent of the population, have diabetes.[5] Type 2 diabetes is epidemic among tribes. American Indians are 2.2 times more likely to develop diabetes than non-Indians; today 16 percent of Native Americans have type 2 diabetes,[6] and 43.7 percent are obese with accompanying complications.[7] Some tribes have been hit especially hard: fully half the adult Tohono O'odham population have type 2 diabetes,[8] and 75 percent of Pimas in Arizona have it.[9] The rate of diabetes on the Osage reservation is 20.7 percent, double the percentage in the United States as a whole, with tribespeople living in a 2,251-square-mile "super food desert," where fresh produce and meats are scarce.[10] The problem continues to grow; in March 2016 the Indian Health Service provided $138 million to tribes and various organizations for diabetes prevention and treatment.[11]

To recap some of these numbers, overall at least 16 percent of Native people in the United States suffer from diabetes and at least 33 percent are obese.[12] Among the Oklahoma population, Indians have the highest rates of heart disease, "unintentional injury deaths," diabetes, and asthma. They eat fewer fruits than whites, blacks, and Hispanics. The Oklahoma Department of Health assigns Native Americans a grade of D for low physical activity and incidence of obesity and an F for "poor mental health" and "poor physical health" days.[13] Of the Cherokees who seek treatment at Cherokee clinics, 34 percent are overweight or obese.[14] As noted, the rate of diabetes on the Osage reservation is double the national rate; it should be no surprise that the rate of heart disease among reservation Osages is double that of those off-reservation. On the reservation 21 percent of Osages live in poverty, compared to 10.3 percent of the U.S. population.[15] Children spend less time playing outdoors, and adults are increasingly separated from the land, resulting in waning interest in the natural world. Smoking and depression exacerbate Oklahoma Natives' health issues.

Using the Oklahoma Choctaws' situation as an example, consider that almost every back issue of the Choctaw Nation's newspaper BISHINIK for the last ten years has at least one article (but usually two or three) about diabetes, obesity, eating right, and exercise—often in a Women, Infant, and Children (WIC) column that features recipes and nutrition information. In response to this epidemic, the Choctaw Nation participates in the "Walk This Weigh" campaign, an annual diabetes awareness walk and run sponsored by the Choctaw Nation Health Care Center, which also sponsors a Youth Wellness Camp and funds a Diabetes Treatment Center that tests and educates Choctaws. In addition, a group of workers with the Diabetes Multi-Resource Task Force travels across the Choctaw Nation to test fifth graders for diabetes and to give presentations about healthy lifestyles.[16]

There is good reason for publishing this information and opening more centers. In February 2002 the Choctaw Nation reported that in 2001, 831 new cases of diabetes were diagnosed, bringing the total number of Choctaws with diabetes in the service area to 3,800.[17] At the 2002 Labor Day Festival in Tushkahoma, Oklahoma, 115 participants in a test to measure fat content revealed that over half of those people were at risk for developing diabetes; of 344 who took a blood test, 35 people had blood glucose levels of 140 mg/dl; and of 64 people who have diabetes and were tested for blood glucose level, 22 had levels above 200 mg/dl. To reiterate the extent of the problem, the Native American Diabetes Initiative asserts that in some tribes, type 2 diabetes has stricken half the tribal members.[18]

The Choctaw Nation has not released recent diabetes statistics. However, one can extrapolate the problem from details about the Choctaw Nation Diabetes Wellness Center, which "was built in 2004 and was remodeled in 2006 and [again] in 2017 to accommodate the growing patient population."[19] As discussed in chapter 3, the Obama administration presented the Choctaw Nation with a Promise Zone award because of the extreme poverty and health problems in some of its counties. The Choctaw Nation—which is worth almost $2.5 billion—has built more diabetes centers and a multimillion-dollar hospital featuring dialysis machines, yet it continues to promote unhealthy eating through its online recipe site, and food-related maladies continue to plague the Nation.

Although individuals may think they are eating right and may have no family history of diabetes, they may be surprised to find they are diabetic because of the types and amounts of foods they ingest. And even if an individual is lean in comparison to most others, that person may have a dangerous body composition. Some skinny people may carry too much fat in comparison to their muscle content.

Very thin people can create high glucose levels if they eat incorrectly. Many believe that consuming sports and fruit drinks and a fat-free diet can make them immune; but even strong athletes with little body fat and high metabolism often eat a tremendous amount of calories. All that sugar and carbohydrate can be turned into more glucose than their bodies can handle. A test can tell you quickly: a blood sugar level greater than 125 is considered diabetic. Abnormal blood-fat levels can put a person at risk, so it is crucial to have a lipid screening. A person is in potential trouble if their triglyceride level is high and HDL cholesterol level is low.

A major contributing factor to developing diabetes is being overly fat.[20] Gaining eleven to eighteen pounds doubles the risk of developing type 2 diabetes. Just gaining ten pounds ups one's risk of heart disease, and gaining twenty pounds doubles a woman's chance of developing breast cancer. Although genetic background accounts for the disposition to being obese, the major culprits are overeating and under-exercising. Many Natives pay little attention to what they put in their mouths and take advantage of the American culture that presents food in extra-large sizes, in cheese-filled crusts, in easy-to-microwave containers, in lattes with heavy cream, and in fast food shops. McDonald's French fries servings have increased in size, as have the sizes of movie popcorn bags and buckets. Restaurant portions and bottles of soft drinks are often large enough for three people and are relatively cheap, mainly because they are made with trans fats and high-fructose corn syrup. *Outside* magazine recently cited a study by psychologist Paul Rozin, who found that despite the French propensity for fatty foods, only 7.4 percent of the French population is obese, compared to 22.3 percent of the American population. He found that an order of regular fries at McDonald's is 72 percent larger in the United States than in France; a Pizza Hut pizza is 32 percent larger; an average chocolate bar is 41 percent larger; an average Coca-Cola is 52 percent larger; an average hot dog is 52 percent larger; and an average serving of ice cream is 24 percent larger.[21]

Corn is produced on such a large scale that it can be sold cheaply as a sweetener, for high-fat and high-calorie snacks such as corn chips, and as feed to create fatter pigs and cattle. One rarely has to use many calories to acquire a meal unless one is a hunter who eschews deer blinds, stands, and ATVs and walks to stalk game; or one is skilled with a blow gun and can track squirrels, rabbits, and birds for hours; or one is a devout gardener who eats only what is grown in the home garden. Americans have adopted a sedentary lifestyle whereby we watch hours of television and play video games every day.

According to the National Center for Chronic Disease Prevention and Health Promotion, approximately 40 percent of the American population are obese and another 31.8 percent are overweight.[22] This problem is so pervasive that consumers can now buy items to fit their bulk: larger caskets and chairs, stronger beds, washcloths on "sticks," and plus-size clothes. A notable example of how Natives are affected by this deterioration in health is found in the 1994 diabetes care study revealing that Pimas in Mexico who ate more of a traditional diet were less fat and suffered less from diabetes than Pimas living in Arizona who ate a westernized diet of fattier foods.[23]

Physical problems associated with obesity are numerous. Overfat children and adults are prime candidates for cardiovascular disease, diabetes, high cholesterol levels, hypertension, orthopedic disorders, pancreatic disorders, respiratory diseases, and various cancers. Obesity also causes a variety of other problems, such as low self-esteem and lack of confidence; and it invites stereotyping.

Alcoholism is another by-product of colonization. In fact, alcohol abuse is the most widespread form of drug abuse in the country. It has touched most Natives either because they personally drink too much, or they have family or friends who do. Alcohol can cause cancers, can damage internal organs, and can cause problems with memory, concentration, judgment, and coordination; it can lead to bleeding gastritis or impotence in men and can damage fetuses and therefore damage the baby—a condition referred to as fetal alcohol syndrome. If alcohol is consumed in cold weather, hypothermia can result from the blood vessels dilating and allowing heat to escape the body. Over-consumption of alcohol can lead to liver failure, meaning the body can no longer process nutrients, and the heart can become weak and damaged. Alcohol inhibits the absorption of medication and adds a significant amount to the drinker's daily caloric intake. And it is not just the alcohol itself that can destroy the body; the effects of alcohol impair judgment, which has resulted in thousands of vehicle (car, boat, and motorcycle) accidents and homicides.

Tobacco, while not a food, is often associated with food. Some people smoke continually, some only sporadically, perhaps to curb their appetite, or they smoke after a meal. Smokers have difficulty breathing and may find walking—and certainly running—difficult. Tobacco is indigenous to the New World, but Indigenous people did not smoke themselves to death. Depending on the tribe, tobacco was and is associated with religion and ceremonies. "Indian Tobacco"—that is, tobacco without any additives (carcinogenic substances like the tar and nicotine found in commercial cigarettes)—is the common name for the plant *Lobelia inflata*, also known as asthma weed, gagroot, pulseweed, emetic herb, frengiotu, lobelia, wild tobacco, and vomitroot. This plant is used for medicinal purposes as an antispasmodic herb and a respiratory stimulant for conditions such as bronchial asthma and chronic bronchitis. The dried herb and the seed can also be used as an anti-asthmatic, diaphoretic (to induce sweating), diuretic, emetic, expectorant, and nervine (for calming) and can be used to treat whooping cough and pleurisy. The plant can be used externally in treating pleurisy, rheumatism, boils, and ulcers. Excessive use, however, can cause nausea, vomiting, and respiratory failure.[24]

The use of commercial tobacco today is a huge threat to Natives. Not only is it addictive, tobacco smoke also contains almost four thousand chemicals, and for every cigarette smoked, that smoker can expect to lose approximately 5.5 minutes of life expectancy. Smoking cigarettes and cigars is the major cause of lung cancer. It reduces fertility, severely damages the fetus, causes cancers of the pancreas, bladder, mouth, esophagus, and cervix. Even if you do not smoke, but someone in your household does, you are still vulnerable to these problems because of second-hand smoke. Dipping snuff can cause a variety of cancers, and vaping is now known to cause serious lung damage.

Some tribes have embarked on agricultural initiatives of various magnitudes in order to revitalize their traditional foods and ceremonies associated with planting, cultivating, harvesting, and eating. The Indigenous SeedKeepers Network, for example, seeks to "rematriate" heirloom seeds back to tribal communities.[25] Unfortunately, not every tribe can revert back to their traditional ways of eating. The Kiowas, Cheyennes, Arapahos, Plains Apaches, and Comanches now in Oklahoma did not farm historically and therefore have no agricultural tradition to revive. They face a dilemma when looking for cultural connections to traditional foods. Comanches, for example, once roamed over a vast area various ecosystems and myriad resources. Historically they ate mainly game meats, but they also relied on a variety of wild fruits and trade items (as well as food they raided, notably for corn, squash, and sheep).[26] The Comanche Nation has founded a diabetes awareness program and an environmental program that monitors hazardous materials in eight Oklahoma counties, but as of November 2017 it has no food sustainability plan. The monthly publication *Comanche Nation News* includes recipes for such foods as patty melts made with one stick of butter and eight slices of cheese; cabbage casserole with butter, Cheez Whiz, and grated cheese; pecan pie with butter, sugar, and dark Karo syrup; cottage pudding with flour, sugar, milk, and shortening; and a host of other recipes that include overabundances of fat, lard, sugar, and salt.[27] Cultural disconnection and the lack of both resources and food initiatives are among the reasons why Comanches suffer from high rates of diabetes and obesity.

It is not only people in Indian Country who feel the effects of environmental degradation, climate change, food-borne illnesses, industrial chemicals, and soil erosion.[28] Water and air are polluted, seafood is overharvested, and the cost of animal feed has risen. All consumers now face prices that are 40 percent higher than in recent years for bread, baked goods, canned vegetables, fruit, eggs, beef, pork, and chicken.[29] Avian flu, the porcine epidemic diarrhea virus, and excessively dry and wet seasons have resulted in sick animals and failed wheat, lettuce, and corn crops. Food sovereignty activists are situated in an economy in which four seed companies, Dow AgroSciences, DuPont/Pioneer, Monsanto, and Syngenta, control 80 percent of the corn market, 70 percent of the soybean market, and half of the world's seed supply.[30] Ten companies own almost every brand of food and beverage.[31] Environmental activist Wendell Berry sums up what we all want: "food that is nutritionally whole and uncontaminated by pesticides and other toxic chemical residues."[32]

All the ailments discussed here should be enough incentive to convince most people who eat poorly to consider a traditional diet, or at least to incorporate parts of a traditional lifestyle into their current unhealthy one. On a positive note, many people are acutely aware that numerous health problems arise from a poor diet and lazy lifestyle. Most people who are overweight, or those who suffer physical ailments because of poor lifestyle habits, are aware that their diets have in large part contributed to their situations. *Parade* magazine tells us that in 1993, one American out of five was on a diet to lose weight. Ten years later, that had risen to one in three. *U.S. News and World Report* states that at any time, 29 percent of men and 44 percent of women are dieting.[33]

But instead of getting thinner and fitter, we are becoming fatter and sicker. How did this happen?

As I have written in elsewhere, the major problems Indigenous peoples face—and still continue to deal with because there is no such thing as "postcolonial"—are many. They include loss of land; loss of population through war, sterilization, disease, policies of genocide, low birth rate as a result of poor health, changing cultures, and removal or relocation; a dependency on material goods that resulted in competition between tribes; alcoholism and other forms of self-abuse; a change of environment that includes a loss of plants and animals; gender role change (the loss of respect for females' important social, political, economic, and religious roles and the loss of men's hunting roles); factionalism within tribes or inter- and intra-tribal differences that lead to "culturalism" and "ethnocentrism"; a dilution and loss of cultural knowledge; dilution of "Indigenous blood" (there are more mixed-bloods than full-bloods today); depression and other mental problems associated with being disempowered; internalizing colonial ideologies that result in feeling confused about identity; feelings of inferiority, apathy, and helplessness; the continued subjugation of Natives because the ideology of Manifest Destiny is still in effect; a loss of intellectual rights (theft of knowledge by scholars and others for the purpose of personal gain); and continued monitoring of tribal governance policies and procedures by the federal government. Native voices are systematically subsumed, dismissed, and devalued in politics, academia, the entertainment industry, and publishing.[34]

The next case study elaborates on these themes by tracing how the forces of colonialism impacted health of tribes in Indian Territory after their removal in the 1830s. While this section focuses on the southern Plains, other tribes also felt the impacts of colonialism.

The previous chapter outlines the extreme change in Natives' health conditions (obesity, diabetes, heart disease, and so on) brought on by regressing from a diet of vegetables, fruits, and game meats and an active hunting/gathering/cultivating lifestyle to a daily routine of sitting still and consuming a processed, fatty, salted diet. We can see this every day around us in our communities and, sadly, in our own homes. The journey to diminished health begins in different places in time.

Kelly M. West, the "father of diabetes epidemiology," argued in 1974 that Natives did not develop diabetes until at least 1940 and probably 1950.[1] This is incorrect. Indians have been suffering from the effects of colonization, including food-related maladies, for hundreds of years. For example, a plethora of historical records—including trading-post and store inventories, boarding school grocery receipts, medical superintendents' reports, tribal languages, medicinal plant descriptions, and reports of resource depletion from environmental destruction—reveal that many southeastern tribespeople moved away from their traditional foods prior to their 1830s removals to Indian Territory. During the latter part of the eighteenth century some Indians in the Southeast began using store-bought sugar, wheat flour, and salt. They began feeling the repercussions of their diets before the Civil War, probably including pre-diabetes or type 2 diabetes. Oklahoma resident Wilburn Hill, who grew up in Indian Territory, summed up tribes' food-related health problems in 1938, stating, "The greatest enemy to the Indians was in the use of salt, fat, flour, sugar or anything else sweet."[2]

Changing Diets

From descriptions of the early explorers, along with early paintings and sketches of vigorous looking Indigenous men and women, one might believe that historical tribespeople did indeed enjoy pristine health. Reviews of medicinal plants used by the Five Tribes, however, reveal that Natives were felled by a variety of diseases, parasites, and wounds. Consumption of alcohol, acquired through the fur trade, also began to take a toll in the seventeenth century.[3] Romans noticed that people suffered from fevers in summer because of "violent heat" and rain. They fell ill during rainy seasons in areas that were converted to swamps for indigo cultivation, "when the air is most prodigiously loaden [sic] with corrupt moist effluvia." Natives also were ravaged by yellow fever in the mid-1760s.[4] Smallpox in particular took a heavy toll on the population, and when weakened tribal groups also faced loss of resources from drought and floods, they became vulnerable to even more illnesses.[5]

The removal ordeal in the 1830s weakened even the physically strongest. Thousands died both en route to Indian Territory and after arrival, from illness, exhaustion, and inadequate food, clothing, and shelter. After the physical and emotional devastation of removal, the Five Tribes struggled to reestablish their governments, farms, and homes, and they managed to do so in varying degrees of complexity and comfort. Affluent mixed-blood Natives had brought livestock with them across the removal trail and could afford to build large homes and to cultivate commercial corn, wheat, and cotton crops.[6] Many increased their stock raising to sell to Fort Gibson and to tribespeople arriving from the east as well as to those desiring to buy cattle to drive to California.[7] In 1837 the agent stated that it was difficult to estimate the number of cattle, horses, sheep, and hogs some of the Choctaws owned.[8]

At the same time that many among the Five Tribes prospered, others succumbed to diseases such as cholera, malaria, and consumption.[9] Five to six hundred Chickasaws and four to five hundred Choctaws died from smallpox in 1838. Others perished after drinking stagnant water when shallow waterways dried up in late summer.[10] In 1844 a large number of Chickasaws were

unprepared for the cold winter and perished.[11] And in spring
the Verdigris River flooded, then left behind "noxious effluvia" that caused "bilious and intermittent fevers" among the
Mvskogee Creeks.[12]

The Five Tribes quickly reestablished their governments,
erecting council houses and schools, and families built homes,
planting gardens and orchards. Tribal councils strengthened
laws and attempted to protect their lands and resources from
intruders.[13] But their socio-economic situation started to change.

As Indian Territory became crowded with non-Native intruders, a variety of complex environmental, social, economic, political, external, and intra-tribal factors accounted for disparities
in access to sustenance. Affluent residents had access to store
foods, while poorer families grew, gathered, and hunted their
own. Residents with incomes traveled to Arkansas to purchase
sundries, while others shopped in Sherman or McKinney, Texas.[14]
In the 1840s Ethan Allen Hitchcock traveled through the western Cherokee Nation and dined at the home of Cherokee High
Sheriff George Lowry. The meal reflected the resources available
to Lowry: bacon, butter, corn bread, chicken eggs, and venison,
washed down with coffee mixed with sugar and milk.[15]

Drought in 1860 and subsequent years caused crops to fail.[16]
During the Civil War soldiers passing through the Nations
destroyed crops, homes, and barns; killed livestock; and stole
clothing and tools. Game was depleted, as were family stores of
dried foods. Natives recalled eating whatever they could find.[17]
Confederate soldier Thomas F. Anderson wrote in 1863 that
his men consumed soup made of snails, screwworms, and bull-
frog legs.[18]

After the Civil War wild, fresh foods were still available, but the
less affluent residents often preferred to trade their homegrown
produce for processed foods. The cattle industry grew rapidly
among wealthy residents (usually mixed-heritage Indians and
opportunistic white men who married Native women), and their
families ate beef, drank milk, and had money to purchase coffee,

wheat flour, and sugared products. One gardener admitted that his preferred diet consisted of meats, bread, milk, and butter.[19]

Some Native families bemoaned their inability to afford store-bought goods, while others used them only occasionally. Many residents liked coffee, but if it was scarce, cooks often substituted parched okra, sweet potatoes, or corn.[20] A few 1880s residents stated that they did not like ground corn flour, and, conversely, some disliked wheat flour and only used it to bake biscuits on Sunday mornings.[21] One Choctaw man believed that white wheat flour was not healthy and did not buy any for his children.[22] A woman stated that when she was a child in the 1880s her family consumed wild game, berries, leaves, roots, and corn, and they never tasted wheat flour. Only after statehood (1907) did she taste beef.[23] Mrs. Greenwood LeFlore's popular boarding-house in the Choctaw Nation reveals the changing diet of her tribe. Her dining hall offered fresh and canned fruit and veg-etables. She also offered pork chops, beef steaks, and roasts in the hot summer months without ice by using a fifty-gallon oak barrel filled with meat and salt brine "strong enough to float an Irish potato."[24] Indicative of the increasing use of sugar is the experience of one white woman who attended camp meet-ings with her Indian neighbors and recalled that "one of their Negro cooks would spend the entire morning making custards or green apple pies."[25] One family ate few vegetables along with meat, but flour gravy and potatoes were their main foods. The mother commented that people used to call gravy "starch," and she often heard the remark, "I have eaten so much starch that I am stiff from it."[26]

"Spirituous" liquor contributed to the growing health and socio-political issues. Whiskey flowed through the tribal nations, resulting in astonishing numbers of murders, assaults, and cases of spousal abuse.[27] Leaders had attempted to stem the liquor tide pre-removal by passing laws against drinking, selling, and making whiskey. Cherokees organized a temperance society in 1845, and every year Indian Territory agents reported the abuse of alcohol and asked the federal government for assistance. Whiskey production never abated. For example, 90 percent of the cases heard at Fort Smith in 1889 had connections to the use of whiskey, and Agent Bennett estimated that at least one person died per day from the effects of liquor consumption.[28] Another favorite drink that could easily be made by Natives and non-Natives was "choc beer," consisting of barley, hops, and a bit of alcohol as the base. Recipe variations included oats, corn, malt, sugar, yeast, and fishberries, a fruit indigenous to eastern India. A constituent of fishberries—picrotoxin—is poisonous, and tribespeople used it to stun fish slightly and make them easy to catch, while another recipe eases nausea in humans. Miners liked choc beer, calling it a "tonic," rationalizing that the brew was preferable to the polluted water they drank around their work areas. Agent Windom called it "a fruitful source of evil, disorder and crime."[29]

Boarding Schools

Schools were also an influence in changing Cherokee diet in the second half of the nineteenth century. Between 1851 and 1909, thousands of young Cherokees were educated at the Cherokee Female and Male Seminaries: tribally created and managed boarding schools that, like colleges in the East, offered courses such as French, Latin, chemistry, and Shakespeare (the first teachers were from Mount Holyoke and Yale).[30] Ironically, unlike at federal boarding schools, which forcibly indoctrinated Native children to the ways of white society, Cherokees themselves established these seminaries in order to acculturate their children.[31] In fact, the curriculum eschewed lessons on traditional ceremonies associated with planting, cultivating, and harvesting, and teachers taught nothing about Cherokee culture except for lessons on the structure of the tribal government.[32] The schools provided small gardens for the students to supplement meals. Some parents traded wild game and unprocessed garden items for tuition, but produce was only available after harvesting and, if dried, into the fall and winter. Because students often came from families who normally consumed fruits, vegetables, and game meats, their systems had to adapt quickly to the vast array of seminary food items, including sugar, canned salted meats, eggs, butter, cheese, cream, table salt, lard, molasses, buttermilk, pies, cakes, and coffee as well as candy and sugar cookies bought during field trips to Tahlequah, the Cherokee capital.[33] Wheat flour and sugar were major ingredients in dishes three times a day. In 1879 seminary officials ordered 7,500 pounds of flour, 60 bushels of corn meal, 4,000 pounds of beef, 2,500 pounds of bacon, and 75 bushels of potatoes. For a one-month period in 1882 the food for 83 students, teachers, workmen, and washers at the seminary consisted of 1,600 pounds of flour and beef and hundreds of pounds of sugar, lard, coffee, rice, and pickles. In one 1887 order, in addition to rice, coffee, prunes, and molasses, school officials ordered 5,000 pounds each of flour and meat and hundreds of pounds of lard and cheese. Another listed 10,000 pounds of flour for 153 people for three months, with receipts for other years revealing similar food amounts.[34] By 1900 seminary officials regularly ordered "barrels" of sugar.[35] After 1901 both schools added to their lists chocolate, butterine (animal fat mixed with other ingredients), Eagle sweetened milk, and flour-based cereals Ralston Breakfast Food and Egg-O-See.[36]

Correspondingly, ailments among the seminarians proliferated in the 1870s as students faced the consequences of a calorie-dense diet featuring fatty, salty, and sugary foods: constipation, hemorrhoids, headaches, diarrhea, rheumatism, jaundice, colic, ulcers, and acne, while the physician became concerned about the girls' weight gain. Dozens of cases of "bowel complaint" appear on every medical report and the frequencies increased each year. In addition, many girls experienced irregular menstrual periods, one symptom of pre-diabetes.[37] In his 1899 annual report the Female Seminary physician stated that he believed their physical problems were due in part to lack of exercise.[38]

Some Cherokees continued their childhood diets into adulthood. One woman in 1969 stated that she had struggled with diabetes, high blood pressure, and "heart trouble" for at least thirty years. She also used tobacco her entire life ("I could chew it, smoke it, and twist it"). Her home meals consisted mainly of corn, but also pumpkins, crawdads, squirrels, hog's head, fried pies, cakes, onions and eggs fried in grease, and sugared grape and plum jelly. As she did not attend the Female Seminary, she had to pack her school lunches and filled her pail with biscuit and gravy sandwiches, or a biscuit and meat with fried potatoes, or fried eggs.[39]

Yet Choctaws had been consuming similar foods even earlier, before their removal from Mississippi and Kentucky. In the 1820s, for example, the Choctaw Academy in Kentucky served students apple dumplings, pies, bacon, butter, beef, coffee, milk, molasses, mutton, and rice.[40] When French military officer Marquis de Lafayette visited Johnson's Indian School at Blue Springs in 1825, the local women made a five-hundred-pound cheese wheel.[41] In the 1840s children at Armstrong Academy learned to make butter and cheese and consistently consumed these food items.[42] A visiting missionary to that academy in 1847 stated that during a dinner they were served plenty of cakes, pies, coffee, beef, and pork.[43] A white woman born in 1881 in the Choctaw Nation often dined with tribal members and enjoyed various corn dishes along with "great stacks of fried pies."[44] Another attended Choctaw dinners consisting of pit-roasted hogs, corn covered in gravy, and sugar-filled egg custards and pies.[45] The effects of such a diet were long term. Boarding school curricula also proved to be influential forces in the loss of tribal culture and language, including traditional Indigenous knowledge about planting, harvesting, plant identification, medicinal plants, and blessings or ceremonies associated with food procurement, thereby severing students' connection to the natural world. After these students left the seminaries, as well as other board-

ing schools, they brought their institutionalized ideas about
diet home with them.

Indians of other tribes likewise moved away from their traditional diets before Oklahoma statehood. A Quapaw woman
born in 1892 in Devil's Promenade grew up on a diet of beef,
flour, and coffee. Her sister was grossly obese and could not
play childhood games, while the tribe's sweat houses would
serve those suffering from rheumatism and dropsy.[46] In 1937
a Shawnee man stated that he grew up in Big Timber Hill in
Craig County, living first in a tipi and later a small cabin, and ate
bison and venison, sugar from maple trees, pumpkins, corn, wild
fruit, black-eyed peas, and goat milk. He prepared dried corn
with "plenty of grease" or "plenty of lard." He does not state
what he ate after adulthood, but by the time of the interview
diabetes had caused him to lose an eye as well as part of a foot.[47]
An eighty-eight-year-old Creek woman interviewed in1970 had
lost both of legs due to diabetes. She regularly consumed fried
pork and she recalled her father purchasing flour six hundred
pounds at a time.[48] Many residents of Oklahoma consumed
(and still do consume) grape dumplings, a dish made of wheat
flour, sugar, and opossum grape juice, but today most use com-
mercially processed grape juice.

Permanent Change?

In 1895 Special Agent John W. Lane commented on the dearth
of old people in the Choctaw Nation. Indeed, by the end of the
century, many older Choctaws, as well as members of the other
tribes, died from ill health. Many were not well educated and had
no access to physicians or to a variety of foods. Lane observed
that Choctaws grew an "abundance" of vegetables, although
most decayed quickly. They also suffered the consequences of
not understanding where to place their outhouses, improper
sanitation, and no dental care.[49] Many Natives had less active lives
than their ancestors. Romans described pre-removal Choctaw
work as "their labor vastly hard, either in the field for cultiva-

tion of corn, or fetching nuts, fire wood and water, which they chiefly carry on their backs . . . generally two or three miles." As children grew up, they wrestled, ran, swam, heaved, and lifted "great weights," and they regularly played the rigorous and often dangerous game of stickball.[50] While many of the less affluent tribespeople continued to stay active by hunting, gardening or farming, hauling water, and chopping wood, the wealthier families often hired workers to tend to their commercial farms and stock raising and did little daily work around their homes.

Medicine men and women continued to treat the more traditional Natives, but they were quickly losing respectability. Some acculturated, Christianized Natives claimed that Indian doctors "were very foggy in their belief."[51] Their practices were regarded as merely "mythical doctoring" or "faith doctoring."[52] Doubters preferred the dubious "tonics" and pills that were advertised in every newspaper and liberally dispensed by white physicians. Ailing residents were not advised to change their dietary habits. In addition, the Indian Territory environment changed. White intruders continued to flood onto tribal lands, taking every resource they could find. Tribes' National Council records show how much tribal land was impacted by human actions, such as fencing, dam building, timber harvesting, mining, railroad building, and the digging of lakes, in addition to drought, overgrazing, and large-scale planting of cotton, corn, and hay on the rich prairie lands. Serious ecosystem changes and resource depletion quickened through the mid- to late 1800s. By the mid-1860s, tribes became so alarmed at the rate at which their trees were being appropriated by non-Native intruders for exportation or for railroads that they passed laws against timber cutting.[53]

In the years preceding Oklahoma statehood, the numbers of intermarried whites and natives who ranched cattle escalated. Comparing modern data on the flora and fauna of Nvnih Chufvk with reported observations from the same area between 1850 and 1880 suggests that despite its relative isolation, many plants and animals on and around the mountain vanished, and the springs dried up, requiring the tribespeople to adjust and innovate.[54]

Tribal citizens had different ideas about the accumulation of wealth, and that necessarily included environmental protection. Tribal house and senate records detail continual amendments to tribal laws from 1830 to 1907 that were designed to protect tribal resources and to avert environmental damage. Of course these laws were also designed simultaneously to protect the investments of wealthy tribespeople.[55] While some Natives and whites killed an abundance of animals, many others were concerned about conservation. One Choctaw said in 1937 that he did not want the smaller animals to be "molested," like the deer, turkeys, and other large animals, so he allowed his boys to hunt for rabbits or squirrels only if someone needed soup.[56] Others also stated that they only killed one animal at a time.[57] Wealthy Choctaw Progressives supported the construction of railroads and mining. Wilson N. Jones, chief from 1890 to 1894, had more fenced cattle land than any other native in all of Indian Territory, and by 1890 he had become one of the Territory's wealthiest men—Indian or white.[58]

By the time of statehood many natives could not procure the varied and nutritious diet they had previously eaten. Flora and fauna depletion disallowed many people from foraging, hunting, and fishing, thus forcing them to barter for canned, salted, sugared, and pickled foods. Some were wealthy and could afford to eat whatever they wanted. Others, however, became desperate. One white man who lived among natives commented, "If a cow got sick or died, all you had to do was notify some of the Indians and they would drag it off, even though it had been dead three days."[59] Many Natives were forced to fill the dietary void with corn after the diminution of gathered fruits, vegetables, and herbs, essentially developing a nutritionally deficient mono-diet. In 1901, for example, U.S. marshal Jasper P. Grady visited Daniel Bell, who represented a faction of full-blood Choctaws, and observed, "The Indians are literally starving . . . they used to have plenty of hogs, cattle and ponies and could kill game, but they now have nothing to live on and are absolutely destitute. . . . A little Tom Fuller, which is nothing but cracked corn, and corn pone, is all the majority of them have to eat."[60] On the other hand, a man who lived with the Choctaws commented that the full-bloods did not care for milk or butter, and the mixed-bloods and whites used dairy products all the time.[61] It appears that many of the poorer families suffered from malnutrition, while others with money faced physical problems from too much food. Tribespeople around the country continued to diminish, especially the poorer individuals. For a variety of socio-economic reasons, including for some the adoption of the mind-set that "white food" was best, natives suffered—and continue to suffer—physically and emotionally.

West's claim that tribes did not develop diabetes until after World War II is important. Of the 202 sources West cites, all but three are from medical, diabetes, and nutrition publications. He used no ethnohistorical data, instead basing his conclusions on the absence of the word "diabetes" in medical records and in interviews he claims to have conducted with Oklahoma Indians. West also stated that he conducted an "extensive review" of the medical reports of civilian and military physicians who treated Oklahoma Indians between 1832 and 1939, asserting that "Oklahoma tribes had, for the most part, considerable medical attention in the 19th and early 20th centuries, often by the same physicians who were finding diabetes common in their white patients."[62] He found no evidence of diabetic Indians within those records. He does not identify the physicians whose records he reviewed, however, nor the tribes they treated, and there are no citations in his paper regarding the nineteenth century.

It is doubtful that he found many reports dated prior to the 1930s. There are many biographies about the lives of Indian Territory physicians, but their accounts of how and why they treated patients are scarce. Data given by military physicians assigned to reservations often lack detail, offering short discussions about the state of sanitary conditions (or lack thereof), statistics about outbreaks such as smallpox, and descriptions of inadequate government rations.[63] Also, among the Five Tribes (Cherokees, Chickasaws, Choctaws, Creeks, and Seminoles), medical records are scarce. In 1890, for example, the special agent in charge of the Choctaw census commented on inadequate record keeping among Choctaws. He stated that many of their census, legal, and health reports had been lost to insects, fire, or unnamed individuals who took them home. The National Records of the Five Tribes at the Oklahoma Historical Society mainly list registers of physicians and license and permit records.[64] In 1926 the Institute for Government Research authorized a detailed study of conditions on Indian lands. The lengthy "Meriam Report" revealed serious problems of poverty; poor health care, housing, and education; and lack of self-determination. The report also found that reservation, school, and hospital physicians did not keep adequate documentation.[65]

West's claim that tribes had "considerable medical attention," at least by white physicians, is also dubious. In the nineteenth century qualified doctors were scarce throughout Indian Territory.[66] In 1874, for example, Agent Breiner stated that within a sixty-mile perimeter of the Seminole Agency at Wewoka there was no physician at all.[67] And a woman born in 1889 who lived near Fort Sill and Tishomingo stated that she "never knew there were such things as doctors" until she was eighteen.[68] On the other hand, when aspiring physician E. O. Barker arrived in Guthrie in 1889, hoping that it would be a good place to start his practice, he found seventy-five men claiming to be physicians were already there. He stated that if anyone in a crowd should call "doctor" that "one third of the audience would answer."[69] However, many who referred to themselves as physicians had only a modicum of training and may not have had the wherewithal to recognize symptoms of diabetes.[70]

Throughout Indian Territory the problem of quacks was so extensive that tribes enacted laws regarding any nontribal citizen who desired to practice medicine in their nations. In 1879 the Chickasaws passed a law requiring that aspiring physicians provide to the governor of the nation three citizen recommendations testifying to his moral character, and a $5 fee, as well as "a recommendation that he is a practicing physician from the board of the county and state from which he came."[71] In 1881 the Cherokees passed a similar law and required a $25 fee.[72] The Choctaw and Muskogee-Creek Nations passed comparable laws in 1884 and 1892, respectively.[73] Dr. E. N. Wright, who served as president of the Indian Territory Medical Association, found that "the ignorance discovered in those exams was appalling" and that many who claimed to be doctors had never even attended college.[74] By 1888, noncitizen physicians in the Choctaw Nation refused to take the medical exam.[75] In 1904 Congress became so concerned that it reiterated tribal laws in a further effort to regulate the influx of pseudo-physicians in Indian Territory.[76]

West makes no mention of tribal medicine, but not every Indian wanted to be treated by someone other than their tribal doctor (that is, medicine man or woman). Numerous Indian agents note the popularity of tribal medicine, such as the Cherokee Agency agent who wrote in 1853 that full-bloods "prefer the roots and herbs of their own native doctors."[77] In 1884 the agent at Osage Agency stated that the Osages "seem wholly under the influence of the medicine men."[78] The commissioner in 1889 expressed annoyance with tribes' "superstitious regard for the grotesque rites of the 'medicine men.'"[79] Creek chief Isparhecher made the news in 1896 after refusing to be treated by a white physician and was only willing to allow a Creek medicine man to heal him.[80] In 1924 the commissioner stated that members of the Five Tribes tended not to seek out medical help when needed, so field matrons and nurses, not doctors, would come to their homes.[81] In 1968 a Cherokee woman commented, "I've known of some white doctors that kind of make fun of the Indians, their Indian medicine."[82] Today some Indians will consult with white physicians, but only in conjunction with medicine men or women;

some prefer tribal doctors exclusively; and some refuse to see any doctor or dentist. Although some Indians agreed to accept medical treatment at the hospital in Lawton, Oklahoma, where West conducted some research, he does not explore the possibility that many Natives in the early twentieth century may not have wanted to be treated there, or at any other facility he mentions.

Medical care is exponentially better today than in 1940 and certainly prior to that time also. Information about diabetes is readily available, yet more than 8 million Americans with diabetes were undiagnosed in 2012.[83] If undiagnosed diabetes is common now, quite possibly there were Indians whose diabetes went unrecognized prior to 1940. West interviewed Indians frequenting the clinic in Lawton, Oklahoma, in 1973 who stated that they did not have diabetes prior to 1936. He also writes that in the twenty-five years prior to the publication of his 1974 essay, he interviewed "several hundred" Oklahoma Indians older than the age of seventy from more than twenty tribes. Unfortunately, West does not provide information about their tribal affiliations, their state of health, the dates of the interviews, or where he spoke to them, nor does he say if he needed translators or whether the elderly subjects were leery of him. In a later 1978 study he again discusses these informants and reveals that he offered one dollar for "any account of diabetes prior to 1940."[84] As a result, depending on how he framed his questions, the interviewees may have simply told him what he wanted to hear. Oral testimonies can be valuable sources of information, but only if one takes into account all such factors. It could be that the informants did indeed know people with diabetes, but they were not diagnosed, or perhaps they categorized their ailment(s) as something else. For example, one diabetic unfamiliar with the word diabetes stated she had a "thirst" and wanted to "drink and drink."[85] As late as 1969 another Cherokee woman commented that she had never heard the term "sugar diabetes" until 1958, so even though she knew of people who probably had it, she described their problem as an "ache."[86]

In 1974 West conducted a blood glucose-tolerance study of 124 Cherokee and 80 Kiowa and Comanche subjects and found that Cherokees had a higher plasma glucose reading. He commented that Plains tribes had been on a "low carbohydrate diet" for centuries, while "starches" made up the majority of the Cherokees' diets.[87] One might take that to mean agricultural groups have higher frequencies of the diabetic genotype than those tribes deemed hunters and gatherers, but these categorizations may not be as clearly defined as some researchers have asserted.[88] In fact, prior to Cherokees' removal in the 1830s, they did not consume only starches. Families cultivated backyard gardens of corn, squashes, green beans, and the European and African-introduced watermelons, black-eyed peas, turnips, and fruit trees, at least, but they supplemented that produce with nut meats (acorn, pecan, walnut, and hickory) and oils as well as deer, squirrels, rabbits, bears, waterfowl, turkeys, quail, pigeons, turtles, and fish; and hogs brought by the Spanish. Segments of the Cherokee population had been eating beef since at least the 1820s. They continued to consume meats after removal. "There were all kinds of game in the woods," one Indian Territory resident stated in 1937. "It was a man's laziness if he did not have any meat."[89]

Second, there were (and still are) physiological differences between members of the Cherokee Nation. Because of racial mixing since the 1700s among Cherokees, whites, and African slaves, as well as freedmen after the Civil War, one cannot generalize Cherokee genetic backgrounds. Then and now, religious adherence, language use, political affiliation, wealth and value of landholdings, and skin and hair color are just some of the possible differences. John Ross, who served as Cherokee chief from 1828 to 1866, was one-eighth Cherokee, while students at the Cherokee Female and Male Seminaries in the 1880s ranged from full-blood to just $1/128$ degree of Cherokee heritage. Even preceding their removal from the Southeast to Indian Territory in the 1830s many full-blood and mixed-blood Cherokees behaved like well-off whites, including having similar diets. Some individuals in the late nineteenth and early twentieth centuries became attorneys, dentists, physicians, and teachers, while others farmed or labored.[90] Furthermore, in 1890 the Cherokee Nation's population was scattered over 7,800 square miles of terrain that included forests, rivers, creeks, rolling hills and valleys, and prairies—not all of it suited for farming. In other words, not everyone had access to the same resources.[91]

Less affluent Cherokees stayed active by hunting, gardening, farming, hauling water, and chopping wood. By contrast, the wealthier residents did little daily work around their homes because they often hired workers to tend to their commercial farms and stock animals. By the late 1830s some tribespeople had started growing corn on a large scale for profit, and in 1856 residents stated that they raised mainly crops of corn, oats, rye, and wheat, followed by peas and potatoes, in addition to large orchards of apples, peaches, pears, and plums.[92] Moreover, many residents frequented well-stocked stores such as J. W. Stapler and Sons in Tahlequah or other trading posts such as the one in Wauhillau.[93] Not every Cherokee could afford to purchase canned salmon, but many saved their money to purchase sugar, flour, and canned goods.

Diabetic Indians recall that they did not eat corn prepared in traditional ways growing up in late nineteenth-century and early twentieth-century Indian Territory. They stated that instead they often ate bowls of dried and ground corn sweetened with equal parts sugar and added animal grease rather than nut oil. Some bought buckets of lard from trading posts for that purpose, and many soaked their corn in cow's milk.[94]

Third, since the early twentieth century, Comanches have been eating much the same foods items as everyone else.[95] Because of both the demise of bison and the men's inability to roam to find game, after their semi-confinement to their reservation in the 1870s they hunted sporadically for only a few decades. Some took to farming and were able to supplement the poor government rations of stringy beef, flour, coffee, and sugar, in addition to occasionally foraging for plants. By the time that West conducted his test in the early 1970s, with few exceptions Comanches and Kiowas had not been hunting bison or other large game animals for over eighty years—about three generations.

Further, the Comanches West studied were not just one group. They initially were part of the Shoshones who lived in the Great Basin, then Idaho and Wyoming, and some moved to parts of the Great Plains. They hunted but also gathered foods nuts, seeds, and roots. Those who became known as Comanches broke from the main group around 1700. Numerous bands roamed on horseback over Comancheria, that is, a vast area with various resources, taking in parts of eastern New Mexico, North and West Texas, western Indian Territory, southeastern Colorado, and southwestern Kansas.[96] Their diets depended on the environments and resources available. Comanches were not known as "Lords of the Plains" for nothing: they stole corn, squashes, and other food resources from Pueblo tribes and Wichitas and also raided Navajos, Apaches, and Utes.[97] During this time they followed game onto the plains, and after settling at Fort Sill, Comanches gathered a number of plant foods, including camas, wild grapes, hackberries, juniper berries, mulberries, onions, persimmons, plums, prickly pear cactus fruit, sumac fruit, nuts, sunchokes, mesquite beans, and lotus.[98] They also have a long history of racial mixing with captives, most notably Mexicans, but also Spanish people, whites, and members of other tribes. Significantly, therefore, their mixed-heritage offspring carry a variety of genetic backgrounds—not only those stemming from hunter-gatherer ancestors.[99]

West's claims about the appearance of diabetes in the mid-twentieth century matter because the causes of high rates of diabetes, obesity, and related maladies among tribes cannot be easily explained. In order to understand health problems in 1974 and today, one must look carefully to the past. There were forces at work besides Indians just eating the wrong things and not exercising. Food-related illnesses and diseases are inextricably interrelated with historical and modern politics, economics, culture, environmental issues, and genetics.

After invaders arrived, diseases decimated Indigenous populations, their lands were systematically reduced, and tribes were removed from their homelands and resources. Children at federal boarding schools lost connections to their languages and religious traditions, including ceremonies associated with foods. Environmental damage in Oklahoma began before the Civil War. The Five Tribes passed numerous laws in efforts to protect their dwindling assets from deforestation, mining, overgrazing, overhunting, mining, and damming. Oklahoma tribes lost even more land through the Dawes Severalty Act.[100] Today many tribal members are educated about nutrition and can afford to eat nourishing foods and to exercise, but they choose not to. Conversely, others want to eat properly but cannot because they are impoverished and lack access to adequate sustenance, or they must contend with pollution, lack of water, climate change, resource depletion, corporate-owned plant pollen that drifts onto tribal crops, and seed-ownership issues that imperil their efforts at seed saving. As discussed in case study 3,following chapter 3, Navajos underwent similar changes. The tribe went from cultivating beans, chilies, corn, melons and squash to heartily accepting the introduction of sheep by the early 1800s. Throughout the first half of that century Navajos continued to consume fruits, vegetables, sheep, and game meats, but by the 1860s the tribe was overwhelmed by the intrusive Americans who proceeded to force them onto a reservation where farming was difficult. They could no longer rely on the land for sustenance and depended on near-inedible government rations, especially meat. Around this time they began consuming lard, sugar, tea, and coffee. Through the 1930s and 1940s the tribespeople also continued to eat fruits, vegetables, and meats, but in the 1950s their diet continued to change when they became dependent on trading store foods such as canned milk, lard, peanut butter, sugar, wheat flour, and soda pop. While many families still raised their own vegetable foods, others continued to consume processed foods that had once been unknown to them.

At the same time that diets were changing, so was the level of physical activity. After being confined to reservations, tribal members were not only too disheartened to "play"; they also were too busy trying to survive on poor food the government provided. Hunting societies of the plains lost the opportunity to hunt rigorously and butcher game animals. Tribes who previously depended on foraging could not range about, either. The exception to the Natives who were unable to move about were some of the students at boarding schools who played on basketball, baseball, and football teams. But even then, their diets were not optimal, and after they left the schools, many had no sports teams to play on. Unless they ran, or worked the family farm or ranch, their level of physical activity dropped.

3. Challenges to Recovering Health

As discussed in the previous chapter, modern Indigenous peoples are suffering from diabetes, obesity, high blood pressure, and other food- and environment-related maladies. Many do not have access to healthful foods, some are not educated about proper nutrition, and everyone is susceptible to the negative impacts of global warming and to the loss of resources.

Organizations made up of determined tribal members have initiated numerous food projects, including educational programs, seed distribution, food summits, farmers' markets, cattle and bison ranches, and community and school gardens.[1] These enterprises are steps toward achieving what many food activists refer to as Indigenous food sovereignty (IFS), though there are various ideas about what IFS is, or can be. Further, there is no universal solution to achieving IFS. Tribal food self-sufficiency involves the coordination of complex social, political, religious, economic, and environmental concerns. Those efforts vary by tribe because tribes adapted to colonization differently and do not have the same access to the resources; consequently their food sovereignty goals—if they even have any—also differ. Many do not have any. British food activist Raj Patel, writing about the idea of food sovereignty in general, comments that "there are so many versions of the concept, it is hard to know exactly what it means," a statement that certainly applies to Indigenous people in the United States.[2] The most complete vision of Indigenous food sovereignty as a concept is defined in the 2007 Declaration of Nyéléni: "The right of peoples to healthy and culturally appropriate food produced through ecologically sound and sustainable methods, and their right to define their own food and agricultural systems." The declaration also asserts that food sovereignty "ensures that the rights to use and manage lands, territories, waters, seeds, livestock, and biodiversity are in the hands of those of us who produce food."[3]

Ideally, then, to be a "food sovereign" tribe would mean that the tribe has the right to control its food production, food quality, and food distribution. It would support tribal farmers and ranchers by supplying machinery and technology needed to plant and harvest. The tribe would not be answerable to state regulatory control and would follow its own edicts, regulations, and ways of governance. Its members would have educational and job opportunities. The tribe would decide collectively if it wanted to purchase foods produced outside its boundaries or to trade with other groups. The tribe would have renewable energy infrastructure, such as solar and wind power.[4] Elders would be honored for their ability to teach language and impart traditional Indigenous knowledge about planting, harvesting, seed saving, hunting, basket and tool making, and ceremonies associated with sustenance. They would remind us about traditions among many tribes regarding female deities who originally brought them sustenance. Rather than viewing environmental resources as commodities for monetary gain, tribal members would show reverence for the land that sustains them. They would protect and respect the natural world because thriving relationships between healthy ecosystems and Indigenous peoples underlie tribal political, social, and religious systems. For Indigenous activists concerned with food injustice, that would be the ideal scenario. But is food sovereignty, defined in this way, possible? Or is food sovereignty just an ideal we will always strive to achieve?

Oklahoma in particular presents opportunities for discussion about challenges Indigenous people face in their quest to achieve food sovereignty, good physical well-being, and the health of the natural world. Oklahoma became a state in 1907. It has a multifaceted, complicated, and tumultuous history. Today the thirty-eight tribal nations in the state face environmental issues, partisan politics, uneven food quality, poor Indigenous health, intra-tribal factionalism, trenchant racism, and the glaring dichotomy between those tribal members who are affluent and those who suffer from extreme poverty.

The reasons for these health changes are complex. Boarding schools, missionaries, and intermarriage with whites contributed to the disassociation from tribal language, religion, and foodways. Particular population groups that were affected include tribal members who were affluent—a group that included full-blooded Native persons, though most were racially and culturally mixed—and Native students at the boarding schools, who were fed white flour and sugar three times a day. These populations developed digestive disorders, with some becoming diabetic or prediabetic. In addition, as non-Native intruders surged into Indian Territory throughout the 1800s, the plants and animals Indians once used for sustenance and medicine diminished. The ecosystems were transformed by dams, mines, deforestation, invasive species, and ranching. Those Native people who could not afford to purchase store goods survived on what they could grow; some suffered from malnutrition. The bison herds diminished, drastically altering the lifeways of Plains tribes. After being placed in Indian Territory in the late 1800s, Comanches, Cheyennes, Kiowas, and other hunters were forced to depend on inadequate rations provided by the federal government.[5]

Many tribal members who do not qualify for government commodities find that stores are not conveniently located, and the products stocked are inadequate. For example, across the 2,251 square miles of the Osage reservation in Osage County there are only four grocery stores, making it a "super food desert." Most of the land is devoted to livestock ranching, not agriculture, and there is no public transportation.[6] Most stores on Indian land sell produce that comes from farms that use genetically modified seeds. These pest-resistant crops grow bigger and more quickly, but they are less nutritious and leave behind eroded and depleted soils.[7]

Among Oklahoma Indians the lack of food, or lack of nutritious food, results from a combination of their having no money to purchase it; being dependent on the government; having no control over resources; and being unable to produce food. Some Indians have eaten their traditional foods, hunted, and gardened their entire lives. Most, however, have not. Natives who take advantage of the commodities offered under the USDA's Food Distribution Program on Indian Reservations (FDPIR) have about one hundred food-buying choices, but often they opt for white flour, lard, cheese, and sugary, and salty items. Notably, food distribution commodities are available to low-income tribal members who live within a tribal nation's boundaries.[8] Yet not all residents on tribal lands are members of that tribe, and given the differing food histories of various tribes, their food choices are likely both to be different and to affect the diets of those around them. For example, the majority of the 233,126 persons residing within the Choctaw Nation are not Choctaws.[9] In addition, in Oklahoma's program, as long as one member of a federally recognized tribe lives in the residence, non-Indians also in the home can receive commodities under the FDPIR. Non-Indians' food choices may not include items that are healthy or culturally connected to the tribe, and their preferences might influence what food is in the house.

"Traditional" Foods

Health and traditionalism intertwine. Tribal members can consume nonindigenous foods and be healthy, but food sovereignty activists are hopeful that a return to traditional foodways will provide something more: empowering links to their cultures and histories. As discussed in case study 3, "Frybread," not everyone agrees on what constitutes their tribes' "traditional" foods. The Choctaw Nation's website and its 2017 calendar, for example, feature some reasons why many tribal members are obese and diabetic: a "traditional" recipes section heavy on unhealthy food items, including sugar, white flour, cheese, and butter, used for making grape dumplings, cheddar and corn chowder, crisp salt pork, cobblers, fried corn, frybread, Indian tacos, and creamed "Indian corn" (sugar, flour, milk, and pork). A sweet potato dish that would be flavorful without any seasoning calls for adding two cups of sugar and one cup of flour.[10] The Chickasaw Nation does the same, with "Chickasaw" appearing in the names of some dishes that lack Indigenous ingredients.[11] Similarly, Osage cooking classes teach young tribal members how to make "Indian food," such as wheat flour rolled out in the "Osage custom"—that is, fried in hot grease—as well as to how to cook chicken and dumplings, and meat with wheat gravy.[12]

One can eat some truly traditional foods and still not become healthy because at the same time that people might eat a nutritious plate of steamed corn, beans, and squash from their garden, they then supplement those healthy foods with fatty meat, sugary drinks and desserts, and greasy sides such as French fries or fatty, mayonnaise-laden macaroni or potato salad. Those same healthy servings of corn, squash, beans, potatoes, game meats and other New World foods are no longer as nutritious if they are prepared with grease, lard, butter, and heavy doses of salt.

If one's goal is to eat only precontact foods, then the menu might include alligator, elk, waterfowl, deer, antelope, wild turkey, and bison. Those animals would have to be hunted or raised, both of which options would require financial planning. Traditional foods are not consistently available, so some food projects and families might use only a few Indigenous foods as symbols of culture. For example, the Delawares were originally hunters and coastal people who were removed several times before settling in Indian Territory in 1867. They no longer have access to marine life, so they stock their ponds with fish, hold annual fishing tournaments, and teach their children to hunt.[13]

Commodities

One way Natives are succumbing to a host of physical problems is because of commodities that are distributed to tribes for those members who live in a certain proximity to their Nations. "Commods" from the FDPIR now include cultural foods such as salmon, wild rice, and blue corn meal, but choices also includes foods high in carbohydrates and trans fats. Natives who take advantage of this program can chose among eighty or so different foods, but if they choose the white flour, lard, cheese, sugared and salty foods, how is this benefiting them? Unless they are educated and select the fresh produce—fruits, vegetables, and meats that are low in fat, sugar, and salt (or can be rinsed and drained)—or supplement the government foods with grocery-bought fresh vegetables, they are well on their way to becoming ill.

Some tribes have vested economic interests in producing foods such as cattle, wheat, hogs, and sorghum, none of them Indigenous. However, supplying traditional foods to their members may not be their goal. Hunting tribes followed bison herds for hundreds of miles each year, and obviously they cannot do that today. The Quapaw Tribe of Indians moved to Indian Territory in 1834 and settled on ninety-six thousand acres in what is now Quapaw County.[14] Traditionally Quapaws hunted, gathered, and farmed, but like other tribes, they were not ranchers.[15] In June 2016 the Quapaw Tribe opened the Quapaw Mercantile, the distribution center for the Quapaw Cattle Company. The store sells beef and bison ribeye steaks, beef bacon, and bratwurst from the tribe's herds in Miami and Quapaw. They provide meat to the tribe's elder center, daycare centers, and the Quapaw and Downstream Casino restaurants. The tribe is in the process of designing its own meat-processing plant and has plans to grow feed for the animals.[16] The Iowa, Modoc, Cheyenne, and Arapaho Tribes and the Cherokee Nation raise bison. Some ranchers crossbreed bison with cattle to create beefalo.

Poverty

Food security has been defined as all members of a household having, at all times, "physical and economic access to sufficient, safe, and nutritious food that meets their dietary needs and food preferences for an active and healthy life."[17] Eric Holt-Giménez writes, "Where one stands on hunger depends on where one sits."[18] Some Natives in the United States are affluent and can buy whatever they want; others are poverty-stricken and have little opportunity for economic or social advancement.

The Choctaw Nation of Oklahoma lands consist of 10,613 square miles of rural area in eleven counties in southern Oklahoma. In 2016 the Choctaw Nation had nine thousand workers on a payroll of $300 million. The tribe operates seven casinos, thirteen travel plazas, twelve smoke shops, two Chili's franchises, a resort in Durant, and document-archiving companies. Along with manufacturing operations, it manages seven Black Angus cattle ranches and provides other management services. In 2018 the tribe's assets totaled $2.4 billion.[19]

My tribe should not be impoverished, yet despite the millions of dollars produced each year, some of the poorest counties in the country are within the Choctaw Nation. A high proportion of residents in Atoka, Coal, Haskell, Latimer, LeFlore, McCurtain, Pittsburg, and Pushmataha counties have high-risk factors such as smoking, obesity, physical inactivity, and low consumption of fruit and vegetables. Those who do find work receive low wages. Recognizing the dire situation, in 2014 President Barack Obama named the Choctaw Nation one of five "Promise Zones." The award entails tax incentives for businesses that invest in the community and promises them "competitive advantage" when applying for federal grants.[20]

After the Promise Zone award was received, the tribe's chief business and economic development officer enlisted several Choctaws with expertise in traditional foods, medicine, and gardening to brainstorm strategies for a farm-to-table agriculture initiative. The focus was to be on nutrition and natural medicines, in addition to Native foods, backyard gardens, "agri-art," farmers' markets, and other endeavors. The new tribal chief elected that year, however, dismissed the business development officer, thereby severing ties with those of us who had contributed a plethora of ideas to the Promise Zone initiative. The initiative's leadership then created the Choctaw Small Business Development Services (CSBDS), which currently offers advice, planning, and counseling for tribal entrepreneurs, but not financial support.[21] One of its stated goals is that "natural, historic, and cultural resources" serve as the foundation for initiatives, including "technology-enhanced traditional farming and ranching," large greenhouses, and training for women business owners.[22] Choctaws did not traditionally ranch, so it is not clear what is meant by "traditional farming and ranching." Indeed, backyard gardens had been among the suggestions initially submitted to the Choctaw Promise Zone initiative. Families desirous of cultivating gardens would have been given seeds, basic tools, soil, and water. The tribe would finance the plowing of land and would provide basic gardening lessons. But that idea was discarded by the new administration. The monthly tribal newspaper, the BISKINIK, includes columns about traditional foods, but other than one large "Choctaw Hoop House," there are no Indigenous gardens or classes to teach tribal members how to grow these foods or gather them.[23]

Part of the Choctaw Nation's plan is to create an educated workforce that can succeed in the business world. This is a crucial initiative, considering that Oklahoma is ranked forty-ninth in the nation in educational services and performance.[24] If that workforce education strategy is to include implementing "traditional" farming methods, the workforce must know how to cultivate traditional foods and how to save seeds. The plan calls for partnerships with Oklahoma State University, Eastern Oklahoma State College, and the Kiamichi Technology Center.[25] However, none of those schools offers courses dealing with Choctaw history and culture.

Some tribes include foodways in their school curriculums, or have started their own healthy lifestyle programs, but they are not always successful in reaching the people who most need the assistance. Unless members are also self-educated from books, magazine articles, and news programs that discuss the correlation between diet and exercise, then more than a few Natives will fall through the cracks in the attempt to fix the health problems we are facing.

For low-income seniors residing in the Choctaw Nation's eleven-county area, the Nation has instituted the Senior Farmers' Market Nutrition Program. Qualified seniors receive $50, and an additional 3,800 participants receive $30, to purchase locally produced foods. Non-Natives over sixty years of age living in a household that includes one enrolled Choctaw are eligible for checks. Funded by both the USDA and the Choctaw Nation, the program is "designed to encourage participants to make better food choices and raise awareness of farmers and farmers markets." Only about half of the ninety-five farmers who sell produce to the market are tribal members, however, which does not advance the purpose of supporting tribal farmers.[26]

An additional concern is lack of data regarding what consumers do with the produce. The Choctaw Nation has a number of health initiatives, but there is little research regarding their success beyond the number of people using the vouchers. The tribal newspaper includes articles about diabetes, obesity, and exercise, and the Diabetes Multi-Resource Task Force travels across the Choctaw Nation to educate tribal members about healthy lifestyles. However, as seen on Choctaw Nation calendars, the nation's website, and at tribal celebrations, the tribe also provides and promotes unhealthy food.

Impact of Diminished Health-Care Funding

As of March 2018, the Trump administration had weakened the Affordable Care Act (ACA) and continues to seek its repeal. Through the Indian Healthcare Improvement Act (IHCIA), which is part of the ACA, Indian health centers can bill third-party insurers, Medicare, and Medicaid. Almost 2.2 million people who use the Indian Health Service (IHS) will be impacted negatively if the ACA is repealed.[27] The IHS could potentially lose more than $800 million in funding from Medicaid programs.[28]

The Choctaw Nation recently completed a 143,000-square-foot regional medical clinic, the first tribal clinic in the United States with an outpatient ambulatory surgery center. The ambitious project provides dental services, podiatry, endoscopy, pediatrics, respiratory therapy, cardiology, and diabetic and pulmonology care in addition to behavioral health services and an on-site laboratory.[29] The tribe paid for the construction of the facility, and the IHS works with Congress to provide funding for staff. Considering that President Trump has called for a 16.2 percent cut in funding for the Department of Health and Human Services, this is cause for alarm.[30] Everyone needs medical and dental care. Nonetheless, to improve physical and mental health and avoid hospital visits to treat maladies caused by poor diet and inactivity, it is key to adopt an exercise regime and a diet of unprocessed and fresh foods, and to quit smoking. Indeed, significant hurdles must be overcome in order to return at least partially to traditional ways of eating (or at least to have nutritious food), to maintain a healthy environment, and to inspire tribal pride through recovering cultural knowledge.

Access to Traditional Foods by Treaty: Hunting, Fishing, and Gathering Rights

Treaties between tribes and the federal government are legally binding contracts that contain assurances of self-determination, health care and educational services, religious freedom, and rights to hunt and fish. The federal government has a responsibility to protect tribal treaty rights, lands, and resources. Those who were forcibly sent to Indian Territory were understandably suspicious of government promises, as are their descendants. Removal treaties guaranteed that tribes would retain their lands, but Oklahoma has a long history of racism and dispossessing tribes of their property—27 million acres during the allotment period. Portraits of men such as Governor Haskell, who stole land from tribes during the allotment period, hang in the statehouse.[31] The discovery in 1897 of oil under Osage lands not only resulted in the murders of dozens of tribal citizens at the hands of unscrupulous whites intent on taking their resources but also caused socio-economic rifts within the tribe.[32] University of Oklahoma students are nicknamed "Boomer Sooners," after the intrepid pioneers who illegally jumped the gun on the Appropriations Act of 1889 in order to claim land belonging to tribal peoples.

Tribes must know how to negotiate the various challenges from outside forces—(such as racism, climate change, and pollution) as they relate to the powers of their tribe, the states, and the federal government—as well as how to negotiate the abrogation of treaty agreements that guarantee water, hunting, fishing, and gathering rights. Several treaties in the 1830s guaranteed the Cherokees "free and unmolested use" of lands not within the bounds of the Cherokee Nation.[33] It was not until 2015 that the Cherokee Nation became the first tribe to sign a compact giving their members hunting and fishing rights in all seventy-seven counties in Oklahoma. Cherokees over the age of sixteen can receive one "dual license" (Cherokee Nation and Oklahoma) and one free turkey and deer tag per year. Beginning in January 2017 Choctaw Nation citizens in Oklahoma did not have to pay for licenses either; the tribes pay a fee for each tag received, and Oklahoma, in turn, receives federal monies for wildlife conservation.[34]

These are indeed important compacts, but one cannot (or should not) just pick up a gun and go hunting. Procuring a deer or turkey requires skill, patience, and knowledge of hunting safety and protocols. Proper equipment and clothing are expensive. Moreover, physical fitness is essential for those who stalk birds all day or who must drag a heavy animal back to camp. Then it must be dressed and butchered. Although some Natives are adept at using traditional blowguns, rabbit sticks, and bows to hunt small animals, it should be recognized that not everyone has the wherewithal to hunt game.

Traditional Foods and Ecosystem Changes

A return to traditional ways of eating requires access to healthy ecosystems and their resources. After the 1830s removal to Indian Territory, serious environmental changes and resource depletion resulted from human activities, including building fences, dams, and railroads; harvesting timber, mining, and digging reservoirs; and overgrazing rangeland, which increased the likelihood of drought. For example, in the 1830s streams of clear water crossed much of the Choctaw Nation's fertile land, making it lush with edible plant foods. After removal my family settled in Atoka County then moved to the Kully Chaha (High Spring) township in the shadow of Nvnih Chufvk (Sugar Loaf Mountain), once deemed by both Choctaws and newspaper reporters an "oasis" of springs, bountiful game, nuts, and berries.[35] Despite the relative isolation of this area, there were losses: nearby cattle ranching, diversion of waterways, and deforestation caused the disappearance of some wild fruit plants, turkeys, deer, and pollinators. Many Natives stated that they were careful not to overhunt, and throughout the Choctaw Nation the complaints were the same: when white intruders arrived on their lands, the herds and flocks declined—some said to the point of "extinction"—mainly because whites engaged in unchecked sport and market hunting.[36] To address severe wildlife depletion, in 1895 the Oklahoma Territorial Legislature created the first game laws.[37] Fish and game shortages and environmental problems remain, however.

Blundering Intruders and Environmental Damage

Nancy Turner and colleagues use the term "blundering intruders" to describe policies and external projects that impede Indigenous peoples' efforts to protect their cultures, resources, and independence.[38] A major blunderer is Oklahoma's fracking industry, which opens fissures into the earth in order to extract oil and gas with high-pressure forcing of sand, liquid, and sometimes chemicals. The waste liquid from fracking often flows into underground aquifers and pollutes water and soil.[39] The rocks fracture because of the force of the injection. Disposal wells holding millions of gallons of liquid cause faults to slip, resulting in earthquakes; the state of Oklahoma has the highest number of induced earthquakes in the country. There were 889 earthquakes in 2015, and 1,055 from March 2017 to March 2018.[40] A September 2016 earthquake damaged the Pawnee Nation's administrative buildings and tribal members' homes. The Nation responded by filing suit against the Bureau of Indian Affairs and Bureau of Land Management in an effort to rid their Nation of drilling permits and oil and gas leases on their land, which the agencies approved without consulting the tribe or adhering to natural resource protection laws.[41]

Fracking is not the only problem. In June 2017 the Oklahoma Department of Environmental Quality warned that fish in fifty-four Oklahoma lakes have high levels of mercury and that consumers should limit their intake of these fish.[42] The Poncas, who were removed to Indian Territory from Nebraska in the 1870s, report that fish in the nearby Arkansas River are contaminated by raw sewage and a ConocoPhillips refinery and other factories in Ponca City. They are also battling air pollution from carbon-black emissions. The Poncas suffer from what Mekasi Horinek, the coordinator of Bold Oklahoma, a former environmental activism group, calls a "tirade of cancer" because of "environmental racism."[43] The problems are so severe that the Ponca Nation will be the first tribal nation to add a statute enacting the "Rights of Nature."[44] Osage oil still causes serious environmental problems because the Bureau of Indian Affairs will not enforce oil and gas drilling regulations.[45] The Cherokee Nation established the Inter-Tribal Environmental Council (ITEC) in 1992 to protect tribal national resources and their environments. The consortium consists of thirty-nine tribes in Oklahoma, Texas, and New Mexico. Recently the Cherokee Nation filed a restraining order against Sequoyah Fields Fuels Corporation to prevent it from dumping radioactive waste into the Arkansas and Illinois Rivers.[46]

Conservationists will continue to resist actors who emphasize economic development over a healthy environment. In February 2017 President Trump appointed Oklahoma attorney general Scott Pruitt to head the EPA. Pruitt's office had previously sued the EPA at least a dozen times in efforts to curb environmental protection regulations, including pollution policies.[47] Since Pruitt's resignation in 2018, his EPA successor Andrew Wheeler, a climate change denier and former coal lobbyist, has rolled back the Clean Water Act, has curtailed scientists' roles on advisory boards, and has reduced the use of scientific data in policy decisions. In 2017 Oklahoma governor Mary Fallin signed into law House Bill 1123, making it illegal for anyone to trespass on property containing a "critical infrastructure facility," which includes pipeline interconnections for oil, gas, and chemicals. Trespassers could receive a $1,000 fine, six months in jail, or both. Those who damage or destroy property might face a $100,000 fine, ten years in prison, or both.[48] The Diamond Pipeline is set to transport almost two hundred thousand barrels of crude oil each day from Cushing, Oklahoma, to Memphis, Tennessee, crossing 491 waterways. Peaceful protesters camped at the Oklahoma Coalition to Defeat the Diamond Pipeline's Oka Lawa Camp (Choctaw for "many waters") in 2017. The camp was located on private, allotted land east of McCurtain, Oklahoma, and from that safe spot protesters educated the country about the pipeline without being harassed.[49]

Poaching, Invasive Species, and Loss of Pollinators

Poachers in Oklahoma illegally take many deer, elk, fish, and other animals every year and trespass onto private land. For example, the Mihesuah family allotment on Little Beaver Creek in southern Oklahoma consists of 180 acres of forest and grassland that the family has hunted and fished since 1902. Multiple times a year my husband hunts for deer, turkeys, and quail, and every time he removes illegally placed deer stands and cameras and contends with poachers, who invariably argue that they were "lost." There is also a problem with runoff from the multitude of cows that graze on ranchland surrounding the allotment. Cows destroy vegetation, contaminate groundwater, and emit methane into the atmosphere. Ranchers often cut trees to provide the pastureland cattle need. In fall 2016 one neighboring white rancher clear-cut an entire swath of cottonwoods to make way for more pasture, thus producing more contaminated drainage. The bass, carp, catfish, crappie, perch, and turtles that used to inhabit Little Beaver Creek are almost gone now.

Nonindigenous flora and fauna such as poison hemlock, Dutch elm disease (a fungus), eastern red cedar (out of control because of fire suppression), tamarisk, Chinese bush clover, musk thistle, and Bradford pear have spread throughout Oklahoma.[50] *Sericea lespedeza*, a perennial legume that was introduced in Kansas in 1900 to control erosion, has spread far beyond that area and is considered a hard-to-eradicate noxious weed. It has overgrown the bison-grazing area in the Seneca-Cayuga Nation, for example, and the animals will not eat it.[51] Many of the more than two hundred lakes in Oklahoma (all but sixty-two of which were created by dams) now contain nonindigenous zebra mussel, bighead carp, golden algae, and hydrilla, among other invasive species. Wild boar, also known as feral hogs, can weigh hundreds of pounds. These aggressive and intelligent animals now inhabit all seventy-seven Oklahoma counties. They reproduce quickly and destroy agriculture, livestock, and ecosystems. Rush Springs, the "Watermelon Capital of the World," is my family's favorite place to acquire watermelons, but feral hogs now destroy multiple acres when the fruit is ripe.[52]

Pollinators—butterflies, moths, flies, beetles, wasps, and hummingbirds—collect nectar from flowering plants and in the process spread pollen. Their activity is crucial to the survival of fruit, vegetable, and nut plants. Residents of Indian Territory and Oklahoma observed healthy populations of pollinators until habitat loss and pesticides reduced their numbers.[53] In recent years Oklahoma has lost more bees than any other state to drought, pesticides, undernutrition, and varroa mites.[54] Natives stated that during the late 1800s they had access to plenty of bee trees and hives in caves and under cliffs, and many men and women kept apiaries. One man recalled finding a hive so big that he collected a "washtub" of honey.[55] In an effort to increase the pollinator population the Monarch Watch Program at the University of Kansas and the Euchee Butterfly Farm in Bixby, Oklahoma, were awarded a $250,000 grant from the National Fish and Wildlife Foundation for planting milkweed and other plants for monarchs and pollinators. Tribal Environmental Action for Monarchs is a coalition of Chickasaw, Citizen Band Potawatomi, Miami, Muskogee-Creek, Osage, Seminole Nations, and Eastern Shawnee tribes that have pledged to plant thirty-five thousand milkweed plants and twenty-eight thousand native wildflowers in the next two years.[56]

Sovereignty and Foodways Systems: Now What?

A common goal among activists is to achieve tribal autonomy and the ability to supply nutritious and affordable foods to tribal members.[57] At the very least this goal requires clean air, uncontaminated water, fertile soil, regular weather patterns, adequate pollinators, clean energy, farm equipment, and a recycling and composting system. There must also be laws to protect the environment and resources.[58] It will be interesting to learn the fate of tribal heirloom seeds. Do any individuals who receive seeds sell theirs to non-Indians? Do any of them work for biotech companies? Many tribes have instituted strict research guidelines in order to protect their intellectual and cultural property, but enforcing a ban on nontribal use of heirloom seeds will be challenging, especially when those seeds leave the tribal nation.[59] In addition, blunders include allowing genetically modified plants to cross-pollinate with fields of heirloom plants. Without biosafety policies, tribal plants will become endangered.

Highly motivated individuals instigate food initiatives, but the tribe as a whole does not always support them. Not every

Indian has an emotional investment in eating traditional foods, and not everyone is concerned about the environment. Many avoid political activism because it can be emotionally exhausting. There are vast socio-economic differences among members of some tribes, and the internal politics can be volatile. Some community-based food autonomy and health endeavors are hampered by inadequate management, shortage of finances, lack of nutritional knowledge, absence of long-range planning, and intra-tribal factionalism. As Hope Radford discovered after an investigation of food sovereignty efforts among seven tribes in Montana, "Tribes are making progress, but many people are still hungry, many people are still unhealthy, and many people are still left without a voice in deciding what their community eats and where it comes from."[60] Anyone familiar with tribal politics knows that one tribal council might approve a project requiring tribal funds—such as a food initiative—but future councils can deny that venture.

Tribes cannot overhaul their foodways without assistance from outside entities and without adhering to governmental laws and regulations. Many business owners need loans, and food project organizers seek aid from Indigenous and non-Indigenous foundations. Institutes such as the Intertribal Agriculture Council, Native Food Systems Resource Center, Seeds of Native Health, and Indigenous Food and Agriculture Initiative at the University of Arkansas School of Law have assisted tribes with heirloom seed distribution, community and school gardens, businesses, and cattle ranching initiatives.[61] However, these organizations in turn are funded by, or partnered with, foundations such as W. K. Kellogg Foundation, American Association of Retired Persons, and Walmart Foundation, among other non-Indigenous entities. The grants and advice offered by these institutes are crucial in helping certain projects flourish, but it takes much more than a few projects to make tribes truly food sovereign.

In order for food initiatives to prosper (that is, to be self-sustaining), there must be long-range plans that take into account available finances and resources and that identify people committed to furthering the goals. Tribal and community discussions are crucial in order to determine what is already being attempted, identify the most critical concerns, pinpoint policies that have negative impact, ascertain what resources are needed and which endeavors are successful, and decide how best to proceed. The decision-making entity should consist of tribal members with knowledge about traditional plants, seed saving, cultivating, harvesting, and animal processing as well as members with political, economic, and scientific expertise. These knowledgeable and culturally connected tribal members (not just friends and political cronies of the current leadership) should have major roles in food education and Native-owned farms.

There are numerous Indigenous food success stories. Schoolchildren cultivate garden plots, more conference papers about traditional foodways are presented each year, Indigenous haute cuisine is a new trend, and more grants are forthcoming. Many Native people are just now rediscovering their traditional foods, and any news story about an Indigenous chef or a successful garden harvest is felt to be a unique and exciting step toward a vision of food sovereignty. It remains to be seen, however, whether schoolchildren will be sufficiently inspired to continue gardening; whether recently formed pan-Indian Indigenous food organizations will benefit communities; and whether Indigenous foodie gatherings and summits will serve only those who can afford to attend them. Moreover, research is needed to determine if the tribal food initiatives that have emerged across the United States improve health. Indeed, gatherings, chefs' cooking demonstrations, food tastings, and philosophizing are easy compared to the work of confronting the political, economic, and social realities of building food sovereignty. That is why the Indigenous food sovereignty movement might stay in a state of "sovereignization"—that is, continual planning and constructing, including negotiation, protest, and debate—until these questions are answered.[62]

"Frybread, the staple of our Native culture. Yep, it just wouldn't be a perfect meal without it!"[1]

"I am so glad to shout from the rooftops that 'Frybread' is not 'our' Indigenous food and I hate that we have allowed it a place of reverence in our communities."[2]

Frybread varies from tribe to tribe in diameter, thickness, and shape but is most commonly a plate-sized disk of flour, shortening, and salt that is fried in grease or oil. "Indian tacos" (or "Navajo tacos" and "Hopi tacos," as they are called in the Southwest) are frybreads topped with ground meat, beans, cheese, lettuce, and sour cream. Dessert frybreads might be crowned with butter, powdered sugar, chocolate, honey, or syrup. Frybread makes its appearance at fairs, tribal commemorative marches, festivals, and powwows and in restaurants. Girls running for the title of tribal princess prepare frybread as their talent component. T-shirts are decorated with the logos "Frybread: Breakfast of Champions," "Powered by Frybread," and "Frybread Power." Frybread enthusiasts are not deterred by *Health Magazine* ranking frybread as one of the fifty fattiest foods in the country.[3]

Many Indigenous food and health enthusiasts argue that eschewing refined wheat flour, along with other unhealthy foods, in favor of traditional tribal foods is the key to eradicating the obesity and diabetes epidemic among tribal communities. Food activism, however, is not without challenges. In 2003 I wrote for the academic journal *American Indian Quarterly* about the repercussions of losing traditional foodways knowledge and opined against the over-consumption of frybread.[4] My bumper sticker, wall clock, buttons, and t-shirt that feature FRYBREAD with a red line through it appeared on Café Press in 2004. As a result I was assailed by frybread fans as "anti-Indian" and "not really Indian."

A year later the director of the Morning Star Institute, Suzan Shown Harjo, reiterated my notions about frybread in the popular online *Indian Country Today*.[5] Frybread fans reacted angrily and the controversy spread across Indian country. Despite Harjo's incorrect reconstruction of frybread's history, her essay has been mentioned in almost every newspaper article about frybread since 2005. That same year, determined Native frybread defenders pressured the South Dakota legislature into designating frybread the "Official State Bread."[6] Elsewhere Kiowa Elder Bronaugh stated: "An Indian person always gets hungry for frybread. Cutting frybread out of an Indian meal would be like cutting out the main ingredient of the entire meal."[7] Gayle Weigle, webmaster of www.frybreadlove.com, declared: "It's like giving up turkey at Thanksgiving. It is a tradition."[8] Recent frybread drama occurred when fitness advocate and *The Biggest Loser* star Jillian Michaels attempted to educate Yavapai Apaches at a 2010 tribal gathering about the dangers of fried flour. She dropped a plate of frybread in the trash, calling it "poison," and in return a tribal member called her an "idiot" and threw a pile of bread at her; she received a poor turnout for her diabetes discussion.[9]

Spokane writer Sherman Alexie has been called a "frybread expert," and he states that "frybread is the story of our survival."[10] But whose survival? Most frybread-focused stories and "traditional Native American recipes" websites proclaim frybread the creation of desperate Diné (Navajos) at Bosque Redondo in New Mexico, also known as *Hwéeldi* ("place of suffering"), where Navajos were confined by the U.S. government from 1864 to 1868. This entrenched legend tells us that Navajo women fried their flour rations in lard and thus supplied their people with enough calories and nutrients to survive the ordeal. There are no government reports, however, of Navajos at Bosque Redondo frying flour. Testimonies of Navajos whose ancestors who lived at Bosque Redondo and survived the Long Walk make no mention of frying flour either.[11]

The late George P. Horse Capture, member of the A'aninin tribe and one-time deputy assistant director for cultural resources at the National Museum of the American Indian, stated about the relation between the Creator and food: "In exchange for all the difficulties we endure, He gave us frybread and June berries." Considering the array of flora and fauna that sustained Natives for millennia prior to contact with Europeans, Horse Capture's reference to the unhealthy frybread as a gift from the Creator to distressed Natives is curious and merits a closer look.[12]

The Frybread Legend: Bosque Redondo

By 1846 Navajos lived in what are now Arizona and western New Mexico and successfully raised horses, sheep, mules, goats and cattle, all brought by the Spanish in the 1500s. Navajos also hunted deer, rabbits, and antelope and cultivated beans, chilies, corn, melons, squash, cactus fruits, piñon nuts, mesquite beans, and peaches that they received from Hopis (who were introduced to the trees by the Spanish). Americans had moved into the Southwest by the 1860s, and Navajos effectively pillaged their settlements. To stop the raiding, government officials planned to settle tribespeople at Bosque Redondo and to transform them into compliant farmers. They charged Kit Carson with gathering the Navajos and forcing them to the reservation, under the eye of the military at Fort Sumner. After an arduous and violent effort that involved much human death and destruction of tribal property, thousands of Navajos surrendered in 1866 and were forced to walk four hundred miles from Fort Defiance to Bosque Redondo. Ultimately about 8,500 Navajos were confined, along with some 500 disgruntled Mescalero Apaches. While they experienced some agricultural successes during their incarceration, there were more failures and difficulties, including drought, floods, seed failure, a plague of worms, inadequate and spoiled rations, the Mescaleros' animosity, and the Comanches' raiding.[13]

At various times Navajos were presented with small portions of salt, cornmeal, mutton, beef, pork, offal, and wheat flour that they did not know how to prepare, and coffee beans that they tried to cook as they would cook common beans. Chiefs occasionally received sugar.[14] Despite claims to the contrary in *Smithsonian Magazine* they received no canned goods.[15] Navajos resorted to digging through horse and mule dung for undigested corn to grind into meal and periodically were allowed to hunt rabbits and gophers.[16] Government buyers contended with open-market prices, and many sacks of spoiled flour contained inedible objects that increased the bags' weight and cost.[17] This was not unusual. At the same time, in South Dakota at the Yankton Indian and Crow Creek Agencies, confined Natives also suffered to the point of dying of malnourishment from flour deemed "very poor," "very coarse," "sticky," and black. Those people ate wolves that had been poisoned, or sick mules, cows, and horses, as well as hooves and entrails.[18] Tough, stringy and spoiled meat sporadically arrived at Bosque Redondo. On one occasion Navajos received a few head of cattle and they used every part of the animals, including the blood, which they mixed with cornmeal to make what the Indian agent optimistically called "nourishing pasta."[19] They were in a dire situation and any rendered animal fat would have been quickly consumed, not saved to fry flour.

Army records mention flour being dropped in ashes to cook, mixed with water and drunk, and eaten "raw." One officer commented that a few Navajos cooked "tortilla-like substances." There were no reports of metal pots and pans and therefore no frying. During the same time period, Civil War soldiers and tribes in the Dakota Territory received "hard tack," an undesirable rock-hard "cracker" mix of flour, water, and salt.[20] Soldiers crushed the hard bread, moistened it with water, and dropped the wad into ashes to create a softer mouthful. This would have been a logical way for Navajos to make use of the unfamiliar flour.

All the army and Navajo reports that mention flour at Bosque Redondo are bleak, conjuring reminders of sickness and death—not of survival. Indian agents wrote that flour was "unwholesome." Navajos became ill from "eating too heartedly of half-cooked bread, made of our flour, to which they were not accustomed."[21] Several Navajos testified in 1975 that their ancestors had spoken of many people dying from consuming flour.[22] It is possible that they perished from dysentery after ingesting Pecos River water that they mixed with uncooked flour and coffee beans.[23] Their symptoms of intestinal distress are similar to those of people suffering from gluten sensitivity, but there is no way of knowing for sure. No nineteenth-century Indian agent's report of celiac disease exists because the connection between a body's inability to digest gluten and the ingestion of wheat was not recognized until 1952.

In 1868 Navajos signed a treaty allowing them to return to their Four Corners homeland, and eventually the reservation expanded to over twenty-seven thousand square miles. Trading posts increased on Navajo lands after 1870 and reached their peak of business between 1900 and 1930. Posts stocked their shelves with household goods, coffee, sugar, flour, baking powder, ginger snaps, oysters, deviled ham, candy, tobacco, popcorn, and canned fruit, tomatoes, and milk. Their animal herds grew exponentially, but in the 1880s Navajos in New Mexico suffered crop failures, and one man stated that "we lived on [goat] milk."[24] In the late 1890s they suffered another failure, and some resorted to eating their animals and cheap flour acquired from trading posts.[25] Robb Redsteer, founder of Naataanii Alliance for Peace, says that was his great-grandparents' time and that frybread was "very rarely made."[26] Photographs of the 1913 and 1914 Shiprock Fair ("the Oldest and Most Traditional of the Navajo Fairs," where frybread competitions had been featured for decades)[27] reveal rugs, livestock, and impressive mounds of produce but no frybread. At the 1920 fair Navajos competed in baking contests, presenting to judges loaves of wheat bread, layer cakes, biscuits and doughnuts, and still no frybread.[28] Navajos again faced economic hardships in the 1940s. The tribe's animal herds decreased markedly, and the people subsisted on "bread and coffee."[29] A 1940 photograph of a Navajo woman with a basket of frybread appears in the Sharlot Hall Museum, perhaps indicating that frybread had become a Navajo food item.[30] By midcentury the tribe recovered economically and consumed mutton, corn, beef, pork, beans, pumpkins, melons, and store-bought goods. They also made baked bread and fried "tortillas" and were not in starvation mode.[31] Throughout the 1950s Navajos ate less garden produce and more canned goods, candy, and coffee. According to Redsteer, in the 1960s frybread was more of a luxury food item. Navajos moved residences with the seasons on account of their livestock, and the heavy containers of lard and bags of flour were too cumbersome to haul.[32]

The Americanized trading post diet had consequences. By 1968 many Navajos were deficient in iron, protein, and vitamin C, and by 1981 nutritional support programs had been established to address the growing cases of deficiencies. A decade later widespread consumption of pizza, cheeseburgers, bacon and mutton fat, sausage, canned meats, mutton sandwiches, sodas, desserts, and fried flour resulted in an obesity explosion.[33] The greasy and delicious frybread had become an everyday food. Somewhere on the vast reservation the Bosque Redondo frybread legend was created—and then spread across the country—to rationalize its mass consumption. The desire for junk food and frybread has not abated. There are only ten grocery stores on the Navajo reservation for three hundred thousand Navajos, in addition to a few gas stations and trading posts, which means residents must plan ahead and buy groceries that will last for weeks. The Diné Community Advocacy Alliance states that 80 percent of those foods are "junk." As a result, one in three Navajos is prediabetic or diabetic.[34]

There are two deviations from the Bosque Redondo story. Some writers assert that Spanish women taught Navajo women how to make frybread in the square shape of *sopaipillas* and that Navajo women instead made their bread round to fit their frying pans.[35] Because the Spanish and Navajos were not friendly and the latter rigorously resisted Spanish attempts to acculturate them, it is doubtful that the few Spanish women in the Southwest and Navajo women cooked together. Besides, one could fry square bread in a round pan. More likely is that Pueblos who lived in the vicinity of Albuquerque observed Spanish cooks making *sopaipillas* from flour and grease and eventually shared that knowledge with other tribes. Most Pueblos, however, baked bread in adobe ovens, and the thin Hopi blue corn *piki* bread is baked on hot stones.[36]

Frybread might have emanated from Canada. By 1789 the Northwest Company traders occasionally used flour to make what they called *galettes* (French for flat crusty cakes or pancakes, although *galettes* are usually made with buckwheat) or to thicken stews.[37] In the Northwest and Canada frybread is sometimes referred to as "bannock." Traditional bannock is dense bread made of oatmeal, barley, or other grain cooked on a griddle (or, in early days, on a heated stone), and it has been made for centuries in Ireland, northern England, and Scotland. Bannock can be made less dense with baking soda, and this form of bread is sometimes made by Natives, but fried bannock takes the form of a modern "Indian taco." Eighteenth-century traders and tribes rendered fat to make pemmican and normally baked breads in ovens or on hot stones, although traders sometimes mixed small amounts of flour with water and fried it in buffalo grease. Their tribal trading partners probably noted that "bannocks" were easy to prepare.[38]

Which Tribes Made Frybread?

Most tribes have always coped with poor government food commodities, including white flour, yet only a few nineteenth-century government reports mention tribes frying flour. In 1891 the physician at the Cheyenne River Agency in South Dakota wrote about the dire health issues of the tribespeople and that "their bread is hardly worth the name."[39] At the Ponca Agency in 1893 the agent observed Poncas suffering from stomach ailments because of the way they prepared their bread: "Flour, water and baking powder, mixing it all together into a stiff dough; they roll it out and fry it in hot lard, making it all a very indigestible mass."[40] Another agent observed "fried bread" at a "Siwash" (probably Chinook) potlatch at Puget Sound; but the tribespeople did not appear to be starving, because they also gave away at their potlatch clams, salmon, venison, potatoes, huckleberries, and apples.[41] One agent wrote in 1892 of "several large fried cakes, made from wheat flour" among Cheyennes and Arapahos north of the South Canadian River.[42] In 1898 the Sac and Fox Indian agent wrote that "nearly everything they eat is cooked in lard." They preferred hot fried cakes, pork, coffee, chicken, turkey, and dog and "relish skunk as a negro does opossum."[43] Francis E. Leupp, commissioner of Indian Affairs from 1904 to 1909, recounted in 1911 that Comanche Quanah Parker told him Quahadis did not like flour because "in our effort to get enough to extract some tastes from it, we filled our mouths, we nearly choked, and then found our teeth and tongues gummed up with a thick paste." So they dumped out the flour and used the bags for leggings.[44]

Some tribespeople did not use wheat flour at all. According to Anishinaabe (Ojibwa) Martin Reinhardt, director of the Decolonizing Diet Project, Ojibwas carried "cakes" made of rice, berries, corn, pumpkin, acorns and meat that were cooked on heated stones.[45] Similarly, after their removal to Indian Territory in the 1830s, the Five Tribes used corn, peanuts, chestnuts, acorns, and bamboo vines to make what English speakers call "breads," but these unleavened grains, nuts, and tuberous rhizomes were boiled or baked. But, to reiterate problems already noted, before long the steady stream of exploitative intruders into Indian Territory caused environmental damage and created an economic class system, resulting in many tribespeople being unable either to purchase foods or to grow enough to sustain their families. While many members of the Five Tribes could afford to buy food, economic disparities caused some poor tribal members to suffer from a variety of ailments brought on from unsanitary conditions and lack of medical care, in addition to depression and frustration. Impoverished tribespeople received little assistance from the government and relied on corn meal, not wheat flour, and the corn mono-diet caused malnutrition. Prior to their removal in the early 1830s, acculturated Cherokees used wheat flour to make pancakes, biscuits, gravy, pie crusts, and cookies but not frybread.[46]

The *Indian and Pioneer Histories* consist of eighty thousand interviews of residents of Oklahoma conducted by Works Progress Administration (WPA) workers in the 1930s. Many of the elderly Native and non-Native interviewees grew up in Indian Territory during the mid-nineteenth century. Only four entries mention "frybread" or "fried bread." Two are about placing biscuits in hot coals; in another, a white man observed Sac and Fox women wrapping "frybread" around raw meat and chewing until blood oozed out of their mouths.[47] The other noted that in Cheyenne, Arapaho, and Kiowa camps there was more "fried bread" than any other food.[48] None of the Native interviewees mentioned frying flour or bread, although some did tell of mixing purchased wheat flour with beans. Choctaws stated they did not like wheat flour and preferred corn meal. If they did use wheat flour, they did not fry it, and some used flour only to make Sunday biscuits.[49] The Cherokee Female Seminary, established in 1852 in Park Hill and rebuilt in Tahlequah after a destructive fire in 1889, served dishes with wheat flour to students every day. Cooks did not prepare frybread, but there is plenty of documentation of physical distress from the girls' diet of excess flour, fat, sugar, and salt. Like Navajos at Bosque Redondo, who had not previously consumed flour and coffee, for the Cherokee children who normally consumed garden produce and wild game at home, the heavy seminary diet of biscuits, gravy, pancakes, cakes, milk, butter, cream, and sugar resulted in a variety of digestive disorders such as "piles," "sour stomach," indigestion, "wind on the stomach," and diarrhea. Lactose intolerance as well as the aforementioned gluten sensitivity were not recognized maladies. Indicative of the cooks' favorite ingredient was the order placed in 1893: sixteen thousand pounds of white wheat flour for fewer than three hundred students.[50] Their health issues continued unabated.

Who Wants "Traditional" Food?

In the 2011 documentary *Good Meat*, Oglala Lakota Beau LaBeau is thwarted in his quest to lose weight with a traditional diet because his family prefers beef over bison as well as favoring processed foods procured from Wal-Mart. Whereas it was once common practice to consume squirrels, venison, and offal, now some tribal elders refuse to eat even the muscle portions of traditional meats such as elk, deer, moose, and antelope. After I spoke at Illinois State University several years ago, a Muscogee told me that his project of "traditional meal delivery" for elders was not successful because his fellow tribespeople associate such fauna with being impoverished and "second class." They prefer fast foods because these are favored fare of mainstream America.[51] Every time I teach "Foodways of Latin America" and "Foodways of Native North America," Native students remark about their dislike of traditional foods such as squash, beans, bison, salmon, and venison. At Indigenous Studies potlucks when I have brought elk stew, those dishes go half-eaten, while cheesy casseroles and desserts are immediately consumed. The answer to why processed foods are more desirable to some Natives is more complicated than frybread tasting better than poke weed.

The topics of traditionalism, cultural change, and food sovereignty reach beyond the scope of this case study, but a cursory overview can help explain why traditional foods are eschewed by some Natives in favor of less healthy fare. There is no monolithic "American Indian" or "Native American" culture. Tribes differed in their religions, languages, gender roles, physiologies, housing, clothing, and subsistence, depending on their environment and their reactions to colonists. One commonalty is that tribes passed socio-cultural information verbally from one generation to the next. Youngsters had the responsibility of listening to their elders and retaining the cosmological and cultural stories instructing them how to behave as a tribal member, how to interact with the natural world, and how to survive. Stories and cultural histories also situate a people's identity within their cultural group and the larger world. This time-tested tribal knowledge, garnered through trial and error, is inexorably tied to tribal lands where ceremonies are performed, where the dead are interred, and where many tribes believed they emerged.[52] Lupton's statement that "food is instrumental in marking differences between cultures, serving to strengthen group identity," is appropriate in this context because, with some exceptions, medicinal and edible flora and fauna were particular to the tribes' homelands.[53]

Tribal foods possessed myriad symbolic connotations, including prosperity, status, wealth, luck, fertility, evil, and poverty. Tribespeople recognized the connection between sustenance and cosmological deities, often female, who presented the people with specific foods. For example, not all tribes grew maize, but among those who did, from the Aztecs in Mexico to the Choctaws and Cherokees in the U.S. Southeast to Iroquois tribes in the Northeast, corn was seen as a symbol of sustenance and fertility. Tribes followed calendars based on weather or harvests. The northern Anishinaabe divided their year into thirteen moons that match the number of sections on a turtle's shell. Their July is *Miin giizis* (berry moon). Tlingits of the northwest coast started their thirteen-month calendar in July, *Xaat disi* (salmon month), when the salmon returned. Choctaws also had a thirteen-month cycle, July and early August being *Hvsh luak mosholi* (month of the fires all out), and Muscogees (Creeks) referred to July as *Hiyucee* (little harvest). The same period is

known among Navajos as *Bii'int'aachili*. Ceremony accompanied
the stages of food acquisition. Late summer for many tribes sig-
nified that corn had reached its roasting stage, and many danced
(and still dance) the Green Corn dance, a thanksgiving festival
that might last several weeks. Senecas, among others, recognized
the importance of other foods with ceremonials, for example,
the Strawberry and Blackberry dances. Navajos performed the
Seeds Blessing and rain ceremonies as well as corn songs and
numerous hunting rituals.[54]

Today, the definition of the tricky and debatable term "traditional" varies from person to person. How people define "traditional" depends on the extent of connection to their tribe, and
how that tribe and their family confronted colonialism and its
myriad socio-economic forces, such as forced education, relo-
cations, influences of Christianity, economic pressures, and
intermarriage with non-Indians. All tribes have been forced to
change, and tribal traditions are continually invented in order
to satisfy the needs of the current generation.[55] In the process
of creating Navajo cultural stability after their Bosque Redondo
experience, their meaning of "traditional" changed every few
years to incorporate accoutrements and philosophies of non-
Navajo societies. They adopted more Euroamerican animals and
foods, learned silver work and blanket making from Pueblos,
and embraced the peyote religion (Native American Church)
from Mexican tribes; they integrated powwow regalia, drumming,
and singing from Plains cultures, learned to carve and sell Hopi
Kachinas, and some participate in the northern Plains tribes'
Sundance. This is not unusual; most tribes adopted cultural
mores from other tribes and other societies. Natives of all tribes
use cell phones, wear jeans, live in homes like other non-Indians,
eat fast food, and watch television; but because they speak their
language, practice religious ceremonies, appear phenotypically
"Indian," and perhaps live on a reservation, they might refer to
themselves as "traditional." For some Natives, tradition equates
with familiarity. For example, David Fazzino conducted a study

of Tohono O'odham foodways in 2003. He discovered that some tribal members considered a food traditional because they recalled eating it as children. Others defined traditional food as their grandparents' food. Still others defined it as food that was personally important to them. Reflecting all three criteria, young adults referred to frybread as "traditional" 37 percent more than did the middle-aged.[56] By asserting that frybread is part of their cultural heritage and therefore traditional, some Natives simultaneously reaffirm their Indian identity and feel justified eating frybread.

Some Natives retain cultural knowledge, while others have little or no connection to their tribal culture. More Natives live off than on reservations, and many participate in tribal activities (such as food sovereignty initiatives) only occasionally or not at all. Indigenous people's dietary choices, therefore, are influenced by multiple and complex factors: finances, availability, politics, religion, educational background, residence, condition of the product (polluted, GMO, farmed vs. wild), physiology of the eater (allergies, diseases, weight issues), ease of acquisition and preparation of the food, historical connection, taste preferences, advertising influences, smell, appearance, and familial and cultural pressures and expectations. Attention is paid to the way food is procured (who buys, grows, hunts, and prepares it), how it is served (who eats first, who is the server, who sits where), and what foods are labeled as taboo. Combine all these elements with how one views the world through the lens of their identities (gender, sexuality, cultural, religious, economic class), and it is not surprising that one Native might declare that frybread is sickening and is not a traditional food, while another cannot name a single food their tribe ate historically, and still another asserts, "I'm Navajo: frybread and mutton are my specialty."[57]

The Persistence of Frybread

In 2012 the Diné Policy Institute surveyed Navajo tribespeople and of 230 respondents from across the Navajo Nation, 90 percent answered yes to the question: "Would you be interested in information about traditional foods if it were available?"[58] Across Indian Country, backyard gardens of heirloom corn, squash, beans, and peppers have sprung up, as have Indigenous food sovereignty projects. Many Anishinaabe (Ojibwas) in Minnesota and Wisconsin attempted to remain true to their foodways and traditions even after the government assigned them to reservations and took away their lands along with their essential *manoomin* (rice) stands. The tribe strategized to use sharing, reciprocity, and communal hunting to harvest wild rice, berries, and maple syrup, to hunt, and to catch fish. Historian Thomas Vennum observed about their wild rice that it "continues to symbolize old Ojibway culture: it is part of the Indian world, distinct from the white."[59] Ojibwa Martin Reinhardt makes it clear that frybread is not part of his "Indian world": "Our traditional Anishinaabe diet never included white flour, white sugar, and Crisco shortening."[60]

In contrast to the Ojibwas' cultivation of *manoomin* is the irony of frybread. Despite tribes' lack of precontact connection to frybread and their dependency on American food manufacturers to provide the ingredients, many frybread advocates associate not eating frybread with not being Indian. Or as one poster asserts in the article "Frybread" at Smithsonian.com: "Your not a real Native if u don't no how to make or eat frybread."[61] Thus while some Natives eat frybread as a way of signifying cultural identity, others connect frybread to the inadequate foods given to tribes by the U.S. government and regard it as a symbol of colonization. Indeed, no ingredient of frybread is indigenous to this hemisphere. Frybread creation requires no cultivating, harvesting, hunting, or gathering. Neither attention to the seasons nor ceremony in procuring the ingredients is required. There is no oral tradition lesson to be taught about frybread, not even about it as a survival food. One can make frybread during any season with goods purchased from Dollar General. For some frybread advocates, it could be that the making, selling, and consuming of frybread under the rubric of it being seen as a "cultural food" is an act of defiance, acknowledging that the ingredients originally belonged to the Other (the colonizer), but also making the claim that item made from the Other's components now belongs to them. Nevertheless, the lack of nutrients and the high fat and caloric content of frybread render it dangerous and undesirable except for the taste, low cost, and ease of preparation.

While some Navajos revere frybread as a symbol of their survival at Bosque Redondo, Natives a thousand miles away with their own traditional foods, specific to their geographic locales, also consume frybread with homage, as if the frybread story is theirs too. This is not too surprising. They want to eat it. Fat, sugar, carbohydrates, and salt can be addicting, and frybread advocates are determined to not give up craveable fare.[62] Historical trauma also accounts for dietary choices. Racism, stereotyping, poverty, and depression are ongoing manifestations of colonization. For tribespeople there is no such thing as postcolonial. The tribes' historical traumas may have taken place at different periods and in different locales, but Natives often put all offenses against tribes into the same category. Their grief is unresolved because they feel the effects of their ancestors' sufferings. Some express their frustrations by abusing drugs or drink or by overeating.[63] Psychologist Billi Gordon explains: "When people are continually battered and abused, they find comfort and shelter where they can; eating satisfies the ancient brain."[64] Many Americans have grown up depending on comfort food such as mashed potatoes and gravy, Cheetos, and ice cream. A lot of Natives have too, and they also feel that way about the easily accessible frybread. Feelings of guilt and depression about having diabetes and other health problems associated with an unhealthy diet can lead people to consume the very foods that are killing them. Indigenous Arizona students in my Northern Arizona University classroom talked about "when" they develop type 2 diabetes, not "if," because every person in their family has the disease. They expect no other outcome than to become sick.

The Yavapai Apaches publish a monthly newspaper that informs tribal members about "Healthy Cooking on a Budget" courses. And as with other tribespeople with access to wellness programs, many Yavapai Apaches choose not to take advantage of such offerings. Jillian Michaels suggests that tribal members might be apathetic, and she has a valid point. Teachers at government-run boarding schools disallowed Native children from speaking their languages, from participating in ceremonies, and from communicating with tribal elders who could teach them cultural mores, including foodway traditions. As a result they lost awareness about how to save seeds, cultivate plants, and hunt game. Every lesson ingrained into them their inferiority to whites, and this "boarding school syndrome" affected not only the children who attended the schools but also subsequent generations who learned from boarding school survivors.[65] Many Natives continue to act on their insecurities by making poor dietary and lifestyle choices. Conversely, Indigenous food activists are hopeful that a return to eating precontact foods will provide Native people with empowering links to their tribal past. Reconnecting with traditional Indigenous knowledge could assist them in finding historic solutions to modern health problems.

Frybread Is Here to Stay

Game meats and organic produce are costly. Frybread ingredients are cheap. Frybread is fairly easy to make at home, albeit potentially messy, and all one needs are the ingredients, basic implements, and an electrical outlet, generator, or camp fire. Cooks from Arizona to Alaska receive national attention from newspapers that feature their versions of the origin and meaning of frybread, and demonstrating one's ability to make good frybread can also bring status, as seen in various Miss (insert Tribe) Princess contests, Pawhuska's annual National Indian Taco Championship, and the American Indian Expositions in Anadarko and as mocked in the wry 2012 film *More than Frybread*. Another use of frybread is that some Natives who do not eat frybread at home will eat it among other Natives for social acceptance. "Wannabes" (non-Indians who cannot prove blood or community connection to any tribe) seeking legitimacy might eat it with Natives in an attempt to prove their connection to tribal culture, even if that identity is vague and "pan-Indian."

Frybread tastes good to most people. Because it is also popular among non-Natives, there is a profit motive to sell it. Dwayne Lewis, owner of the now-defunct Arizona Native Frybread in Mesa, Arizona, sold frybread because, as he said, "Everybody wants it."[66] Indian tacos are marketable to crowds looking to connect with Indian cultures, and frybread hawkers cater to Americans' taste for greasy, salty, and fatty foods. The Annual Haskell Indian Art Market in Lawrence, Kansas, for instance, offers frybread from numerous vendors, all of whom cater to perpetually long lines of customers. At my university down the road from Haskell, the instructor of the Indigenous studies "Grant Writing" graduate course eschewed lessons in actual grant writing and focused on how to organize Indian taco sales. Representatives from the Houma Nation (not federally recognized) sell frybread to non-Indians at the New Orleans Jazz Festival every year, using 150 pounds of flour, twelve gallons of milk, and twelve dozen eggs per day. Cook Noreen Dardar claims that making frybread is her "tradition," yet frybread was not a food among southeastern tribes.[67] The company Navajo Frybread is owned by non-Indians and produces six hundred thousand 25-pound bags of Blue Bird flour each year. Owner Trent Tanner states: "We wouldn't be in business without the Navajo people. It's our philosophy that it's their flour and we make it for them. Sales go up especially in the summer when kids get home from boarding school."[68] Indeed, it is not uncommon to see Native shoppers fill their carts at a Safeway market in Flagstaff, Arizona, with bags of the refined flour. Some cooks rely on the mystical element to attract buyers. Although some frybread makers advise poking a hole in the dough so that the edges will fry evenly, one cook clearly caters to non-Indians looking for an "authentic Native

American" dish. Clark "Little Bear" Oxendine, a member of the Lumbee Tribe (another group not recognized by the federal government), cooks frybread at powwows and tells customers and reporters of the cryptic, yet unsubstantiated tribal custom that making a hole in the bread will "let the evil spirits out of it, so it'll taste good."[69]

What Is "Native American Food"?

If one searches for truly traditional Native American recipes on the web or in published materials, the results are hit or miss.[70] The marketing and selling of so-called traditional recipes take advantage of the reality that most people know little about tribal foodways. Hobsbawm and Ranger define "tradition invention" as a "set of practices . . . which seek to inculcate certain values and norms of behavior by repetition, which automatically implies continuity with the past," and note that some of these "traditions" are "established with great rapidity."[71] Many "traditional" recipes contain more nonindigenous ingredients than anything else; but because Natives have been using some recipes (such as grape dumplings) repetitively for decades, some deem them traditional and market them as such. The regular "Native Recipes" column in *Indian Country Today* illustrates the misrepresentation of nonindigenous recipes as "traditional."[72]

With the popularity of chef's memoirs and foodie shows, the media have fervently jumped on the fryer wagon. Reporters romanticize frybread as an "American Indian" culinary delicacy and apply enthusiastic imagery to its preparation: "The sound of fresh dough being tossed and flattened melds with the sharp sizzle as it hits hot oil to create a pleasing culinary rhythm."[73] "Hot canola oil pangs off a stainless steel tub under the watch of a local frybread master."[74] "In this comforting Father's Day dish, homemade frybread gives the stacked entrée an indulgent foundation from which to grow."[75] And so forth. The publicity given to the stories told by frybread makers has contributed to its reputation as a bona fide "Native American" food.

Natives also take advantage of the burgeoning interest in Native foods. It is obviously the featured item of the Frybread House in Phoenix, a restaurant owned by Tohono O'odham people who advertise their restaurant as serving "Native American food," but the menu choices are nontraditional: fried potatoes, refried beans, beef and burro plates, along with butter, powdered sugar, and honey to adorn the frybread. The James Beard Foundation honored the Frybread House as "beloved for quality food that reflects the character of the community."[76] And that is the problem. At least half of Tohono O'odham adults have diabetes, and it is not because they are consuming their historic diet of corn, squashes, beans, and cactus fruit.[77] The Frybread House is owned by a few people who aim to make money. On the other hand, the opposing goals of the tribe's "Healthy O'odham People Promotion" and "Tohono O'odham Community Action" are to encourage physical activity and the consumption of traditional foods.[78]

One of the first Natives to market "Indian foods," Osage Raymond Red Corn, started HA-PAH-SHU-TSE (Red Corn) Indian Foods in Oklahoma in 1975 because, according to Raymond in 1981, "young people don't know our cooking anymore." Osages traditionally hunted, gathered wild foods, and cultivated gardens, but like every other tribe they did not traditionally use wheat, beef, or dairy products. Originally, the Red Corns served food at their establishment, including beef chuck meat pies and "Osage purple dumplings" made of flour, baking powder, shortening, butter, sugar, and Welch's grape juice.[79] Now the company is called Red Corn Native Foods and sells only frybread mix. Selling frybread has also spread to Alaska, where Indigenous peoples have never grown wheat. The Native-owned Garfield's Famous Frybread does a brisk business selling frybread to Tlingit tribal members, to the tune of 175 pounds of dough a day, along with toppings of margarine, powdered sugar, and Hershey's chocolate syrup.[80]

In 1987 Wooden Knife Company of Interior, South Dakota, began selling a pre-made frybread mix, marketed as "the original Sioux recipe," although what the latter might be is unclear. According to government reports, tribes in the Dakotas received the same goods as Navajos. There are no reports of them frying flour, and despite claims to the contrary on the Wooden Knife frybread site, there are no entries in the journals of Lewis and Clark stating that tribes fried *timpsala* (prairie turnip) flour. When Wooden Knife owners started making frybread, they added ground *timpsala* as flavoring, but they can no longer do so because of sustainability issues. Today, the company markets the ordinary frybread mix in "a version of the Native American pouch bag" because "this option gives a small look into the Sioux Indian culture."[81] This is an odd keepsake; Sioux tribes did not use wheat flour while they "migrated with the buffalo," that is, as they followed one of their main foodstuffs.

In 2010 the *Atlantic* featured the "American Indian eatery" Tocabe. The owners of the restaurant state: "Our mission is to become the Industry Standard of American Indian cuisine. . . . We need to help push it."[82] The only Indigenous ingredients offered on the Tocabe menu, however, are bison, tomatoes, beans, and possibly *wojape*—depending on how it is made (real *wojape* is made of fruit only, no sugar). Tocabe's menu prominently features nonindigenous nachos and frybread with toppings of beef, chicken, cheese, sour cream, or powdered sugar as well as chips and sodas. The Kekuli Café, with locations in Merritt and Westbank, British Columbia, was inspired by owner's "First Nations roots." The slogan is "Don't panic, we have bannock!" with one "bannock taco" dish described as "piled teepee high."[83] Besides bannock, frybread, and local Saskatoon berries featured as "Indian food," the offerings are purely North American.

Like Tocabe, the Mitsitam Native Foods Café at the National Museum of the American Indian features an even longer list of nonindigenous ingredients, some of which are the focal point of the pricey dishes. The restaurant claims: "Each menu reflects

the food and cooking techniques from the region featured";
but the Mitsitam menu features numerous foods that were not
traditionally used by tribes: crabapple, carrots, chicken, apple
cider, beets, cabbage, bacon, cheese, almonds, Spanish olives,
macaroons, Brussels sprouts, celery, cherries, wheat flour tortillas, sour cream, wheat rolls, leeks, saffron, cauliflower, goat,
fennel, oxtail, okra, cilantro, cookies, and tarts. The adjoining
Mitsitam Espresso Coffee Bar serves Tribal Grounds Coffee, a
product that is grown by unidentified "Indigenous farmers."[84] Coffee plants are not indigenous to this hemisphere. The problem
with Mitsitam is that it misrepresents a foundational feature of
tribal cultures—food—while housed in a world-famous museum
that is supposed to educate visitors about Indigenous peoples.

Cookbook authors aim their coffee table publications at those
who can afford to purchase them. and those buyers usually
are not tribespeople. Recipes in the aforementioned *Foods of
the Americas* include nonindigenous items, among them flour,
butter, milk, ice cream, beef, cilantro, plantain, chicken, and
pork. The same can be said of *Spirit of the Harvest: North American
Indian Cooking*, which renders some "Native recipes" unrecog-
nizable because of a myriad of nonindigenous items. *Foods of
the Southwest Indian Nations* alternates between traditional and
thoroughly nonindigenous dishes.[85] By including ingredients
such as heavy cream, milk, butter, flour, peaches, cinnamon,
chicken, and many other European-introduced items, authors
miss opportunities to showcase truly traditional tribal cooking.
Instead, many "Native" cookbooks present dishes made mainly
of European-introduced ingredients mixed with a few native
North American ones.

Granted, frybread is only one cause of poor health. I know
healthy and active Natives who eat small amounts of frybread at
tribal events, not out of homage to a "cultural food" but because
it tastes good, as does cheesecake. Occasional indulgences do
no harm in an otherwise conscientious diet. Some Natives, however, eat frybread and other processed foods multiple times a

day, even during foodways ceremonies such as the Green Corn dance. At the Choctaw Nation's festivals the always crowded midway features donuts, butter-slathered corn, corn chip pie, funnel cakes, fried Twinkies and frybread. Next to this array of junk food stands the extensive "Healthy Living Expo," ready to assist Choctaws with their diabetes, obesity, and high blood pressure. Some festival organizers obviously can identify traditional foods such as *banaha* and *tanfula*. Still, despite my suggestion that they move *banaha* and *tanfula* to the main midway, these dishes are relegated to the "cultural demonstration" area with *ishtaboli* (stickball) games and bow and blow-gun making.

Tribal Food, Tribal Health

So what is the harm of the "tradition invention" of dishes that contain only a few Indigenous items, or sometimes none at all, and marketing them as "Native American" foods? Those who profit will argue there is nothing wrong with it. For others, promoting traditional foodways is integral to becoming aware of their tribes' history, learning their language, and becoming politically active in ways that will contribute toward building pride and shaping their identity as Indigenous people. And while many activists urge youngsters to engage their elders, not all elder Natives are aware of their foodways. Fazzino comments that it is not constructive to expect tribal elders to know how to identify, cultivate, and prepare traditional foods. Many Natives have adapted to what has been available to them. Expectations of a know-it-all elder could be a detriment to modern food security because the assumptions "obliterate the processes of adaptation to and learning from one's elders and environment through rituals, experiences and just plain work under the desert sun."[86] Indigenous food activists would agree. Besides the issue of many Natives' inability to distinguish between traditional and nontraditional foods, Indigenous food activists have no quarrel with the adoption of nourishing, nonindigenous plants and animals into tribal foodways, nor with new techniques for food sustainability, such as the Choctaw Smallwood brothers' aquaponic farming system.[87] After all, broccoli (indigenous to the Mediterranean and Asia Minor) is more nutritious than frybread. Rather, the concern is with the overall deteriorating health of tribal peoples, their dependency on nontribal entities to supply their foods, and the lack of interest many have for community-based food sovereignty and health endeavors.

Many Natives are attempting to revitalize their cultural foodways and have altered their diets to focus on tribal foods. Navajo Robb Redsteer, for example, says: "I personally experienced all the illnesses but overcame them with a good diet and exercise. Frybread has to be eliminated," and now he grows traditional plants inside the Navajo BioEnergy Dome. Martin Reinhardt agrees: "Indian communities are in a state of emergency regarding obesity, diabetes, heart disease, and high blood pressure. Frybread has no place as part of a healthy daily diet in Indian Country."[88]

4. What Are You Ingesting?

The study of how Natives' diets changed from meals of fresh fruits and vegetables and game meats to a poor diet of processed, fatty foods and sugary drinks can assist students in understanding why Natives suffer from an epidemic of diabetes, obesity, and other problems associated with these diseases. Many people would like to begin a healthy lifestyle but are not certain how to proceed. Here is one way to understand the health of your diet. Keep a diary of what you eat for one week. Use a nutrition book or app to make a chart so that you can determine how many calories and how many nutrients each item provides you. Purchase a basic nutrition book to help you understand the caloric value of foods in addition to the functions of vitamins A, B, C, D, E, F, K, biotin, folic acid, para-aminobenzoic acid (PABA), calcium, magnesium, sodium, potassium, and so on.

Also document how much exercise you get per day and calculate how many calories you use on exercise. This is an intensive project and can be confusing, but it gives a reality check, not only as to what nutrients you are and are not taking in, but also in terms of how many calories you are ingesting versus how much energy you expend. I did this for one month in high school, and I have never forgotten how important it is to keep close tabs on what you eat and drink. If you have ever considered your diet or calculated what you are eating and drinking, it is daunting and humbling. However, we must take responsibility for our health and for the health of our children and those who cannot make reasonable choices for themselves.

These measures of calories, protein, carbohydrates, sodium, fat, fiber, and cholesterol are only part of the analysis we should consider. In order to be healthy, we must also consider how

Table 1. Sample diet for one day

Food	Calories[1]	Protein[2]	Carbohydrates[3]	Sodium[4]	Fat[5]	Cholesterol[6]	Fiber[7]
BREAKFAST							
1 T grapeseed oil	120	0 g	0 g	0 mg	Sat. 1.5 g; poly. 10 g; mono. 2.5 g	0 mg	0g
2 eggs	150	12	2	280	5	424	0
½ c mushrooms	9	1	1	1	.1	0	0
¼ c red pepper	20	1	5	3	.3	0	3
2 green chilies	36	2	8	3	.1	0	1
2 corn tortillas	120	2	25	35	.5	0	2
4 T salsa	16	0	2	320	.1	0	0
1 c carrot juice	70	2	15	16	0	0	1
1 c decaff coffee	4	0	1	4	0	0	0
1 T skim milk	5	.45	.65	6.5	0	0	0
1 pack Stevia	0	0	0	0	0	0	0
LUNCH							
½ turkey sandwich:							
1 slice wheat bread	60	3	11	125	1	0	2
1 slice turkey breast	40	8	0	24	.5	17	0
1 spinach leaf	1	0	0	0	0	0	0

mustard/no salt	14	1	1	10	1	0	0
10 Triskets	240	6	40	280	9	0	6
DINNER							
½ grilled zucchini	22	2	4	5	.5	0	2
½ grilled squash	30	2	7	3	.3	0	3
½ grilled red pepper	20	1	5	3	3	0	3
½ baked potato	106	2.5	25	8	.2	0	2.5
2 c spinach (raw)	14	2	2	48	.1	0	1
5 cherry tomatoes	31	1	7	13	.5	0	2
3 spring onions	10	.1	1	.3	0	0	.1
½ c sweet corn	70	2	15	175	1	0	1.5
3 T no-fat Italian dressing	24	0	6	575	0	0	0
1 baked skinless chicken breast	150	29	0	85	1.5	75	0
2 T Teriyaki sauce	30	2	4	1,220	0	0	0
DESSERT							
1 c low-fat yogurt	120	8	22	120	0	5	0
1 banana	109	1	28	1	.6	0	0
1 can drained Mandarin oranges	70	0	15	15	0	0	0

Food	Calories[1]	Protein[2]	Carbohydrates[3]	Sodium[4]	Fat[5]	Cholesterol[6]	Fiber[7]
SNACKS							
apple	73	0	19	0	.4	0	2
1 16 oz. Diet v-8 Splash	20	0	3	25	0	0	0
2 Diet Pepsi	0	0	0	70	0	0	0
3 33.8 oz. Propels	120	0	36	315	0	0	0
Totals	1,804	91.05	310.65	3,932.8	25.6	521	30.5

CALORIES EXPENDED

8:15–9:30 a.m.: mountain running/hiking (steep hills)   500 calories

5:30–6:00 p.m.: gardening   150 calories

many vitamins and minerals our foods contain. For example, in table 1, I eat a lot of vegetables that may not contribute significantly to my protein or caloric intake, but a half cup of cooked spinach, for example, provides a full day's supply of vitamin A and more than 25 percent of the daily requirement of folate. It also contains 419 mg of potassium, in addition to vitamin C, riboflavin, and vitamin B6. Carrot juice provides me with 700 percent of my daily need for vitamin A, in addition to vitamin C, calcium, and iron. See discussion of vitamins and minerals below for information about getting enough of what you need.

1. A food calorie is the amount of energy needed to change the temperature of 1 kilogram of liquid water (a volume of 1 liter) by 1 degree centigrade. Calories are essential for all body functions. Taking in too many calories result in fat storage. Taking in too few calories causes one to lose fat; too much fat loss can be deadly.

2. Protein is essential for growth and development. Deficiency results in mental and physical inefficiency. My protein mainly comes from beans, lentils, chia seeds, nut butters, potatoes, dark green vegetables, plant-based cheeses, game meats (venison, turkey, and fish), and our hens' eggs.

3. Carbohydrates are our sources of fuel and are necessary for normal body functions. They are found in fruits, vegetables, grains, nuts, and seeds. It is recommended that 50–55 percent our daily calories should be complex, low glycemic index (GI) carbohydrates that take longer to digest and cause a slower rise in blood sugar. Do not go "no carb"; we all need at least 130 grams of carbohydrates per day.

4. Sodium may be too abundant. Adults need no more than 2,400–3,000 milligrams per day, depending on activity level. It is needed for maintaining fluid balance and transporting nutrients across cell membranes. Sodium is found in a myriad of processed foods; most of us ingest too much sodium and should be aware of our limits.

5. Fat should be limited to less than 30 percent of the daily intake: less than 90 grams per day. There are two types of fat, as discussed in chapter 6. Saturated fats include many nonindigenous items, like beef, lamb, pork, chicken skin, lard, butter, and cream. Unsaturated fats include Indigenous foods: avocados, peanuts and peanut butter, sunflower and corn oils, salmon and mackerel. Go to the American Heart Association's homepage and type in "fat" in the search block: https://www.heart.org /en/healthy-living/healthy-eating/eat-smart/fats/dietary-fats.

6. Cholesterol is necessary for bile production, sex hormones, vitamin D, and nerve sheaths. Diet accounts for 20 percent of the body's cholesterol, and the liver produces 80 percent. It is found in animal products. Exercise, genetics, and gender all play a role in how the body processes cholesterol. All cholesterol attaches itself to lipid-carrying proteins: LDLs or lipoproteins carry two-thirds of it and tend to deposit the cholesterol in artery walls, while HDLs (high-density lipoproteins) take cholesterol from the artery walls and deliver it to the liver to be metabolized. Foods that raise cholesterol include vegetable shortening and hard margarine, cookies, cakes, pastries, full-fat dairy products, cream cheese, marbled beef, bacon, hamburgers, salamis, and cold cuts. Foods that may lower cholesterol include whole wheat breads and whole grains, fruits, vegetables, nuts, seeds, and nonhydrogenated oils. A test can determine if people have too much cholesterol in their system. If there is too much, the diet must limit fat intake to 20 percent or less of total calories and limit saturated fats to 7 percent. See https://www.heart.org /en/health-topics/cholesterol/about-cholesterol for detailed information about cholesterol.

7. Fiber is supposed to amount to about 30 grams per day. It can assist in preventing colon cancer and lowering blood cholesterol levels. Not enough fiber results in digestive disorders, such as constipation and diverticulosis. Too much fiber can cause bloating and abdominal pain and can interfere with the absorption of some minerals. Indigenous foods high in fiber include

avocados, strawberries, raspberries, black beans, lima beans, quinoa, chia seeds, and sweet potatoes. High-fiber introduced foods are broccoli, lentils, apples, spinach, and whole grain breads. Some essential vitamins and minerals follow.

Vitamin A: Often measured in USP units or International Units (IU). Men need 3,330 IU per day and women need 2,664 IU, or 900 and 700 micrograms (mcg), respectively. It is necessary for proper growth, eyesight, and resistance to infections and aids in secretion of gastric juices. Depletion results in eye inflammations, night blindness, frequent colds, rough and dry skin, and other skin disorders. Too much will result in headaches, fatigue, appetite loss, blurred vision, cracked skin, hair loss, and birth defects if taken before and during pregnancy. Vitamin A is found in Indigenous foods such as goosefoot/lamb's quarters, red bell peppers, sweet potatoes, papaya, and pumpkins. Nonindigenous sources are beet greens, kale, mustard greens, yams (which are from Africa and are not in the same plant family as sweet potatoes), carrots, spinach, apricots, cantaloupe, pistachios, dairy products, and fish liver oils.

Vitamin B1 (thiamine): Men need 1.2 mg per day and women need 1.1 mg. This is necessary for protein metabolism, protects the heart muscle, prevents constipation, promotes appetite, and stimulates the nervous system. Depletion results in edema, poor circulation, weakness, constipation, and depression. Too much results in other B vitamin deficiency. Indigenous sources are potatoes, salmon, trout, black beans, acorn squash, and sunflower seeds. Nonindigenous sources include beef, milk, oranges, oats, pork, eggs, and breads.

Vitamin B2 (riboflavin): Men need 1.3 mg per day and women need 1.1 mg. This burns starches and sugars and assists in adrenal functions. Depletion results in loss of appetite. Too much can interfere with cancer chemotherapy. Vitamin B2 is found in Indigenous foods such as quinoa, salmon, tomatoes, sunflower seeds, and clams and in introduced foods including beef liver, oats, spinach, apples, and dairy products.

Vitamin B3 (niacin) is necessary for healthy eyes, hair, and skin. It may prevent cataracts. Depletion results in bloodshot eyes, mouth inflammations, lip cracks, and dull hair. This vitamin is found in Indigenous foods such as turkey, salmon, peanuts, and avocado; it is also present in chicken breasts, pork, beef, and whole wheat.

Vitamin B6: Men aged 19–50 need 1.3 mg per day; men 51+ need 1.7 mg. Women of 19–50 need 1.3 mg; those aged 51+ need 1.5 mg. This vitamin is necessary for food assimilation, contributes to antibody production, prevents skin disorders, contributes to protection against diabetes and heart disease, relieves premenstrual edema (swelling), regulates the balance between sodium and potassium, and is required for absorption of vitamin B12 and for producing hydrochloric acid. Depletion results in anemia, depression, headaches, irritability, kidney stones, and swelling. Too much results in nerve deterioration. It is found in Indigenous foods like avocados, green leafy vegetables, green peppers, peanuts, pecans, sunflower seeds, turkey, wheat germ, walnuts, and tuna as well as in nonindigenous pork, carrots, spinach, eggs, and milk.

Vitamin B7 (biotin): Adults need 30 mcg per day. This is necessary for metabolism of fats and proteins and for healthy hair and hair growth. Depletion results in eczema, dandruff, hair loss, fatigue, depression, and hallucinations. Biotin is found in Indigenous peanuts, salmon, avocado, and sweet potatoes and also in eggs, beef liver, and dairy products.

Vitamin B12: Adults need 2.4 mcg per day. Vitamin B12 is necessary for blood and nervous system formation. Depletion results in anemia, nerve weakness, and sore tongue. It is found in Indigenous trout, tuna, and salmon, in addition to occurring in nonindigenous lamb liver and kidneys, beef, dairy products, and eggs.

Vitamin C: Adults need 60 mg per day. This is necessary for healthy gums, wound healing, and resistance to infections. It assists in absorption of iron. Depletion results in scurvy and bleeding gums. Excess vitamin C results in diarrhea, kidney stones, urinary tract irritations, bone loss, and an increase or buildup in iron. Vitamin C is found in chile peppers, guavas, American persimmons, pawpaws, tomatoes, and green peppers as well as thyme, parsley, kale, kiwis, citrus fruits, and broccoli. Vitamin D requirements vary by age. Both men and women of ages 19–51 need 200 IU or 5 mcg daily; ages 51–70 need 400 IU or 10 mcg; and ages 70+ need 600 IU or 15 mcg. This vitamin is necessary for preventing rickets, for formation of teeth and bones, and for absorption of calcium and phosphorus. It is also needed for the proper function of the thyroid and parathyroid glands. Depletion results in rickets, tooth decay, osteoporosis, and retarded growth in children. Vitamin D is found in Indigenous salmon, perch, trout, and oysters, also in nonindigenous spinach, kale, okra, collard greens, and oatmeal.

Vitamin E is necessary for blood oxygenation. Men need 14.9 IU per day and women need 11.92 IU, or 15 mg for adults. This dilates blood vessels, prevents scar tissue, is an anti-coagulant and anti-thrombin, provides protection from pollutants, and is used in the treatment of asthma, emphysema, heart disease, hypoglycemia, reproductive disorders, and varicose veins. Depletion results in acceleration of heart disease, strokes, sexual disorders, miscarriages, and degeneration of red blood cells. Too much vitamin E results in excessive bleeding. It is found in Indigenous sunflower seeds, pine nuts, geese, peanuts, avocado, trout, salmon, and crayfish. It also occurs in nonindigenous almonds, wheat germ oil, mangos, and turnip greens.

Bioflavonoids strengthen the capillary walls and prevent hemorrhaging and coagulation. They protects vitamin C from oxidation. Depletion results in arteriosclerosis, eczema, hemorrhoids, hypertension, psoriasis, and varicose veins. Bioflavonoids are found in fruits and vegetables, especially Indigenous papaya, the white core of green peppers as well as in broccoli, eggplant, and the white pulp of citrus fruits.

Calcium is needed for developing bones and teeth. Adults aged 19–50 need 1,000 mg per day; those older than 51 need

1,200 mg. Calcium assists in muscle contraction and blood clotting. Depletion results in osteoporosis. It is found in Indigenous lamb's quarters, chia, salmon, amaranth, and beans in addition to dairy products, lentils, almonds, collard greens, and figs.

Copper: Adults need 900 mcg daily. It is necessary for iron metabolism, nervous system and bone health, and hair, eye, and skin pigmentation. Copper is found in Indigenous potatoes, cacao, black pepper, animal liver and kidneys, spirulina, and lamb's quarters, and in shellfish and whole grains.

Iron: Aged 19–50, men need 8–10 mg and women need 15–18 mg per day; both need 8 mg after age 51. Iron is necessary for red blood cell formation and function. Depletion results in anemia. Iron is found in Indigenous potatoes, beans, quinoa, turkey, pumpkin seeds, shellfish, organ meats, and red meats as well as in tofu, cashews, spinach, broccoli, and enriched grains and cereals.

Folic Acid: Adults need 400 mcg daily. Folic acid is crucial to the formation of red blood cells and the production of RNA and DNA. It is found in Indigenous potatoes, avocado, papaya, beans, sunflower seeds, and liver as well as in broccoli, chickpeas, lentils, spinach, beets, soybeans, and okra.

Iodine: Adults need 150 mcg daily. Iodine is essential for normal thyroid function, growth, development, and metabolism. It is found in iodized salt, seaweed, cod, tuna, shrimp, and lima beans, plus eggs, dairy products, and prunes.

PABA is para-aminobenzoic acid, which promotes metabolism and fights aging (skin wrinkles and graying hair). It soothes burns and skin disorders. Deficiency results in fatigue, gray hair, anemia, and infertility. PABA is found in organ meats, mushrooms, spinach, molasses, and enriched grains.

Magnesium is needed along with calcium to maintain strong bones (density). Depletion results in nervousness, tension, and fatigue. This is found in Indigenous dark chocolate, avocado, hazel nuts, chia, pumpkin seeds, and salmon in addition to legumes, tofu, whole grains, and bananas.

Manganese: Adults need 2–5 mg per day. This is needed for development of skeletal and connective tissues and assists in metabolizing carbohydrates. It is found in Indigenous foods such as pecans, pinto beans, mussels, sweet potatoes, pine nuts, and lima beans and nonindigenous foods including almonds, legumes, oatmeal, spinach, and pineapple.

Pantothenic acid: Adults need 5 mg daily. Useful as an antistressor, it helps to keep away infections and reduce premature aging. Depletion results in fatigue, infections, gray hair, depression, stress, constipation, weakness, insomnia, cramps, and low blood pressure. Pantothenic acid is found in Indigenous avocado, organ meats, sweet potatoes, and nuts, and nonindigenous broccoli, kale, eggs, legumes, milk, and chicken.

Phosphorus: From age 19 adults need between 800 mg and 1,200 mg a day to maintain strong bones and teeth. It assists in energy metabolism and enhances the use of other nutrients. Phosphorus is found in Indigenous beans, salmon, tuna, quinoa, and trout as well as in dairy products, poultry, eggs, whole grains, nuts, seeds, fish.

Potassium works with sodium to maintain body fluid balance; it may assist in lowering blood pressure. It is found in Indigenous lima beans, pinto beans, sweet potatoes, zucchini, pumpkins, tomatoes, halibut, and trout in addition to citrus fruits, legumes, avocados, and bananas. Athletes and heavy sweaters need to pay attention to their sodium and potassium intake to prevent dehydration and cramps.

Selenium: Men need 70 mcg per day and women need 55 mcg. This is necessary for use of iodine in thyroid function and for growth and development. It is found in Indigenous sunflower seeds, turkey, and Brazil nuts as well as in spinach, oats, beef, eggs, dairy, and bananas.

Water: Adults need 8–10 cups of water per day, in addition to the 4 cups one ingests from foods throughout the day. Those in hot climates need to drink more fluids.

Zinc: Men need 11–15 mg per day and women need 8–12 mg. Zinc is an essential component of over 100 enzymes that are involved with wound healing, digestion, metabolism, and reproduction. It is found in Indigenous squash and pumpkin seeds, pine nuts, and peanuts as well as in eggs, meats, liver, fish, almonds, cashews, and whole grains.

5. Calories, Exercise, and Recovering Fitness

People who have access to nutritious food, who exercise, and do not smoke possess more energy, think clearly, can deal with stress more adequately, are successful in work and their personal lives, and often serve as role models for others who want to improve their quality of life. There are many things we can do as consumers to ensure that we get quality foods, from protesting misleading and deceptive ads to campaigning for nutrition education in our schools, demanding nutritious meals for children eating at school cafeterias, educating others about diet and exercise, and becoming environmentalists to make certain our water, air, and soil are clean and free of pollutants. We can also become aggressive in our efforts to eat well and to exercise; in so doing, we become role models for others. Not one of the suggestions is bizarre or difficult. They are common sense ideas that I hope will inspire readers at least to try some of them. A complete return to hunting, gathering, and cultivating in the same ways our ancestors did is not usually practical, but all of us can make small adjustments to our lifestyles that can contribute to overall well-being.

Our metabolism slows as we grow older, which means that adults on the average gain two pounds per year. And this goes for those of us who are careful about our intake. To make the situation more difficult, in order to make foods taste better, dishes are cooked with cream, fat, lard, grease, salt, and sugar. When we are tired or stressed, it is easier to buy a bag of corn chips than it is to prepare the corn-based Choctaw foods *banaha* or *tanfula*. It is challenging even to walk into Starbucks for a cup for coffee because of the amazing array of goodies that one can add to a 10-calorie serving of Joe: 130 calories for whipped cream, 270 calories for whole milk, mocha caramel at 25 a pump, and so on. The Java Chip Frappuccino contains 650 calories and more grams of fat than a McDonald's Big Mac. Without question, the more choices we have, and the easier it is to find something to eat when we're hungry, the more we tend to eat, and we eat what we want instead of what we should be eating. As the years go by, our health problems are compounded by the reality of bad food choices, slower metabolism, loss of enthusiasm to stay active, and the fact that it is easy to become discouraged as the scale shows added pounds.

Figuring how many calories you need per day takes a bit of calculating. You must take into account your height, gender, and activity level. The easiest way to find out what you need is to log on to a website that can quickly calculate all the factors pertaining to you. There are several sites that where you can calculate your caloric and nutritional needs. Try Calculator.net: https://www.calculator.net/calorie-calculator.html.

If you want to calculate yourself how many calories you need per day, get a calculator and bring some patience to the table.

Step One

CALORIES PER DAY

Men: multiply your body weight in kg (kg = pounds divided by 2.2) by 24 to equal calories per day. Example: 190 pounds divided by 2.2 = 86.36 kg × 24 = 2,073 calories per day.

Women: multiply your body weight in kg (kg = pounds divided by 2.2) by 23 to equal calories per day. Example: 150 pounds divided by 2.2 = 68.18 kg × 24 = 1,636 calories per day.

Step Two

BASAL METABOLIC RATE

Next, calculate your basal metabolic rate (BMR)—calories needed if sedentary.

Men: BMR = 66 + (13.7 × weight in kg) + (5 × height in cm) - (6.8 × age in years). Explanation: add 66 to 13.7 times weight in kg, then add to 5 times height in cm (inches times 2.54), then subtract 6.8 times your age in years: 66 + (13.7 × weight in kg) + (5 × height in cm) - (6.8 × age in years). Example: 66 + (13.7 × 86.36 kg) + (5 × 177.8 cm* [= 70 in. × 2.54]) - (6.8 × 42) = 66 + 1,249.13 + 889 - 285.6 = 1,918.53 BMR for a 5'10", 42-year-old sedentary male. *cm = inches multiplied by 2.54 (i.e., 70 inches × 2.54 = 285.6 cm).

Women: BMR = 655 + (9.6 × weight in kg) + (1.8 × height in cm) - (4.7 × age in years). Example: 655 + (9.6 × 68.18 kg) + (1.8 × 285.6) - (4.7 × 47) = 655 + 654.52 + 514 - 220.9 = 1,662.62 BMR for 5'10", 47-year-old sedentary female.

Step Three

ACTIVITY FACTOR

If you exercise:

Men: 66 + (13.7 × weight in kilos) + (5 × height in cm) - (6.8 × age in years) = BMR. To determine your total daily calorie needs, now multiply your BMR by the appropriate activity factor, as follows:

> If you are inactive (little or no exercise): BMR × 1.2
>
> If you are lightly active (light exercise/sports 1–3 days/ week): BMR × 1.375
>
> If you are moderately active (moderate exercise/sports 3–5 days/week): BMR × 1.55
>
> If you are very active (hard exercise/sports 6–7 days/ week): BMR × 1.725
>
> If you are extra active (very hard daily exercise/sports and physical job or 2× day training): BMR × 1.9

Women: 655 + (9.6 × weight in kg) + (1.8 × height in cm) - (4.7 × age in years) = BMR. To determine your total daily calorie needs, now multiply your BMR by the appropriate activity factor, as follows:

If you are sedentary (little or no exercise): BMR × 1.2

If you are lightly active (light exercise/sports 1–3 days/
week): BMR × 1.375

If you are moderately active (moderate exercise/sports 3–5
days/week): BMR × 1.55

If you are very active (hard exercise/sports 6–7 days/
week): BMR × 1.725

If you are extra active (very hard daily exercise/sports and
physical job or 2× day training): BMR × 1.9

To Lose Weight

A pound of fat contains 3,600 calories. If you want to lose one pound of fat, you must expend 3,600 calories. If you want to lose ten pounds of fat, you must expend 36,000 calories, and so forth. The healthiest way to lose weight is to expend 500 more calories per day through both exercise and food consumption.

What solves many health problems is a diet heavy in vegetables, fruits, nuts, seeds, and lean meats, plus daily exercise, no smoking, and minimal use of alcohol. Not everyone has time or the desire to lift weights or to run every day, but almost everyone can manage walking and lifting light weights. Some activists argue that we should only perform "traditional" exercise. That is not always possible, especially if we consider the Raramuris (or Tarahumaras, as they were called by the Spanish), who live in northwest Mexico. They live simply, in remote areas in cabins or in caves. They eat what they have always eaten: beans, corn, potatoes, fish, herbs, rabbits, and more recently beef and goat. The amazing aspect of the Raramuris is that they can run for a hundred miles at a time. One of their traditions is "foot throwing," a competition that involves a small wooden ball "thrown by the foot" by teams in a multi-day race. Matthew Karsten's article "Running with Mexico's Tarahumara Indians" is among the many articles and videos about the Raramuris.[1]

To be sure, few people desire to participate in extreme running. But it is not always possible to garden, hunt, gather, or play stickball every day either. Good health does not come easily. Unhealthy foods abound in fast food places, stores, and restaurants. Pollution, deceptive advertising, and low prices make for unhealthy meals. What can we do that is manageable?

Educate yourself about nutrition. Buy or check out books that inform you about nutrition and fitness.

Attend your tribal council meetings and pressure your elected council to make certain there are healthy food choices for all tribal members. Better yet, run for tribal office so you can help make crucial economic, political, and social changes that will allow your tribe to have control over its food production.

Companies and organizations like McDonald's, Domino's Pizza, Campbell's Soup, the National Livestock and Meat Board, and the National Potato Board serve as sponsors of educational materials. When your children take healthy lunches to school and get kidded about what is in their lunch boxes, teach them to say, "I like it," and when asked why they don't eat junk food to say, "I don't like it."

Take a stand at home and limit the amount of time the kids (and you) watch TV, play video games, or surf the web. Make rules and stick with them. When my kids watched TV for half an hour, they had to play outside for half an hour. The only snack allowed in front of the TV was fruit.

Learn about the food your tribe once consumed. Ask yourself why you cannot also start eating like this. What are the drawbacks? What is the expense?

Many food advertisements are deceptive and manipulative. Question what you are buying: check labels and do not buy foods that you now know are fatty, greasy, salty, and sugary.

At restaurants, ask for doggie bags, ask the waiter to take away the bread basket, and do not eat everything on your plate.

Buy healthy food for your family. Children usually do not have the luxury of picking out what they want, but you do.

Do not give your children lunch money when there is a chance they will buy soft drinks, cookies, and French fries. Spend some money and make their lunches. The investment is well worth it.

Campaign with your school board or tribal council for healthier food at schools.

Volunteer to be an educator about health and fitness at schools, tribal council meetings, or neighborhood meetings.

Start an exercise and diet group among your friends. Meet often at designated times to walk and to talk about healthy recipes. Have potluck dinners—no junk allowed.

Organize a cookbook of your tribe's traditional meals.

Start a community garden where everyone can pitch in and help and later reap the rewards.

Show by example. If you start eating right and exercising, others will see what you are doing, and they will do the same. Be prepared to answer questions.

There are works to turn to if you want more information about what to eat, the politics of food production and marketing, and how to maintain a healthy lifestyle. National magazines such as *Time, Newsweek,* and *Consumer Reports* consistently feature articles that tell us of the latest discoveries about nutrition. Another source of information is *Outside* magazine, which often features articles on health and fitness.[2]

I recommend several recent eye-opening books, most notably Kelly Brownell and Katherine Horgen's *Food Fight,* Greg Critser's *Fat Land,* Eric Schlosser's *Fast Food Nation,* and Marion Nestle's *Food Politics;* a book I have turned to for forty years is Gaylord Hauser's *Diet Does It.*[3]

Do you exercise? If so, how and how much? What sports do you like to watch? Do you park your car as close to store fronts as you can? Do you take the stairs?

The best recipe for success is to choose an activity that you like and look forward to; if it feels like a chore, try something else: walking, swimming, basketball, softball (you get the benefits from training, mainly), or bicycling.

Weight lifting builds muscle, and muscle burns more energy than fat, even at rest. So the more weight-resistant exercise you do, the more calories your body will burn at rest.

A return to playing stickball on a regular basis and practicing enough to keep us strong and our body fat low is another option. It can be done; when my son was in elementary school we tossed and caught in our yard. We always took our sticks to the gym and used the racquet ball courts for throwing balls against the wall. While this is not exactly the traditional way to play, it does provide the opportunity to work on skills and hand-eye coordination. This, in combination with running and lifting weights, is an effective workout.

Include your friends and family in your fitness plans. Learn to play stickball and invite friends to join in weekly games. Start a walking group with your friends or neighbors. Go to the YMCA, walk around a mall, or look for aerobic classes in your town and take a friend for motivation.

Learn to swim like your ancestors. Hundreds of thousands of Natives lived by the coast, rivers, and lakes and there is no doubt that swimming was part of their lifestyle. As artist George Catlin observed in the early nineteenth century, "The art of swimming is known to all the American Indians; and perhaps no people on earth have taken more pains to learn it, nor any who turn it to better account. There certainly are no people whose avocations of life more often call for the use of their limbs in this way; as many of the tribes spend their lives on the shores of our vast lakes and rivers, paddling about from childhood in their fragile bark canoes, which are liable to continual accidents, which often throw the Indian upon his natural resources for the preservation of his life."[4]

Learn to canoe like our ancestors. Tribespeople who lived near water not only swam; they also paddled canoes. While your ancestors may have used canoes they made themselves from trees, you can purchase a metal or fiberglass canoe to save you the backbreaking trouble (or, satisfying work, depending on how you look at it) of building your own craft. I learned to manage a canoe at age eight and get into one whenever I can. Your local Red Cross might offer courses that teach you the basics of canoeing. The beauty of it is that it is like riding a bike—you never forget how. Paddling can be strenuous and even dangerous, depending on the waters you choose, but in calm water even little children can help you along. As they grow older, their strokes become more powerful. Invest in a canoe and you can take it on trips to lakes, rivers, streams, and ponds.

Run Like Your Ancestors

How do you start running?

Our ancestors often ran barefoot, without running shoes, Gore-Tex, socks, or fanny packs holding water bottles and iPhones. So there is no reason for you to avoid giving it a try. And if you cannot run, then walk. The cost of running is less than for most sports. You will need to invest in a good pair of running shoes that will be appropriate for your feet (high or low arches, pronation, supination), body type (weight, knee condition), type of activity (racing, walking, cross training), and running surface (street, trail). Socks are also important; if you use thin socks you will get blisters. Buy thick socks (such as Thorlos) that will protect your skin and absorb perspiration.

Walk first. Start with fifteen-minute walks every day for a week and work up to thirty minutes. Once you are comfortable with a fast walk and your doctor says you are healthy enough for more rigorous exercise, then try slow jogs. Walk when you are winded, then jog again after you recover. Don't go too fast or far the first few months. Once you feel comfortable, then extend your outings by fifteen minutes.

Take water with you. "Tough" coaches used to go by the adage of withholding water in hope that their athletes would become stronger, but this has proven to be physically damaging and sometimes fatal. You must stay hydrated on walks and runs; take a bottle with you and drink every twenty minutes. Then drink another glass when you get home. When you become thirsty, you are already dehydrated.

Buy a small fanny pack that will hold a water bottle. You can also clip your cell phone and mace to the waist band and store lip balm, sunscreen, money, Kleenex, and other sundries in the pockets. I have packs for every outing: a light fanny pack for short runs that holds just the preceding items; one a bit larger for longer hikes and runs in the mountains, where I might need more water, extra socks, a knife, food, band aids, and so on; and a larger shoulder pack for all-day outings.

Buy a hat or visor and sunglasses and wear them for sun protection.

New mothers often find it difficult to find time or energy to exercise. Try what I did with both my children: I bought a baby jogger (not a cheap stroller that cannot withstand much use; even my joggers with shocks wore out after a year) and went out for six-mile walks until my body was ready to run, and we went out every day. You don't have to go as far, of course, but I've been a runner for more than forty-five years. I took along diapers, bottles, and sunscreen (get a jogger with a shade); and a fanny pack to carry water, Kleenex, and money for stopping at garage sales; and extra clothes in cold weather. Both my kids basically grew up in the joggers; along the way they learned about trees, birds, and squirrels, and once we moved into the woods they got to see deer, elk, porcupines, and hawks.

Fitness and Your Children

When your children are old enough to walk distances, take them with you. Even if they are so small that they can only manage half a block, take them, then drop them off at home (with a sitter, of course) and continue your walk or run. Take them swimming; teach them how to shoot hoops and to throw and catch. Organize games for the children in your area so they all can be active.

Volunteer to be a coach when the soccer, basketball, or cross country season comes around. Add a few more workouts and tell team members about healthy eating. Tell parents that no junk food is allowed as after-game snacks.

Have your children play sports. Focus on their learning the game(s), not on winning. Children who start a sport early learn valuable lessons they will carry with them the rest of their lives: what it takes to become fit; how to maintain that fitness and skill level; that achieving something takes work and perseverance; how proper eating enhances physical performance; and that it is easier to maintain fitness than to stop being active and then try and regain that after a period of inactivity and poor eating habits. My children started playing basketball and soccer on formal teams at age four for fun and fitness. They also hike extensively and run. My daughter was able to hike eight miles for three days straight at Zion National Monument when she was six. Both my son and daughter ran cross country and track in high school, and my son ran at university for four years. Children will do these things willingly, especially if they see you doing them.

For students, completing a degree can be stressful. Studying for exams, keeping up with readings, and meeting assignment deadlines is difficult enough without the student also having to face racism and prejudice. Indigenous students, along with other marginalized students, are often emotionally charged just by being on campus. Having to travel to keep up with community duties and ceremonies, dealing with family responsibilities, and worrying about finances can be overwhelming. Many people turn to alcohol or drugs to relax, while others watch movies or try and forget the daily drudge by sleeping. According to the NAU Native American Student Services office that deals with Native dropouts, many students simply stop going to class or "stop-out"; that is, when the going gets tough they leave school and return when they feel like it. How can Native students combat this stress?

One's attitude can be improved almost immediately by walking to classes instead of driving or taking the bus; by forgoing processed, fried, and fatty foods in favor of fruits, vegetables, and lean meats; and by stopping bad habits such as smoking and drinking. Not only is one's physical state improved, but just making the changes is greatly empowering and can inspire students to face the challenges thrown at them in school. And one can take those strategies a few steps farther. Along with proper diet, students can find easy ways to exercise by focusing on other things. For example, buy a book about animal tracks, in addition to small pocket guides to insects, trees, clouds, and so on, and make it a point to visit trails several times a week and try to identify what you see. Taking plenty of water and food, plus clothing appropriate for the weather, means you can stay outside for hours, not only exercising but also learning about the natural world at the same time.

Burning Calories and Becoming Fit

You burn calories throughout the day, and the more you move, the more you burn. There are many calculators on the web for counting calories burned. The numbers below are based on a 150-pound person exercising for one hour.

Aerobics (high impact): 420+
Aerobics (low impact): 320
Basketball game (entire): 490+
Basketball (wheelchair): 400
Bicycling (10 mph): 250
Bowling: 180
Canoeing (easy): 250
Canoeing (6 mph, vigorous): 700+
Car repairs: 180
Child care (active): 180
Chopping firewood: 430
Circuit weight training (minimal rest): 475+

Construction (shingling, nailing siding, installing porch, etc.): 350+

Cooking (grinding corn is about 50–100 more per hour): 150

Cross-country machine: 500

Cross-country skiing (moderate speed): 490

Cross-country skiing (vigorous): 550+

Dancing (including ballet, modern, powwow): 360+

Darts: 150

Driving: 110

Eating: 90

Farm work (milking, baling hay, etc.): 490

Fishing in boat: 150

Fishing in waders: 350

Football and baseball (catch): 150

Football (touch): 490

Frisbee: 207 (more for your dog)

Gardening: 250–400

Golf (carrying your clubs): 325+

Handball: 700+

Hiking: 350

Hiking (mountain): 600

Horse grooming: 350

Horse riding: 300+ (more for the horse, of course)

House cleaning (light): 220

Hunting: 300+ (depending on weather, terrain, amount of sitting, tracking, dragging, etc.)

Ice skating (recreational): 430

Kayaking: 300

Lacrosse or stickball: 500+

Martial arts: 590

Mountain biking: 500+

Mowing lawn with push mower: 330

Racquetball: 600

Raking leaves: 250

Rock climbing (ascending and rappelling combined): 650+
Rollerblading: 500
Roller skating: 430
Rugby: 600
Running (10 mph/6 min. mi.): 950
Running (6 mph/10 min. mi.): 590
Running (5 mph/12 min. mi.): 480
Running (cross-country): 550
Sewing or knitting: 90
Shoveling snow: 360
Sitting: 85
Skateboarding: 300
Skiing (snow): 440+
Sleeping: 60
Snorkeling: 320
Soccer (casual): 430
Softball: 320
Squash: 720
Stair machine (not leaning on arms): 370
Swimming (laps): 500
Tennis: 400+
Typing: 140
Walking (slow, 2 mph): 150
Walking (fast, 3.5 mph): 350
Walking (very fast, 4 mph): 357
Walking ("power," fast and using arms): 500
Water skiing: 350+
Weightlifting (moderate effort): 190
Weightlifting (vigorous): 400+
Yoga: 250

Finally—do not let anyone discourage you from your goal of becoming fit. Often spouses, friends, and children are wary of something new, and it is not unheard of for those close to us to try to sabotage our intentions.

6. Changing What We Eat

A radical option is to give up all foods that are not indigenous to this hemisphere and to prepare only native plants and animals in the same ways that our ancestors traditionally ate them. From March 2012 to March 2013 Martin Reinhardt, associate professor at Northern Michigan University, along with some of his students and colleagues, did just that for one year. For two years prior to the venture Reinhardt had researched foods of his Anishinaabe (Ojibwa) ancestors before embarking on the challenging year-long diet of precontact foods only, all from the Great Lakes Region.[1] Not everyone would be enthused about eating only unrefined and unprocessed foods, and even if they were desirous of participating in the challenge Reinhardt undertook, there is no guarantee that their precontact resources would be available.

Historically Natives were constantly active. They did not breathe polluted air, drink polluted water, or eat foods made from genetically modified organisms (GMOs). And therein lies a catch: today much meat and fish is contaminated with polychlorinated biphenyls (PCBs) and other toxins, and much of what we consume involves GMOs. Many of the foods tribes gathered are no longer available or are on private property. Diets of people in one century may not necessarily be practical for those in another century, and the reality is that today there are many more variables to consider. This pertains especially for northern tribes who depended mainly on blubber and meats. For example, some researchers write that some the animals—and especially parts of the animals like the kidneys, beaver tail, the harbor seal's deposits of fat, and sheep intestines—are high in saturated fat—as much as 65 percent—and Natives consumed this fat on a regular basis.[2] While tribespeople did eat more parts of the deer, elk, moose, and bison than we night today, they were consistently active and did not eat processed or toxin-laden foods that would have devastated their health, like a modern diet has affected us. But we can try to eat in a similar fashion. According to the Mayo Clinic, three ounces of deer meat, for example, contains 134 calories, as opposed to 259 calories for the same amount of beef. (This is a composite of all cuts that have been trimmed and cooked.)[3] Other types of venison (elk, reindeer, moose, caribou) also are lower in fat than beef.

Few of us are willing to give up all sweets, milk products, chips, and pizza. Some argue that we don't have to abstain from processed foods to stay healthy, but we must eat them only in moderation. Regardless of arguments over the intricacies of nutrition, many Native activists advocate educating ourselves about our histories in order to take a stand against colonization, and that includes studying the way our people used to eat. One symptom of accepting colonization is adhering to the typical American diet even while it is killing us.

Many have come to the conclusion that an "Americanized" diet is the best diet. Some, on the other hand, never think about what they eat at all. This attitude stems directly from what I call the boarding school syndrome, a psychological problem that plagues thousands of Natives. Symptoms include apathy toward racism, stereotypes, and other forms of discrimination. Sufferers feel no desire to fight against prejudice or the colonial ideology that Native culture is inferior to white, Christianized, "civilized" culture (as defined by those who believe they are superior). The syndrome is a result of generations of young Natives being forced to endure racist teachings at boarding schools that told the students their languages, religions, clothing, hairstyles, world views, and foods were inferior. Students were dressed like Americans and were fed Americanized, salty, greasy, fatty, and wheat-laden dishes. These teachings were then brought back to their families, and what we see today are Natives who make minimal or no effort to regain their cultures. Eating the foods this society presents without questioning the contents of those foods, or the damaging effects of those foods, is one of the manifestations of the boarding school syndrome.[4]

As we have seen, some Natives see traditional tribal foods as "second class" foods, and others claim that fried white flour is "traditional."[5] To illustrate: at a Department of Indigenous Nations Studies potluck I brought elk stew, and at a recent family (Comanche) reunion I brought venison and pinto bean chili. Both were the least-consumed dishes at long tables of cheesy beef casseroles, fried chicken, chips, and desserts. Recall that, as discussed in case study 3, Beau LeBeau finds losing weight difficult because his household prefers chips and sodas.[6] His family especially dislikes bison, once a mainstay of their ancestors' diet.

A "clean" lifestyle that includes a diet free from (or with minimal use of) processed foods, combined with moderate drinking and daily exercise, will bring many rewards. Proper living will keep our weight down, our blood pressure normal, and our energy high. Even twenty minutes of exercise per day, three days a week, can reduce the chances of developing diabetes. Studies reveal that a reduction of 5–10 percent of body weight in obese individuals can reduce the chances of developing cancer by 58 percent.

By gaining good health we also gain confidence—pride in ourselves and in our tribe's rich traditions. Even small steps are greatly meaningful. Contact members of your tribe and exchange traditional recipes. Try to make one traditional meal per week, then begin incorporating two or three per week. Walk around the block each morning.

One thing to keep in mind is that everyone is different. Some cannot properly digest milk products or gluten. Some are allergic to certain foods. Some are able to eat many eggs and other animal products per week without a change to their cholesterol level, while others have difficulty when they eat even few animal products. Others have high blood pressure even though they exercise and are careful about their diets. My father, for example, was an exceptionally thin distance runner who was obsessive about his diet, yet he inherited and retained high blood pressure. People also metabolize foods at different rates. Do not try to eat as much as your larger and more active spouse or friends.

Suggestions for Transitioning an Unhealthy Diet

Keep in mind that there are many reasons why we continue to be tempted by foods that we know are bad for us. Taste is the main factor. Sweet, salty, greasy, and sour flavors are favorites (think of kids eating the huge, sodium-laden dill pickles that are sold at pow wows, sporting events, and even school functions). In *Fast Food Nation,* Eric Schlosser discusses what goes into making foods like milkshakes, burgers, and French fries taste good; if the list of artificial ingredients that go into a Burger King strawberry shake doesn't make you queasy, then perhaps nothing will.[7] Even if the food you eat from a fast food joint would smell rather rank in its truly natural state, a dose of a food additive that makes it smell good will ensure that you never know the difference. How ironic that many of the foods Natives now prefer are artificially colored and "odorized," when the natural foods that we could be eating are underutilized. It is a sorry state of affairs indeed if a person thinks McDonald's fries smell and taste better than grilled salmon, or turkey breasts and vegetables spiced with garlic and peppers, or elk steaks smothered in green chilies.

It is not the purpose of this discussion to provide medical advice about "curing" diabetes or obesity. A person with diabetes must consult with a physician. One thing a diabetic needs to be aware of, however, is how to count carbohydrates. Away to educate yourself is to look at the NIH/National Institute of Diabetes and Digestive and Kidney Diseases website.

"Carb Counting" at Carb Counter.net is a web page that gives you a formula for calculating how many grams of carbohydrates you may consume, depending on how much insulin you use. And the Native American Diabetes Project has a Diabetes Wellness Connection web page for information on how to control and prevent diabetes.[8]

The *Atlantic* reported in 2016 that more than half of what Americans eat is "ultra processed."[9] Because our society is faster moving than ever, those who responded said they buy such foods for several reasons: preparation time is brief; they are too tired to cook; they find the convenience foods taste good, and they believe the convenience foods are nutritious (the reality is that you do have to pick and choose carefully). Nine out of ten adults eat dessert at least once a week. The favorite snack is chips (almost seventeen pounds of potato chips per person, per year), followed by popcorn, fruits, cookies, and ice cream.

Dropping hamburgers, fries, and milkshakes and substituting fruit, vegetables, lean and game meats, in addition to daily exercise, can make a tremendous difference in body fat percentage and sugar levels.

For those who like bread but do not want to deal with the consequences of celiac disease, look for substitutes. Gluten is not in corn, rice, or potatoes. You can make substitute gluten and wheat with arrowroot, corn (flour, meal, and starch), potato starch flour, rice flour, and tapioca.[10]

Use Indigenous greens, such as goosefoot or lamb's quarters, which often pops up unexpectedly in gardens. I freeze goosefoot and use it as a staple. If you do not have access to this plant that many people consider to be a weed, use nonindigenous spinach. Your picky kids won't notice it much, either. You can add it to pizza and baked potatoes as a topping and put it in scrambled eggs, soups, casseroles, salads, tacos, etc.

Consider adding non-GMO brewer's yeast to your diet. It contains the B vitamins, zinc, and protein. You can take brewer's yeast as tablets or add powder to drinks (it tastes strong, so try it with tomato juice or v-8).

Learn to like foods that are high in fiber and nutrients but low in calories and with a low glycemic index. Foods with a high glycemic index cause your blood sugar to rise and fall quickly, making you hungry. Those with a low number allow your blood sugar to fall more slowly, thus satisfying your hunger for longer. High GI foods are cakes, pies, muffins, breads, cereals, cookies, potatoes, rice, candy, and sugars. Lower GI foods include most vegetables and fresh, whole fruits (not juice).

If you are a milk drinker, add a tablespoon or two of organic nonfat dry milk to your cup of milk in order to increase your intake of protein and calcium. Add beans, chia seeds, and amaranth cereal to your diet to increase your calcium intake.

Go to the grocery store with your children or a friend and pay attention to every food in the fruit and vegetable section. What foods do you eat regularly and which ones have you never tried? Many groceries have "cards" or recipe books located close to the scales. Take a small tablet with you and look through the recipes. Write down the ones that sound appealing and try making them.

If you don't buy an item, you reduce your chances of eating it. When grocery shopping, grit your teeth and pass by the chips, candy, and sugary drinks. If you only have fruits, vegetables, yogurt, and lean meats in your basket, those will be your choices at home. If you avoid buying Oreos, candy, pop, and pie, then your children will not be eating those things either. Children can be sneaky when they know goodies are in the kitchen; they will find the tempting items (and believe me, spouses will, too).

Try ground turkey (without the skin) instead of hamburger and "turkey dogs" (with white meat) instead of hot dogs.

If you eat gluten, buy whole grain bread, not just wheat bread. The latter is often no more nutritious than white bread and may have been dyed with caramel coloring to look like whole wheat bread.

Eat yogurt that contains *Lactobacillus acidophilus*, a bacterium that helps break down food and extract more nutrients.

There are fifteen thousand species in the legume family. A nineteen-year study shows that men and women who eat legumes four times a week have a 22 percent reduction in the risk for heart attack.[11]

When the bran layer is removed from grain, 80 percent of the nutrients are lost. Eat whole grains. They keep you fuller longer. Beware, however, of bran muffins, which are very high in fat and calories.

Wild rice is Native to North America. Stop eating white rice (and certainly fried rice at Chinese restaurants) in favor of wild rice. Add zucchini, chile peppers, or cranberries to the mixture.

Use nutrient-rich lamb's quarters, dandelion leaves, and other deep greens instead of iceberg lettuce.

Stop eating your children's leftovers. Either pack leavings for later or feed them to the chickens.

Use vegetable or nut oil instead of lard. I like to cook with grape oil.

Trim all visible fat from red meats and fowl and after cooking, and drain and blot off any more excess fat from bacon, sausages, and breads with paper towels. Chill canned meat so that you can remove the layer of grease that accumulates on the top. Stop eating fried foods; roast, broil, bake, or steam instead.

Reconsider hot dogs and luncheon and canned meats. Factory farms are often cruel to cattle, swine, chickens, turkeys, rabbits, and fish. In addition, these meats usually contain too much sodium and fat. Look for "white meat," "low fat," and "low sodium."

Be careful about buying fish. Find out where your fish came from. Farmed fish are less nutritious, and the farms destroy the marine environment. Many fish contain PCBs (which have shown up in breast milk among Iroquois women) and mercury (which appears even in fish from small freshwater lakes). As with beef and poultry, remove any visible fat, and don't eat the skin.

Likewise, be careful about purchasing soy products. Vast swaths of jungles have been cleared to make way for soybean fields, thus creating soil compaction and erosion. Soy production has destroyed ecosystems and displaced animals, and it exploits workers.[12]

Buy an easy-to-use crock pot (slow cooker). You can put, for example, a venison roast, potatoes, tomatoes, mushrooms, chilies, onions, and spices in the pot in the morning, and the hearty meal will be ready for dinner. Crock pots are inexpensive, very easy to use and clean, and they last well.

Eat smaller portions, and eat slowly. Use a smaller plate or bowl and put down your utensils between bites.

If you have difficulty consuming enough fiber, try chia seeds (make certain to drink a lot of water).

Stop using salt and try herbs instead. Drain and rinse canned vegetables to get rid of salt, and do the same for fruits to lose the sugar syrup. You do not need salt to cook pasta, rice, or oats.

If you need something sweet on oatmeal, try Stevia, an extract of the stevia leaf that is three hundred times sweeter than sugar and is safe for diabetics. Stevia can result in abdominal pain, headaches, and other physical issues, so use it only in small amounts.

You can lessen the carbohydrate and calorie count of a sandwich or hamburger by removing the top half of the bun or one piece of bread.

University students must beware of the "freshman fifteen," that is, the average amount of weight students gain during their first year at school. The main culprits are keg parties and high carbohydrate and fatty foods such as chips, cookies, breads, fast foods, and sweets. Walking to classes each and eating salad instead of French fries, and fruit instead of cookies, can hugely improve a student's health, as can drinking a glass of water after every glass of beer.

Curb or stop yourself from drinking colas. Even diet drinks can be problematic because they erode your teeth and they can make you crave sweet foods. The artificial sweetener Aspartame is known to have negative side effects for some people.[13]

Start checking your foods for "high-fructose corn syrup" (HFCS), an inexpensive ingredient that appears in everything from Cool Whip to Special K cereal. HFCS does not stimulate the creation of insulin and leptin that can tell you when you've had enough to eat. You don't feel full when consuming large quantities of HFCS. It is recommended that if a food you're about to purchase at the grocery has more than eight grams of sugar, and if HFCS appears first or second on the list of ingredients, then buy something else.[14] Remember that sugar also goes by these names: corn syrup, crystalline fructose, dextrose, fructose, fruit-juice concentrates, glucose, high-fructose corn syrup, high-maltose corn syrup, honey lactose, invert sugar, lactose, malt, maltose, molasses, sucrose, and syrup.

That Hidden Death Trap: Trans Fats

Trans fat lurks in thousands of foods, but manufacturers are not required by law to include on their list of ingredients whether it contains trans fat. In fact, the Food and Drug Administration did not require this ingredient to be listed until 2006. Most people have heard that there are different kinds of fats: *monounsaturated* fat (in olives, olive oil, canola oil, peanut oil, cashews, almonds, peanuts, and most other nuts, avocados); *polyunsaturated* fat (in corn, soybean, safflower, and cottonseed oils, fish); *saturated* fat (mainly animal fats: in meat, seafood, whole-milk dairy products such as cheese, milk, and ice cream, poultry skin and egg yolks, and in some plant foods—coconut and coconut oil, palm oil, and palm kernel oil); and the bad one—*trans* fat, or *trans-unsaturated fatty acids*. If you see the words "hydrogenated" or "partially hydrogenated" in the ingredients, then the product contains trans fat. This ingredient helps to increase the shelf life of food, but it has disastrous effects on our bodies.

The first two are "good" fats (although that does not mean you can eat all you want of them). Saturated fat can be a "bad" fat, but luckily, when you eat too much of it your body converts it to monounsaturated fat (a good fat). Trans fats from partially hydrogenated vegetable oils are a serious problem. Trans fats cause a lowering of your HDL (good) cholesterol and an increase in LDL (bad) cholesterol. Trans fats lurk in most margarines; vegetable shortening; partially hydrogenated vegetable oil, deep-fried chips, many fast foods, and most commercial baked goods. This list can include waffles, "chicken tenders," fish sticks, cheese and cracker sandwiches, Ramen noodles, Chex party mix, pizza, biscuits, tater tots, margarine, nondairy creamers, popcorn, and apple pie. The list is a long, scary one. Unfortunately, trans fat is not listed as an ingredient on some food labels.

If you drink a glass of wine or beer, drink a glass of water while considering whether you really need another glass of alcohol. Try no-alcohol wine and "near beers," those brews with less alcohol.

Roasted green chile peppers can serve as a garnish or side dish for any meal. Because they are roasted, the skins come off easily. We put them in stews and on pizza, sandwiches, eggs, and baked potatoes, and when they are freshly roasted, I eat them plain. Beware of eating too many, however; because they are members of the nightshade family you can get headaches. Take it slowly until you know your tolerance level (and start with the "mild" variety, not "hot").

Plain baked potatoes have only around 100 calories and are filling. But when you add butter, sour cream, bacon, and cheese, you can easily add up to 500 or more calories. Better yet, have a sweet potato for a sweet taste and much vitamin A. Potatoes are primarily carbohydrates, which means they are converted into sugar very quickly. Diabetics must beware of eating too much of these.

Stop eating canned meats and soups and cold cuts unless the label says "low sodium."

Eat the entire fruit instead of just drinking the juice. Juice may contain some nutrients but is high in calories and sugar. Eating a whole apple instead of drinking apple juice provides you with fiber and a feeling of satisfaction. And remember, Sunny Delight is not fruit juice.

Dieters can save money by paying closer attention to how grocery stores market their products. Check unit prices; for example, sometimes you can get cereal at a lower price in a larger box than a smaller one because the "unit price" is different. Pre-cut vegetables and salads cost more than individual fruits and vegetables. The healthier, cook-it-yourself "plain" oatmeal is cheaper than the individual "sugared" packets. Store-brand products are usually cheaper than national brands, and many of the former are now organic. Small bags of products such as snacks sold next to the check-out stands are more expensive than large bags of the same thing. Organic cereals on the bottom shelves are often cheaper than those higher up and at eye level. Items on the ends of aisles are not necessarily on sale. Warehouse clubs such as Sam's Club are not always full of bargains, and you have to buy enormous quantities of some items to get a good deal (and unless you're having a party or have a large family, who can eat that case of mangoes before they spoil?). Coupons and store cards do help cut costs.

Take a tip from Dolly Parton, who stands five feet tall. "I just eat small portions of what I like," says Dolly. She admits, "You just have to watch it when you're this short and have an appetite this big."[15]

At airports, do not buy from the food stands. Cinnabon, Pizza Hut, and other fast food restaurants only offer carbohydrates that will leave you feeling hungry a short time after eating. Instead, bring your own food. I either bring "roll ups"—lean meat (turkey, usually), cheese, lettuce, tomato, and mustard wrapped in a spinach tortilla—that I pack in a flat, insulated lunch box that fits easily in my kids' backpacks, or I go to Subway beforehand and get turkey subs with everything on them (375 calories for a six-inch sub with cheese; 330 without cheese). For snacks we eat nuts and jerky. In a tight pinch, we might buy a turkey sandwich on whole grain bread, which is around 450 calories. This is a much better choice than a Whopper with cheese (at 760 calories and 1,380 mg of sodium), and certainly better than Double

Whopper with mayo (1,010 calories and 1,460 mg of sodium). Do not order French fries. Even a small unsalted portion adds 250 calories and 480 mg of sodium to your intake. A small chocolate shake will add another 330 calories to this list. Have water from your reusable bottle (most airports now have water bottle filling stations) and a kiddie nonfat yogurt (88 calories) from TCBY instead.

As the above preceding listings of calories and sodium illustrate, it is crucial that all of us concerned about nutrition check the ingredients of our meals. This is easier than you might think. You can access specific restaurant nutritional analysis at Nutritionix.com.[16]

Instead of dumping dressing onto your salad, ask for dressing on the side and dip the ends of your fork into the dressing before skewering your greens. You may find that you don't need dressing as much as you thought. Try fat-free dressings. My favorites are salsa and balsamic vinaigrette (this, instead of fattening butter and sour cream, goes on the baked potato as well). You can completely ruin a low-calorie and low-sodium salad by adding 500 calories or more of dressing.

Do not feel as if you have to eat everything on your plate. Eat only until you are full. More is not better. Just because corn, avocados, and potatoes are traditional foods, that does not mean you can eat as much of them as you want. It's as simple as controlling the portion size. As we grow older, our metabolisms change and become slower. In high school I could eat a huge breakfast, a good lunch, and devour an entire pizza for dinner by myself, but at that time I was a teenager, ran every day, and rode my bike eight miles to and from school. I had to adjust the amount of food I took in at age thirty, then again at forty and sixty. I still log in fifty miles a week, swim, lift weights and garden, but I cannot eat nearly as much as I could ten years ago. You can't eat as much as your teenage athlete children, either. So unless you are a marathoner or work construction every day, don't attempt it. If you are not hungry, settle for fruit, yogurt, or a smoothie. Just because everyone around you is eating does not mean you have to do so. Consider that eating five to six small meals a day is easier on your body than three large meals. You are better able to monitor how full you are if you eat smaller portions.

Unless I am very hungry and know I can handle everything on my plate, I use the following strategies to make sure I don't overeat and to make sure that what I eat is healthy:

At restaurants:

Order an appetizer instead of an entrée (perhaps a shrimp cocktail, chicken sate, bowl of soup, or dinner salad).

Drink plenty of water with lemon so you won't be tempted to order a calorie-filled drink.

You and your partner order an appetizer and split an entrée.

Ask the waiter to take back the bread or chips basket. If it's not in front of you, you can't eat it.

Do not fall prey to servers who encourage ordering desserts and drinks. Say up front that you do not want to see the dessert tray. Say no and mean it.

Eat only half your meal and ask for a doggie bag. I ask for one as soon as the food arrives, so I can put half the meal in the container immediately and not be tempted.

Ask the waiter to remove any food you do not plan to take home so you won't be tempted to pick at it.

Never order dessert. Or if you must eat dessert, share it. If it is a special occasion, or you have been very active that day, order one dessert and split it with the rest of the table. Our family may indulge in, say, Key lime pie, but we divide one serving among four people. A dessert that we eat guilt-free is yogurt topped with chia seeds, blueberries, raspberries, pecans, and banana.

Do not order drinks unless they are diet drinks or unsweetened tea. Considering how expensive tea bags are at restaurants these days, drinking water helps your pocketbook.

At home:

Use small bowls and plates instead of your large ones. This
helps you psychologically: you don't feel as if you are
being deprived.

Make only enough dinner for one helping per person. If
you make more than that, eaters are tempted to keep
going back for more.

Make more vegetable and fruit dishes than the heavier
main course (unless your main course is free of unprocessed foods, heavy fat, and salt). In other words, make
less chicken and dumplings, steak, and lasagna and
more salad, grilled vegetables, and fruit mixtures.

Desserts, if any, should be limited to a few bites, just enough
to enjoy. A small tube glass filled with frozen yogurt is
satisfying. Taking a half gallon of ice cream to your chair
with you while you watch TV is mindless eating.

At parties and potlucks:

Have an apple or a small cup of vegetable soup before leaving the house so you won't be tempted to eat everything
you see.

Tell yourself ahead of time that you will not eat the frybread, potato or egg salad, chips, cookies, cakes, or pies.
Tell yourself you will eat the healthier alternatives: the
mayonnaise-free vegetable salads, fruit, beans, a hamburger with only half the bun, and just half of a dessert
(I like oatmeal cookies). It helps a lot to have a companion with you who follows the same strategy.

One way to solve the unhealthy potluck problem is to
being healthy foods yourself. If you bring to events
sliced vegetables with ranch dip, a variety of cut-up fruit,
a crock pot of vegetable stew, or a large salad (I always
bring my "Everything Salad," Choctaw *tanfula*, or elk
stew), then you know you will have things to eat.

On the road:

If you are traveling any distance in a car, invest in an ice
chest. Pack healthy foods for your family so you can
either bypass the fast food restaurants or use your own
food to supplement "road food."

Take yogurt, fruit (it helps to put fruits in plastic containers so they don't bruise), containers of applesauce,
low-calorie drinks, cheese, peanut butter, whole grain
bread, sliced low-fat meat, condiments, plastic glasses,
paper towels, and dinnerware. Think ahead about all the
things you normally use at home that can be taken on
the road, so that when you take a break at rest stops or at
hotels you'll have everything you need.

If you plan on frequenting restaurants, order vinaigrette
or Italian dressings instead of fattening ranch, thousand
island, and blue cheese dressing. Take your own Stevia
packets instead of using Sweet 'N Low in coffee and tea.
Fill up on salad, get low-calorie appetizers, split entrees,
never order dessert, and always request fruit instead of
fries (this is really important for children, who are often
stuck with greasy choices on the kids' menu). You will
not only save money; you will also be proud to discover
that you have not gained any "vacation weight."

With relatives:

Many Native people say that they cannot change their diets
because they were raised eating tortillas, frybread, and
fried potatoes. Their parents and grandparents cooked
with lard, grease, and sugar, and they ate large amounts
of food. Many people say they feel pressure to continue
that tradition, especially during holidays, visits, and ceremonies. Parents and grandparents, aunts and uncles,
cousins and siblings want to feed you when you visit. You

can deal with unhealthy food for a day or two, but for extended visits you may need to take matters into your own hands. Tell them you would like to contribute to the meals. Go to the local grocery store and buy ingredients for a large salad that includes lean meats and a light dressing; this is a meal by itself. For other meals make skinless chicken breasts, squash, corn and cornbread, or perhaps grilled catfish, spinach salad, sweet potatoes, and corn tortillas. Breakfasts can be oven-baked potato slices, with egg white omelets filled with sautéed vegetables and lean meat. Buy fruits, cheese sticks and vegetables to snack on.

When family members come to visit you, use the same healthy ideas for meals, but add one dish per meal that they like. For example, if your family insists on white flour tortillas, make sure that these are supplemented with fruits, vegetables, and lean meats. Try new ways of preparing green chilies. You do not need ice cream and cake for dessert. Yogurt, fruit and nuts can satisfy almost anyone, especially when placed in a fancy cup or dessert flute.

Regarding Children

Breastfeed your babies. Human milk and cow's milk are different in their protein make-up and antibody make-up. Breastfeeding provides protection against infections and promotes closeness for mother and child.

When we went to a salad bar or buffet, my children had to get at least six "colors" on their plates; one was to be red (tomato or bell pepper) and two were to be shades of green (perhaps spinach and kiwi); the colorful candy options were not allowed.

Provide your children with a nutritious lunch rather than depending on the questionable menu at their school. My kids' boxes were filled with the following:

A small, reusable ice pack to keep food cool

Half to whole sandwich of whole wheat bread with either peanut butter and a thin layer of plum jelly, or a slice of lean turkey or chicken breast with a slice of cheddar cheese and mustard

Fruit (an apple, pear, peach or banana; cut up in a small plastic container)

Small baggie of pretzels

One squeeze-tube-style yogurt

Baggie of cut-up carrot or celery sticks with hummus

Small container of chocolate milk

An organic fruit and nut bar for after-school snack. Also try Tanka Bars made by the Native-owned Native American Natural Foods, LLC.

They rarely got soda, candy, or donuts. Occasionally they might get a bag of tortilla chips, but they split a small bag between the two of them.

1. I learned about gardening at an early age. Here I am with my grandfather, Thomas Abbott, in front of his Muscogee garden in 1960. Note the corn plants, potato plants, green beans, and interspersed flowers. Author's collection.

2. (*above*) Hopi woman grinding corn. Photograph by Marie L. Olson, 1919. Northern Arizona University, Cline Library, nau.ph.516.62.

3. (*opposite*) A Hopi runner. Photograph by Leo Crane, 1920. Northern Arizona University, Cline Library, nau.ph.658.289.

4. Hopi men plant a cornfield by using planting sticks, as their ancestors have for centuries. Photograph by Bill Belknap, 1970. Northern Arizona University, Cline Library, nau.ph.96.4.14.16.

5. Creek man pounding corn to make sofky, 1890–1916. Frederick S. Barde Collection, Oklahoma Historical Society.

7. Importance of Backyard Gardens

Tribes need to be providing provide healthier food for all their members. The challenge is to produce enough of it in a safe and sustainable manner. Historically tribes did raise crops in just that way, but it required a community effort. Today larger farms invest in machinery and other technologies that make production easier, maximize profits, and minimize costs.[1] Many of those large-scale agricultural endeavors, however, use technological innovations such as fertilizers and pesticides that result in multiple environmental consequences.[2] This is not how tribes farmed historically.

The long, complex history of Native agriculture is beyond the scope of this book, but it is important to know that Mesoamerican cultures were cultivating plants at least seven thousand years ago. Corn, squashes, pumpkins, beans, and peppers made their way northward and were planted by Natives in the Southwest between 3500 and 2500 BC and around 1000 BC in the eastern part of the United States.[3] By the time European colonizers landed in North America many tribes were adept farmers. They dug canals for irrigation; created baskets and pottery as food and seed vessels; organized trade networks to share plants, animals and textiles; and used crops (corn, especially) as a commodity. They divided farming tasks by gender and incorporated ceremonies into their religions for planting, cultivating, and harvesting. However, tribes did not just domesticate food plants. Most tribes that farmed also hunted, gathered, and fished, although tribes that practiced hunting, gathering, and fishing did not always farm.

Anthony "Chako" Ciocco, national program coordinator of the Ancestral Lands Program on the Navajo Nation and former communications coordinator for the Mvskoke Food Sovereignty Initiative in Okmulgee, believes: "Our agricultural practices are a major part of who we are. If we were really sovereign we'd be living in the Mvskoke way."[4] What does he mean?

Historically, the Five Tribes cultivated large community gardens under strict protocols. Roles were delineated by gender and age, and everyone participated in planting, maintenance, and harvesting. For example, prior to the removal of the Muscogees in the 1830s, each town worked a large garden divided into family parcels. Everyone worked there: women cared for the small family gardens, and in summer, when men did not hunt, they helped women tend the larger community gardens. At other times women provided the bulk of the labor with the assistance of older men who could no longer hunt.[5] One man blew a conch to call the men to work. They arrived at the garden with their hoes and axes while the women arrived with food for the day. William Bartram, who observed them farming in the eighteenth century, described them as "marching in order to the field as if they were going to battle." Those who did not work were fined. The farmers sang as they worked, usually through early afternoon, when they sometimes broke to play games. Children sat in small shelters that were interspersed in the fields in order to scare away pests such as birds and raccoons. Men patrolled the fields at night to deter deer, which were especially fond of potato vines, while bears and raccoons targeted young corn "that is filled with a rich milk, as sweet and nourishing as cream."[6]

When it was time to harvest, all tribal members received a share of the community garden produce. Individual families also cultivated separate backyard gardens, sometimes called "patches," "roasting-ear patches," or "roasting patches," growing favorite foods and medicinal plants. Each family gathered plants from their parcel and donated a portion of their corn crop to the "king's crib," a cache of corn for use in hard times, for guests, and for war parties.[7] During times of drought, or over-trading of produce from the community gardens, the family gardens provided those in need with sustenance.

Their main foods were corn, sweet potato, rice, squashes, and pumpkins as well as the nonindigenous watermelons. Muscogees pounded, boiled, and then strained hickory nuts to extract the oily, sweet liquid to use in corn dishes. In addition to produce, they consumed waterfowl, rabbits, turkey, venison, alligator, bear, deer, trout, catfish, sunfish, bream, and softshell turtle as well as European-introduced beef, goat, and pork. Muscogees had festivals every month, almost all of which were dedicated to hunting or agriculture; their principal festival, called the "feast of first fruits," took place when the corn crops matured in August.[8]

After removal to Indian Territory many families continued to maintain small gardens around their houses, and Muscogees reestablished their smaller gardens; some also farmed on a large scale for profit. By 1873 they cultivated sixty thousand acres of corn, wheat, oats, rice, sweet potatoes, and Irish potatoes. Backyard gardens featured more European-introduced foods: lettuce, turnips, peas, and mustard. Many cultivated apple, peach, and plum trees as well as grape vines. Some of the farmers along the North Fork and Arkansas Rivers grew cotton and tobacco, and ranchers raised horses, cattle, mules, sheep, goats, and hogs.[9]

As discussed in case study 1, prior to their removal, Choctaws also used a plethora of wild flora and fauna, including acorns, alligators, blackberries, chestnuts, chinkapin, corn, deer, fish, geese, wild grapes, hickory nuts and oil, mulberries, mushrooms, pecans, persimmons, wild plums, potatoes, pumpkins, strawberries, sunflowers, squirrels, sweet potatoes, turkeys, walnuts, and wild onions.[10] Choctaw families were responsible for their own sustenance and cultivated backyard gardens. Men and women both procured game. Families often lived far from each other, but feasts and religious ceremonies brought families and clans together.[11]

After their removal to Indian Territory families continued to plant their traditional crops, to trade seeds, and to explore new planting innovations. Some family gardens were large. One Atoka family that moved to Indian Territory from Mississippi in the late 1880s maintained an ambitious garden of corn, potatoes, pumpkins, beans, peas, and peanuts, together with an orchard of apple, peach, plum, pear, and cherry trees as well as berry bushes and grapevines. They managed cattle, hogs, and horses, along with chickens, turkeys, and bees. Another resident cultivated five acres of corn, peas, beans, and pumpkins. When planting corn he dropped a minnow into each hole to fertilize the corn kernel.[12] The variety of cultivated plants allowed farmers to recycle nutrients and organic matter. Choctaw seed savers took great pride in saving the best kernels and stringing cobs in a dry place.[13] If people lost kernels or seeds or had a poor growing season, they could trade something of equal value with a neighbor for more seeds.

After the Civil War, Choctaws cultivated sixty-five thousand acres of land. They raised cereal grains and planted home gardens that included tobacco as well as apple, peach, pear, and cherry trees. They raised enough cotton to ship bales by train and steamboat to St. Louis and New Orleans, and they sold cattle. Ranchers raised goats, sheep, hogs, mules, and horses. As did the Cherokees by this time, Choctaw farmers used the axes, plows, hoes, harrows, scrapers, shovels, spades, threshers, mowers, and reapers.[14] Others did not need sophisticated equipment; Choctaw Peter Alexander commented that the Choctaws could "grow anything that one would wish to raise" and that as long as he possessed a six-inch turning plow along with a double shovel or Georgia stock, plus a heavy hoe made of bone or wood, "he had all the farm implements that he needed."[15]

These backyard gardens allowed tribes to survive in a rapidly diminishing environment. Natural resources became depleted. Many game animals were overhunted, cattle overgrazed the land and the polluted water, dams diverted waterways, and forests were clear-cut. The few trading posts were stocked with wheat flour, sugar, candy, canned sugared drinks, heavily salted meats, and brined pickles. During the Great Depression, when many people suffered economic hardship and could not afford to purchase foods from stores (when there was food in the stores), some Natives continued to cultivate their gardens as they always had, and they had enough. Ironically, some of those successful gardeners and farmers were from non-agricultural tribes. Full-blood Comanche Joshaway Mihesuah was forced to Fort Sill Indian School as a child, where his braids were cut off and he was disallowed from speaking Comanche. At the school Joshaway learned how to farm, and during the hard times of the 1930s he provided produce to neighboring whites and hired children of freedmen to work his fields.[16] The late Alfred Zeigler, a Lower Brule Sioux, also kept his gardening traditions and was able to harvest enough corn, potatoes, and squashes to last through the Depression winters, also making sauerkraut from cabbages. Food preservation was crucial, because as he recalled, "Even if you had the money, you couldn't go to the store and buy fresh vegetables; there weren't any."[17]

Then and now, backyard gardens may only supply a portion of the sustenance necessary for an entire family, but they are greatly symbolic and provide a direct link to one's culture. Gardening traditional plants, seed saving, and investigating historic planting methods has proven to be inspirational, educational, and greatly empowering. Cultivating even small plots contributes to physical fitness and teaches children about the natural world. Despite the Cherokees, Choctaws, and Chickasaws amassing hundreds of millions of dollars annually from various enterprises such as casinos, tourist plazas, and golf courses, there are few tribally financed gardens. There are, however, many thriving neighborhood and backyard gardens that are maintained by grass-roots coalitions of concerned tribal members and individuals.

I recount the importance of family gardens as a lifeline to cultural, emotional, and physical survival through multiple generations in my first novel, *The Roads of My Relations*.[18] After removal, my ancestors, like many other Choctaws and Chickasaws, cultivated backyard gardens that supplied a good portion of their diet. Understanding the seasons and knowing when to plant and harvest were crucial to survival. My parents had a variety of plant foods growing around their home, but I have duplicated the large garden my grandparents cultivated in Muskogee, which was a copy of what their ancestors had cultivated.[19] As I write this in August 2019, produce from last fall remains in one of our freezers: peppers, okra, dried tomatoes, and squash soup as well as venison, a wild turkey, pheasants, quail, and catfish from our pond. Our modest greenhouse and inexpensive cold frames allow me to start planting in early spring and to keep plants going into the cool fall and cold winter. Since spring 2019, we have harvested potatoes, herbs, carrots, beets, spinach, bok choy, kale, broccoli, raspberries, mulberries, and strawberries. Corn, peppers, green beans, okra, squashes, and another round of potatoes are yet to come. We save seeds, make compost, use rain barrels, and maintain pollinator gardens around the property. Not all the foods are Indigenous, and the gardens do not supply us with everything we need. Still, this kind of gardening provides quite a bounty and is realistic for families willing to spend time outside and to exert themselves. If tribal members are physically unable to garden, the tribe should provide a workforce to do it for them. Growing backyard gardens was just one of the suggestions submitted to the Choctaw Promise Zone initiative. Families desirous of cultivating patches, a small backyard, or a kitchen garden need access to seeds, basic tools, soil, and water. The tribe could have financed the plowing of land, a load of soil, seeds, equipment, and lessons on how to farm for tribal members interested in starting a patch.

Planting and cultivating gardens large enough to feed our families and to keep us active is one option, and the inspiration for planting is multifold. Working in a garden allows people of all ages to participate in the various stages of cultivation. Research has shown that garden-grown produce (from seeds of traditional, native plants) is more nutritious than market or grocery produce. Even if we don't have yard space or adequate ground for a garden, we can garden in pots. We would need many pots to have enough food for a family for the fall after cultivation, but even a few pepper, tomato, herb, and squash plants can be greatly empowering and symbolic.

You do not need acres of land to plant a productive garden. Properly prepared and maintained, even a small plot of land can yield vegetables you like. It initially takes some work and determination to get the garden started, but the better prepared the garden is, the less maintenance it will require. Numerous websites provide instructions on how to start a garden. For example, see Common Sense Home's "How to Start a Garden: 10 Steps to Gardening for Beginners."[20] Bookstores offer many books for in-depth information. Excellent resources for starting a school garden include Jane Kirkland's *No Student Left Indoors*, USDA's *Start a School Garden: Here's How,* and Eartheasy's *How to Start a School Garden: Your Complete Guide.*[21] Be aware that while gardening is satisfying work, our efforts can fail from drought, too much rain, pests, and taking on more than one can handle.

Visit your local nursery and you will find numerous people willing to talk to you. These are the steps that have worked for me. Other gardeners will no doubt have a variety of strategies that also work for them.

You will need:

Gloves (it only takes a few minutes of working with dirt to split fingernails)
Shovel
Spade
Hoe
Hose (I prefer a soaker hose that you can bury and then turn on and off, so as not to have to spray each row yourself)
For tall plants like tomatoes, a metal cone the plants can lean on

For cold environments, "Walls of Water," plastic wrap with tubes you fill with water that encircles the plant to keep it warm

Tall stakes for pole beans to climb if you do not plant corn

Either a rented rotor tiller to break up the hard soil and mix fertilizer, or a strong back that can to the same with a shovel

Steps to a Garden

Find the place in your yard that has afternoon sun. If possible, it should be a place where you can see it from your house in case birds and animals decide to eat your crops.

If you know that you have rabbits, deer, elk or other animals that will be attracted to your garden, it will be necessary to fence it. You do not need an expensive chain link fence. You can use six-foot wood or metal poles that you place it the ground one foot. Use a post hole digger to make sure the hole isn't too wide and will make the poles wobbly. Instead of cement to secure the poles, you can pack the hole with dirt and water. Slowly add water to the dirt as to pack the soil firmly around the base of the pole.

If you live in an area with deer, rabbits, and other animals that like garden produce, check local used building supply stores for pre-owned fencing. In Flagstaff we put up an eight-foot fence to deter elk. To keep out digging animals, get a roll of chicken wire and bend it in half lengthwise. On the outside of the fence, have half the wire rise vertically up the fence and lay the other half horizontal on the ground. This keeps skunks and rabbits from digging underneath. Keep in mind that raccoons and opossums can climb and that deer and coyotes (omnivores that will sample your fruits and vegetables) can jump low fencing.

Some people plant without taking into account their soil composition, and they may have good luck initially. After a few years, however, the soil "plays out" and they have poor yields of vegetables. If you decide to become a gardener, you will need to check to see what type of soil you have. Serious gardeners will take their soil in to a soil laboratory to find out how much sand, clay, loam, etc., their soil contains. You can also check with local nurseries, where staff will probably know this information about your area from other gardening customers. Many nurseries sell soil-testing kits.

One way you can find out for yourself is to take a sample of soil from your garden area about eight inches into the ground. Add soil to a quart jar that is two-thirds filled with water until the jar is filled. Add one tablespoon of water softener. Put on the lid and shake the contents. Sand will settle to the bottom, then silt, and clay on top. After two to three hours, look at the layers:

Sandy: less than 5 percent clay
Sandy loam: 5 to 10 percent clay
Medium loam: 10 to 20 percent clay
Clay: 25 to 30 percent clay; more than that is heavy clay

So what does this mean? Loam is the best soil. If you have too much sand or clay, add organic mix so that you have almost one-half of your soil consisting of organic matter. You can buy bags of organic matter at nurseries. Be certain that you tell the nursery staff as much as you can about your environment and bring in a soil sample with you.

You can start your own compost bin so you will have organic material each year for your garden. Use a garbage bin, preferably a plastic one. Drill holes along the sides so that air can circulate. Add food scraps (no meat or walnut shells), straw, grass clippings, coffee grounds, and chicken and pigeon droppings to the can (no dog, cow, or cat waste), and periodically add water and sawdust shavings and do your best to mix it up. Cover it with a lid and let it set for a year, or until it looks and feels like soft loam. Don't add "hot" material to your garden until it is decomposed. Adding chicken waste too soon, for example, will rob your plants of nitrogen as it breaks down.

Prepare your soil by moving rocks, pulling weeds (by the roots, to ensure they won't re-grow), and tilling. Either use the rented rotor tiller or shovel through the dirt thoroughly. Add your organic matter to mix the materials.

Smooth your garden soil, stand back, and decide what to plant.

If you live in an area with a short growing season, you can do one of two things: plant seedlings in indoor containers and wait until it is warm enough to transplant them outside. Or buy plants that are already three to five inches high from a nursery. I have planted watermelon, pole beans, radish, and sunflower seeds before the danger of frost has passed, but I cover the area with a tarp to keep in the warmth.

Squash and zucchini will spread out, so make sure you plant them with a distance of four feet between rows and at least two feet between plants in the rows.

Peppers, green beans, okra, onions, and radishes only need a two or three feet between rows and a foot or less between plants.

Tomatoes will need support, so buy metal cones and place them around the tomatoes when the plants are young; if you wait until they are two feet high, the stems with break if you bend them.

I used to use a garden hose to water the plants, but that proved to be wasteful Now I bury a soaker hose next to the plants and my rows "snake"; that is, at the end of one row, the hose turns a corner and I plant seeds or plants around that corner alongside the hose. I have very little wasted space.

I water once a day for fifteen minutes initially (in the evenings after the sun begins to set), and when the summer weather heats up, I water again in the mornings. If you have a soaker hose, then just turn on your faucet. I use an egg timer to remind me to turn it off.

The first year you may need no fertilizer. The second year I did not add organic material to the garden and used Miracle-Gro every two weeks instead.

Depending on your environment, sometimes the plants at the end of your soaker hose don't get as much water as they need, which is why you should plant the plants that need a lot of water (squash, melons, tomatoes) toward the "beginning" of the hose and place peppers toward the end. To make up for this deficit, I use "Aqua Cones," which are plastic cones about six inches long that you place into the ground with a two-liter soda bottle attached to each cone. After cutting the bottom out of the soda bottle, add water, and the water goes directly to the plant roots. You can order them at Gardeners Supply.[22]

Recruit your family to assist you in pulling weeds. The more you water, the more weeds will proliferate.

Planting the Three Sisters

The "Three Sisters" are corn, squash, and pole beans, which were grown by many tribes and were symbiotically grown together in mounds by tribes in the U.S. Northeast. Mesoamerican farmers have grown corn, squash, and beans in the same fields, called *milpas*, for thousands of years. Although they planted pole beans next to corn, the three plants were not planted in the same symbiotic fashion as the Three Sisters in the Northeast. Recently, the Three Sisters have emerged as a catch phrase and as the most notable garden produce. My tribe (Choctaw) did not plant in this manner, yet I have found the companion planting useful. A properly maintained garden of Three Sisters can help ward off nighttime visitors such as raccoons, deer, and rabbits because of the densely grown vegetation (although I have found that prairie dogs and moles are apparently undeterred, even by fencing that extends two feet under the ground), and it provides a shelter for birds. When I lived in Flagstaff, sparrows, yellow finches, woodpeckers, Steller's and piñon jays, and nuthatches especially enjoyed the damp shade from the sun when the soaker hose was turned on.

I plant the Three Sisters in different ways. One way is in rows, so that each plant is separate from the others (although this is not the "interactive" way to plant them). Another is to follow these instructions from NativeTech:[23]

1. In late May or early June hoe up the ground and heap the earth into piles about a foot high and about twenty inches across. The centers of your mounds should be about four feet apart and should have flattened tops.

2. First, in the center of each mound, plant five or six corn kernels in a small circle.

3. After a week or two, when the corn has grown to be five inches or so, plant seven or eight pole beans in a circle about six inches away from the corn kernels.

4. A week later, at the edge of the mound about a foot away from the beans, plant seven or eight squash or pumpkin seeds.

5. When the plants begin to grow, you will need to weed out all but a few of the sturdiest of the corn plants from each mound. Also keep the sturdiest of the bean and squash plants and weed out the weaker ones.

6. As the corn and beans grow up, you want to make sure that the beans are supported by cornstalks, wrapping around the corn. The squash will crawl out between the mounds, around the corn and beans.

Another way to plant pole beans is to use long green poles to form what looks like a tipi frame and plant pole beans at the base of each pole. By August my kids have a dense "wall" of green bean vines and leaves to hide behind.

I also plant pole beans and cucumbers at the end of the rows at the base of a tall circle of range fencing; the soaker hose curls nicely around the base, and the plants can latch on to grow up the fencing.

Gardening with Pots

Not everyone has land to cultivate a garden in the ground. When space is scarce or if the ground is rocky, polluted, or otherwise undesirable, you can use pots to grow many plants. Container gardening conserves water and adding nutrients is easier. Containers also make it easy to spot and pull weeds; moles, gophers, and other annoying pests cannot dig into the pots; you can arrange the garden in whatever way you want and according to the sunlight availability as the plants grow; and you can move the pots from outside to inside in case of cold weather or hail.

You will need:

A spade (a cheap one from a discount store) or a large, heavy spoon that won't bend.

Light gloves to protect your nails and skin.

Plastic pots, five-gallon paint buckets (cleaned, of course), or whiskey barrels. The latter will fall apart after about five to seven years, however. Get your children into the activity by allowing them to paint the containers with waterproof paints.

Small pebbles to add to the bottom of pots before adding the soil and plant (you can find pebbles in your yard or by a creek, or you can buy a small bag of them).

If you're indoors, buy the "saucers" that the pots sit in so that water won't drain all over your carpet or floor.

Unless you know you have fertile soil (that is also free of bugs and parasites), purchase a light potting soil.

Drill three to five holes in the bottom of pots that have no drainage holes.

Most plants require a five-gallon container. Squash, cucumbers, and climbing beans need a half barrel.

Decide what plants you want to grow. I have grown peppers, eggplant, tomatoes, and many herbs in pots: mint, parsley, bay, basil, oregano. It is difficult to grow root vegetables such as potatoes in small containers, and squash, zucchini, and melons require much space and water. A half whiskey barrel might work with squash, cucumbers, gourds, and melons, although their "arms" will spill out.

To plant:

Depending on where you live, you might have to buy plants if you have a short growing season. In warmer climates you can plant seeds after the danger of frost is over.

Put newspaper under your pot so you don't make a mess. Then put pebbles in the bottom of the pot and add soil to cover the pebbles.

Gently remove the plant from its container.

Place the plant in the middle of the dirt and gently spoon soil around the root ball. Don't pack the soil; drop it in so that the soil is two inches from the top of the pot.

Water gently; don't use the garden hose unless it is turned down to low. A watering pail with a sprinkler end to the spout works best.

Intersperse your vegetable and herb pots with colorful flowers for beautiful décor.

If deer are a problem, put a circle of range fencing around your pots.

Curriculum Guide

One might think that teaching and writing about Indigenous foods is simple. Granted, Indigenous foodways really *are* easy to teach if one provides only lists of what tribes ate historically. In most "American Indian" or "Native American" history courses, what tribes ate and how they procured sustenance are usually incidental to the main topics. We get English colonists arguing that northeastern tribes were "uncivilized" because they did not farm, even though they produced millions of bushels of corn per year. We get no clear indication that the decimation of bison herds by non-Indians was a purposeful act designed to deny the Plains tribes their main food source. Then there is the romanticized first Thanksgiving. Even instructors who stereotype that event as one big happy multi-cultural feast at least get one thing right, and that is to recount some of the Western Hemisphere's bounty: turkey, venison, squashes, and potatoes. There was, however, much more, including cacao, cranberries, elk, bison, tomatoes, salmon, peanuts, vanilla, and manioc.

Providing students only with catalogs of flora and fauna misses opportunities for more thorough discussions about social, political, religious, and economic aspects of tribal life and Indian-white relations. The issues swirling around hunting, gathering, and growing food are complex. The production and sharing of food provided social cohesion and identity. Everyone had to eat, and in order to procure food they had to understand and respect the natural world. Therefore their emotional, spiritual, cultural, and physical well-being depended—and still does depend—on the condition of the environment.

As a historian, I connect the past to the present in my writings and teachings. In any course dealing with Indigenous issues it is crucial to remind students that colonization is not simply a memory from the misty past. Natives are still alive and contending with a multitude of oppressions, including suffering from food-related maladies such as diabetes, obesity, and heart disease, and like everyone else, they must contend with the effects of climate change and pollution. How did this happen and what can be done about it? That question is the foundation of the classes I teach on Native North America and Latin America foodways. Environmental degradation, poverty, and the adoption of processed foods—in addition to the loss of knowledge of how to save seeds, plant, cultivate, and harvest according to the seasons and ceremonial prescriptions—are ongoing results of colonization and have caused tribespeople to develop unprecedented health problems. Today many are attempting to revitalize traditional foodways. In order to accomplish that, they have to contend with environmental pollution, climate change, treaty rights, racism, and impoverishment. Teaching about foods and health, therefore, requires a complex meshing of social, economic, political, religious, environmental, and ethical topics.

Colonialism has shaped the attitudes of tribal groups in the United States toward food and eating, and the relationships between ethnicity, religion, culture, and food choices offer many opportunities for classroom discussion.

What follow are lessons that can be modified for K–12 classes in addition to college-level courses. Keep in mind that there are differences between an introductory course and upper-division and graduate classes in which students are expected to have prior knowledge of Native North American tribes, ethnobotany, and nutrition. All discussions and research assignments require critical thinking; we can expect that in some of the lessons, aspects such as the meaning of the terms "traditional" and "sovereignty" are controversial, and not everyone in the classroom will agree. Remember: traditional and modern tribal foodways are complex topics. In order to impart information to students, anyone who teaches such a course needs to explore the vast amount of information in the fields of history, anthropology, literature, religion, law, political science, and nutrition. This is a crucial topic and should be taught more. Food is a necessary part of Indigenous concepts of decolonization, empowerment, and nation-building.

For a course on Indigenous foodways, there is a plethora of topics to address:

Precontact diets of tribes, including cultivation of crops; hunting, fishing, and foraging methods; food preparation and seed preservation.

How foods were brought to tribes as told through cosmological stories.

How the influences of social, economic, cultural, religious, environmental, and psychological factors have affected the attitudes of tribal groups in the United States toward food, eating, and the environment.

The relationship between ethnicity, religion, culture, and food choices and respect for the natural world.

Policies and ideologies that caused the cultures to alter their ways of eating, resulting in health problems and environmental degradation.

Challenges to achieving food sovereignty and food security.

Strategies for health recovery, including traditional ways of governance, a return to egalitarianism (so that women have more of a say about food and meal preparation), language recovery, and the use of oral traditions to maintain cultural knowledge and pride.

Course objectives might include:

Delineate foods of Native North America by tribal nations.
Explain the historical and modern cultural importance of
   Indigenous foods.
Critically assess the social, political, religious, and environ-
   mental impacts cultivation of the foods has on peoples
   in the modern world.
Delineate foods of Native North America by geographical
   regions.
Explain the historical and modern cultural importance of
   Indigenous foods.
Explore local grocery stores and farmers' markets and
   examine Native foods for sale.
Identify the nutritional aspects of precontact foods.
Explain the connection between good health and unpro-
   cessed foods.
Critically assess the social, political, religious, and envi-
   ronmental aspects of the Indigenous food sovereignty
   movement.
Identify the causes of the decline of health among Indige-
   nous peoples.
Describe Indigenous food sovereignty initiatives.

The course description might look something like this:

This class will spur discussions about how the significant differences in tribal foodways and interactions with the natural
world relate to tribal cultures, beliefs, religions, gender roles,
economies, worldview, and environmental changes. Because
tribes historically did not experience the food-related maladies such as obesity, high blood pressure, type 2 diabetes, and
related maladies that they suffer today, this course necessarily
explores the connection between good health and traditional
ways of eating, and the effects of colonization on how modern

Indigenous peoples procure and prepare foods. The course also addresses the destruction of flora and fauna from environmental degradation and explores challenges to Indigenous food sovereignty initiatives. In so doing, the methods used to examine tribal foodways enable students to explore their own ancestries and the impact of socio-economics, religion, politics, and identity on their attitudes toward foods, eating, and the environment. This course is multidisciplinary in approach. Lectures mesh archival data, oral testimonies from tribal individuals, and scientific data in order to present more complete versions of the past.

Foundational topics to include:

Terminology
Indigenous food sovereignty and food sustainability
Precontact foods of the Americas
Foods introduced to the Americas
Importance of place
Connection of food to culture
Women and tribal foodways
Tracing the decline of Indigenous people's health
Influences of boarding schools
Environmental issues

Possible texts:

Sophie D. Coe, *America's First Cuisines* (Austin: University of Texas Press, 1994).
Nelson Foster and Linda S. Cordell, *Chilies to Chocolate: Food the Americas Gave the World* (Tucson: University of Arizona Press, 1992).
Robert B. Kent, *Latin America: Regions and People* (New York: Guilford Press, 2006). This work is for Latin America foodways courses.

Emory Dean Keoke and Kay Marie Porterfield, *Encyclopedia of American Indian Contributions to the World: 15,000 Years of Inventions and Innovations* (New York: Facts on File, 2002).

Robin Wall Kimmerer, *Braiding Sweetgrass: Indigenous Wisdom, Scientific Knowledge and the Teachings of Plants* (Minneapolis: Milkweed Editions, 2013).

Winona LaDuke, *All Our Relations: Native Struggles for Land and Life* (Cambridge: South End Press, 1999).

————, *Recovering the Sacred: The Power of Naming and Claiming* (Cambridge: South End Press, 2005).

Devon A. Mihesuah and Elizabeth Hoover, eds., *Indigenous Food Sovereignty in the United States: Restoring Cultural Knowledge, Protecting Environments, and Regaining Health* (Norman: University of Oklahoma Press, 2019). There are study and discussion questions for each chapter at the end of the book.

Devon G. Peña, Luz Calvo, Pancho McFarland, and Gabriel R. Valle, *Mexican-Origin Foods, Foodways, and Social Movements: Decolonial Perspectives* (Fayetteville: University of Arkansas Press, 2017).

Enrique Salmón, *Eating the Landscape: American Indian Stories of Food, Identity, and Resilience* (Tucson: University of Arizona Press, 2012).

Online resources:

American Indian Health and Diet Project, http://www.aihd.ku.edu/.

Bizarre Foods with Andrew Zimmern (in particular the episodes about Central and South America), https://www.travelchannel.com/shows/bizarre-foods.

Culinary Dictionary, https://whatscookingamerica.net/Glossary/A.htm.

Decolonizing Diet Project (Facebook).

Decolonizing Diet Project, http://decolonizingdietproject
.blogspot.com/.

Food Sovereignty Is Tribal Sovereignty (Facebook).

From Garden Warriors to Good Seeds, https://
gardenwarriorsgoodseeds.com/.

"Gather," http://indiangiver.firstnations.org/nl180506-01/
?fbclid=IwAR3MYzpVMSh_3YDo7tyDp3fwWKkmZPaZrXfb
-7fWlZNxFllsLbAqoaS_EGw.

Indigenous Eating (Facebook).

Intertribal Agriculture Council, http://www.indianaglink
.com/our-programs/technical-assistance-program/.

"Medicinal Plants Used by the Five Tribes in Indian
Territory," http://www.aihd.ku.edu/health
/MedicinalPlantsoftheFiveTribes.html.

*Native American Ethnobotany Database: A Database of Foods,
Drugs, Dyes and Fibers of Native American Peoples, Derived
from Plants*, http://naeb.brit.org/.

Native Food Systems Resource Center, http://www
.nativefoodsystems.org/about.

Native Seeds SEARCH *Catalog* for plant photography, https://
www.nativeseeds.org/collections/catalog.

Seed Savers Exchange, https://www.seedsavers.org/.

Seeds of Native Health, http://seedsofnativehealth.org
/partners/.

Seeds of Native Health Campaign, https://
seedsofnativehealth.org/.

"25 Best Food Documentaries," compiled by Academy of
Culinary Nutrition, https://www.culinarynutrition.com
/best-food-documentaries-to-watch/.

University of Arkansas School of Law Indigenous Food and
Agriculture Initiative, http://indigenousfoodandag.com
/about-us/.

Kyle Whyte's articles about climate and environmental
justice and Indigenous environmental studies, http://
kylewhyte.cal.msu.edu/articles/.

YouTube videos cover every aspect of Indigenous foodways, including seed saving, harvesting, preparing dishes, planting, and harvesting. Here are some that focus on Indigenous foodways: https://www.youtube.com/playlist ?list=PLnxoEF9zAcruknB5AhOOU834S3RSCb92S.

The lessons that follow are in the order that I generally teach. I have added many resources for each lesson, and it is up to teachers to choose which ones suit their class plans.

Lesson: Precontact Foods of the Americas

Prior to colonization peoples of the Western Hemisphere had access to a vast array of edible flora and fauna in mountains, deserts, rivers, lakes, oceans, and forests. A basic activity is to have students list as many precontact foods as they know—you might be surprised that they are familiar with only a few of these and often include on their lists nonindigenous foods such as chicken, beef, and asparagus. A lesson that makes an impression on students about the importance of these nutritious foods is to discuss how the flora and fauna changed the population of the world (chapter 1). Several class sessions provide overviews of where tribes lived and what they ate based on the resources available to them. As discussed in chapter 1 and the case studies, the geographical areas I use are the Southwest, Northeast, Old Northwest (or Great Lakes), Alaska, Canada, California and Northwest, Plateau, Northern and Southern Plains, Arctic, Southeast, Indian Territory, and Hawaii. Within these areas, however, tribes and cultural groups are culturally different, and there are multiple ecosystems that determined how the people lived.

Tribespeople historically ate foods that many students have not tried, so find out your school's rules about bringing food into the classroom. I usually bring something in every day for students to taste. For example, peoples of the Southwest often consumed insects, and today insect consumption is common in Mexico. I purchase insects from Educational Innovations, but you can also purchase insects from other sources. Just be sure they are labeled "safe for consumption."

OBJECTIVES

List the precontact flora and fauna that tribes of the Western Hemisphere used for food and medicine.

Delineate the precontact foods by tribal nations.

RESOURCES

Chapter 1, "Traditional Diets and Activities," this volume.

Appendix A, "Precontact Foods of the Western Hemisphere," this volume.

Foods of the various geographic areas at the American Indian Health and Diet Project website, http://www.aihd.ku.edu/foods/index.html.

Alan Davidson, *The Oxford Companion to Food* (New York: Oxford University Press, 2006).

Sean Sherman and Beth Dooley, *The Sioux Chef's Indigenous Kitchen* (Minneapolis: University of Minnesota Press, 2017). Note that many cookbooks feature Indigenous dishes, but most of them also include introduced foods and therefore are not as helpful for this lesson. This applies especially to Latin American cookbooks.

ACTIVITIES

Delineate from a list of one hundred flora and fauna food items (not dishes) from around the world that fall into pre- and post-contact food lists.

Create a list of foods from your tribe, of if not Indigenous, from a local tribe.

Keep a food diary for a week and identify all precontact foods. See chapter 4.

Create a menu of precontact food. Show three meals per day that include only ingredients *indigenous to this hemisphere*. Each meal must include a drink, a protein, a grain, a fruit, and a vegetable. Do not just list the one food as a dish. For example, you must have at least three ingredients per dish and, dishes must be different. You may only use ingredients one time.

Alternatively, create a menu of precontact food of a specific tribe.

Lesson: Precontact Foods of Latin America

A section on precontact foods of Latin America is important for students to understand the origin of important U.S. tribal foods. Corn, for example, is considered a major food plant of tribes in the Northeast, Southwest, and Southeast. It was developed from a grass called teosinte about seven thousand years ago and then spread north from Mexico. Today tribes grow several kinds of corn: dent, flint, flour, pop, and sweet. Chile peppers, many kinds of squashes, and sunflowers also originated in Mexico. Tribes organized trade networks throughout the continent to acquire resources from various environments.

SPECIFIC INDIGENOUS FOODS

I chose the following plants because they originated in Latin America. Follow the same format for any of the foods listed on the American Indian Health and Diet Project, http://www.aihd .ku.edu/foods/western_hemisphere.html.

The activities for corn, peppers, squashes, and beans are similar:

Visually differentiate between the types of corn, peppers, squashes, and beans and explain how each is used.

Compose a paper about the dangers of genetically modified plants.

Compile a list of products that contain corn, peppers, squashes, and beans.

Go to the Native Seeds/SEARCH page and download the catalog: http://www.nativeseeds.org/pdf

/seedlistingcatalog.pdf and the page https://www
.chilipeppermadness.com/chili-pepper-types/. Look at
the pictures of corn, peppers, squashes, and beans and
identify the specific plants you have and have not tried.
Separate the types of corn, peppers, squashes, and beans
by their geographical origins.

Cacao

Objectives

Demonstrate your knowledge about the history and cultivation
of cacao.

Compare the tastes of almost pure cacao with processed chocolate and compose your thoughts about them.

Consider the environmental, economic, and social impacts
of cacao cultivation and discuss your thoughts about the problems associated with chocolate production. This includes the
issue of forced child labor.

Resources

Coe, *America's First Cuisines,* 50–58, 101–3, 129.

Foster and Cordell, *Chilies to Chocolate,* 105–22.

Sylvia A. Johnson, *Tomatoes, Potatoes, Corn, and Beans: How
the Foods of the Americas Changed Eating Around the World*
(New York: Atheneum, 1997), 95–109.

Cameron L. McNeil, *Chocolate in Mesoamerica: A Cultural
History of Cacao* (Gainesville: University Press of Florida,
2009).

"Senators Call for Crackdown on Cacao Imports Made
with Forced Child Labor," *Washington Post,* July 16, 2019,
https://www.washingtonpost.com/business/2019/07/16
/senators-call-dhs-crack-down-cocoa-imports-made-with
-forced-child-labor/?utm_term=.7d62a38e2c59.

Slavery in the Chocolate Industry (46:31), http://www.youtube
.com/watch?v=ZNpwIzeyjKQ.

Activities

Purchase a dark chocolate bar that is at least 90 percent cacao. These are available at most stores. If you do not know what a basic candy bar tastes like (Snickers, Hershey's Kiss, etc.) buy one of those. Compare and contrast the tastes. Write an essay discussing what you think about the two bars. Historic peoples in Mexico used 100 percent cacao mixed with honey. Do you think you would like that? Teachers: purchase cacao nibs and distribute only a few to students. They are pretty strong!

Discuss your thoughts about the problems associated with cacao production, including child labor.

Corn/Maize

Objectives

Chronicle the origin of corn and how it spread from Mexico north to the United States.

Define the types of edible corn and how each type was and is used among tribes.

Understand the social, political, economic, and religious significance of corn to tribes.

Assess the nutritional value of corn.

Investigate the repercussions of genetically modified corn.

Resources

Michael Blake, *Maize for the Gods: Unearthing the 9,000-Year History of Corn* (Oakland: University of California Press, 2015).

Johnson, *Tomatoes, Potatoes, Corn, and Beans*, 7–25. Suitable for grades 7–10.

King Corn (film), http://www.kingcorn.net/the-film /synopsis/.

Muriel H. Wright, "American Indian Corn Dishes," *Chronicles of Oklahoma* 36 (Summer 1958): 155–66.

There are many corn curriculums online, such as this one produced by Missouri Corn: http://www.mocorn.org/resources/education/corn-in-the-classroom/. Be forewarned that many of these are also promotions for the use of corn as ethanol.

Peppers

Objectives

Interpret the Scoville Heat Scale.
Assess the importance of peppers as food to Latin Americans and to the modern world.

Resources

Coe, *America's First Cuisines*, 60–65.
Foster and Cordell, *Chilies to Chocolate*, 81–94.
"Heat, Drought Make for Potent Peppers," http://www.nbcnews.com/id/48257563/ns/weather/t/heat-drought-make-potent-peppers/.
Johnson, *Tomatoes, Potatoes, Corn, and Beans*, 38–50.
Kraig H. Kraft et al., "Multiple Lines of Evidence for the Origin of Domesticated Chili Pepper, *Capsicum annuum,* in Mexico," *Proceedings of the National Academy of Sciences of the United States of America* 111, no. 17 (2014): 6165–70, doi:10.1073/pnas.1308933111.
Peppers curriculum by the Urban and Environmental Policy Institute (younger students), http://www.farmtopreschool.org/states/documents/F2PHOTM_Peppers_000.pdf.
"Peppers History and Nutrition" (4:50), http://www.youtube.com/watch?v=8YhNheYaw68.
Maricel E. Presilla, *Peppers of the Americas: The Remarkable Capsicums That Forever Changed Flavor* (New York: Penguin–Random House, 2017).
Scoville Heat Scale, https://www.alimentarium.org/en/magazine/infographics/scoville-scale.

Potatoes

Objectives

Organize the historical events leading to the worldwide importance of potatoes.

Discuss the reasons why potato cultivation decreased after Spanish invasion.

Assess the causes of the potato famine.

Resources

"Bizarre Foods Chuños" (5:17), https://www.youtube.com /watch?v=AHekHgFIKHM.

Coe, *America's First Cuisines*, 19–26, 29, 93, 127, 139, 162, 182–83, 224.

Foster and Cordell, *Chilies to Chocolate*, 4–5, 10–14, 96–97.

"Impact of the Potato," http://www.history-magazine.com /potato.html.

Johnson, *Tomatoes, Potatoes, Corn, and Beans*, 64–83.

"Potatoes," in documentary *Botany of Desire*, https://archive .org/details/BotanyOfDesire2009.

"Sweet Potatoes: History and Nutrition" (6:00), http:// www.youtube.com/watch?v=zEB0NqZD8s8.

"Year of the Potato," https://web.archive.org/web /20060718230841/http://www.cipotato.org/pressroom /iyp.asp.

Squash

Objectives

Assess the nutritional value of squash.

Indicate where and how squash was and is cultivated.

Resources

Coe, *America's First Cuisines*, 37–41.

Foster and Cordell, *Chilies to Chocolate*, 18, 68, 147, 155.

Beans

Objectives

Identify the nutritional values of beans.

Define the various nutrients present in beans.

Resources

Coe, *America's First Cuisines*, 80, 90, 118.

Foster and Cordell, *Chilies to Chocolate*, 61–80.

Johnson, *Tomatoes, Potatoes, Corn, and Beans*, 26–37.

Lesson: Insects and Offal

Tribes also ate offal, that is, brains, entrails, kidneys, tongue, and marrow, animal parts that many people in the United States consider undesirable because they have access to other cuts of meat. There are exceptions, of course, and mentioning those exceptions helps students to understand the importance of those foods. For example, ingredients in hot dogs span the spectrum of animal parts. Some restaurants offer expensive organ meats as haute cuisine entrees. Many families use turkey giblets in their Thanksgiving gravy, and liver and onions remains a popular dish. Menudo is a staple in many Latino homes.

OBJECTIVES

Identify countries that extensively use offal and insects.

Evaluate the nutritional and economic value of insects.

RESOURCES

Can Eating Insects Save the World? (58:57), http://www
.youtube.com/watch?v=Acxbx-DUkL4.

Coe, *America's First Cuisines*, 99–100, 159, 178, 249.

Go to the Eat Me Daily site at http://www.eatmedaily.com/ and in the search box type "offal." Go through the various entries and read the ones titled "Offal of the Week."

"Edible Insects" (3:12), http://www.youtube.com/watch?v=
r9M2JPscbmQ.

"The Future of Food: Eating Insects" (6:42), http://www
.youtube.com/watch?v=F2sDrJ8AOzU.

"Nutritional and Sensory Quality of Edible Insects,"
https://www.sciencedirect.com/science/article/pii
/S2352364616300013.

ACTIVITIES

Compose a paper discussing what offal and insects you would
be willing to eat and what you absolutely will not try (and why).
Mention the creatures in *Can Eating Insects Save the World?*

Geographical Areas

These lessons do not include resources for tribal histories. Basic
resources are:

Anton Treuer, *Atlas of Indian Nations* (Washington DC:
National Geographic, 2014).

Carl Waldman, *Atlas of the North American Indian* (New York:
Checkmark Books, 2009).

ACTIVITIES FOR ALL AREAS

Identify tribes in each area who lived there pre- and postcontact.
List flora and fauna used by cultures in each region.
Trace how their foodways and health changed through time.
Identify environmental problems that negatively impact food
resources in each area.

Southwest

Resources

"Arizona's Tepary Beans Preserve a Native Past, Hold
Promise for the Future," https://www.npr.org/sections
/thesalt/2018/02/21/586420523/arizonas-tepary-beans
-preserve-a-native-past-hold-promise-for-the-future.

John F. Doebley, "'Seeds' of Wild Grasses: A Major Food of Southwestern Indians," *Economic Botany* 38, no. 1 (January–March 1984): 52–64.

"Nutritional and Sensory Quality of Edible Insects," https://www.sciencedirect.com/science/article/pii /S2352364616300013.

J. M. Reid et al., "Nutrient Intake of Pima Indian Women," *American Journal of Clinical Nutrition* 24 (1971): 1281–89.

"The Resiliency of Hopi Agriculture: 2000 Years of Planting" (4:12), https://www.youtube.com/watch?v= 28gAFESNGMU.

Dennis Wall and Virgil Masayesva, "People of the Corn: Teachings in Hopi Traditional Agriculture, Spirituality, and Sustainability," in Mihesuah and Hoover, *Indigenous Food Sovereignty in the United States*, 209–22.

Northeastern Tribes and Great Lakes (Old NW)

Resources

Decolonizing Diet Project, https://share.nmu.edu/moodle /course/view.php?id=33.

"Foods at Risk in New England," http://www.slowfoodusa .org/downloads/raft-new_england_risk.pdf.

"Foods at Risk in the Great Lakes Foodshed," https://www .albc-usa.org/RAFT/images/Resources/great_lakes _foods_at_risk.pdf.

S. K. Wertz, "Maize: The Native North American's Legacy of Cultural Diversity and Biodiversity," *Journal of Agricultural and Environmental Ethics* 18 (2005): 131–56.

California and Northwest Tribes

Resources

M. Kat Anderson, *Tending the Wild: Native American Knowledge and the Management of California's Natural Resources* (Berkeley: University of California Press, 2017).

Gerald Clarke, "Bringing the Past to the Present: Traditional Indigenous Farming in Southern California," in Mihesuah and Hoover, *Indigenous Food Sovereignty in the United States*, 253–75.

"Manoomin: The Food the Grows on the Water," https://theways.org/story/manoomin.html.

Jay Miller, "Salmon, the Lifegiving Gift," https://www.nps .gov/olym/learn/education/upload/Salmon-the-Life -Giving-Gift-Essay.pdf.

Ann M. Renker, "The Makah Tribe: People of the Sea and the Forest," https://tadubois.com/US_indigenous/US _indigenous_subpage_makah.html.

Tending the Wild (1:00:04), https://www.youtube.com /watch?v=TbxLv9EEzs8.

"Wild Rice," http://www.mpm.edu/content/wirp/ICW-36.

Michael Wilken-Robertson, Deborah Small, Don Bartletti, and Rose Ramirez, *Kumeyaay Ethnobotany: Shared Heritage of the Californias* (El Cajon CA: Sunbelt Publications, 2017).

Plains Tribes and Texas

Resources

Sarah E. Colby, Leander R. McDonald, and Greg Adkison, "Traditional Native American Foods: Stories from Northern Plains Elders," *Journal of Ecological Anthropology* 15 (2012): 65–73, https://pdfs.semanticscholar.org/f682 /11b11430e7eb227045b50c4cea0e3c693038.pdf.

Devon Mihesuah, "Comanche Traditional Foodways and the Decline of Health," in Mihesuah and Hoover, *Indigenous Food Sovereignty in the United States*, 223–52.

Gary Nabhan and Kelly Kindscher, "Renewing the Native Food Traditions of Bison Nation," https://garynabhan .com/pbf-pdf/Bison.pdf.

Indian Territory

Resources

"The Comanche and the Horse" (5:22), https://www
.youtube.com/watch?v=MRXXvm-zKTY&fbclid=
IwAR38rqD-dDXixXLjLl_p-338B6gK8HP47nDWKqB
-bOZijt0ot_MuNeBaxOE.

Julia A. Jordan, *Plains Apache Ethnobotany* (Norman: University of Oklahoma Press, 2008).

Kelly Kindscher, *Medicinal Wild Plants of the Prairie: An Ethnobotanical Guide* (Lawrence: University Press of Kansas, 1992).

"Medicinal Plants Used by the Five Tribes in Indian Territory," http://www.aihd.ku.edu/health
/MedicinalPlantsoftheFiveTribes.html.

Arctic

Resources

Bruce E. Johansen, "The Inuit's Struggle with Dioxins and Other Organic Pollutants," *American Indian Quarterly* 26, no. 3 (Summer 2002): 479–90.

Melanie Lindholm, "Alaska Native Perceptions of Food, Health, and Community Well-being: Challenging Nutritional Colonialism," in Mihesuah and Hoover, *Indigenous Food Sovereignty in the United States*, 155–72.

Canada

Resources

Priscilla Settee and Shailesh Shukla, *Indigenous Food Systems: Concept, Cases, and Conversations* (Toronto: Canadian Scholars, 2020).

Lesson: Personal Views about Foods

OBJECTIVES

Document the role that food plays in your life.

Learn from knowledgeable men and women in your cultural group about your food traditions.

RESOURCES

For an overview of food studies: Carole Counihan and Penny Van Esterik, *Food and Culture: A Reader* (New York: Routledge, 2013).

Kimmerer, *Braiding Sweetgrass.*

Devon Mihesuah, "Nephi Craig: Life in Second Sight," in Mihesuah and Hoover, *Indigenous Food Sovereignty in the United States*, 300–319.

Salmón, *Eating the Landscape.*

"Voices from the Indigenous Food Movement," in Mihesuah and Hoover, *Indigenous Food Sovereignty in the United States*, 26–56.

ACTIVITIES

Read statements by Indigenous food activists in "Voices from the Indigenous Food Movement," and "Nephi Craig" and compose an essay explaining your interest in Indigenous foods.

Food is a major part of any culture. What is your "family food culture"? That is, does your family participate in ceremonies associated with foods? Do you always eat certain foods on particular holidays? Birthdays? In the past, some students have commented that they still eat something on special occasions that their mother or grandparent makes even though they do not like it. Does that happen to you?

Do you have goals to participate in any Indigenous food sovereignty initiatives?

As you read *Braiding Sweetgrass,* answer these questions developed by the Longwood Gardens Library and Archives staff:

https://longwoodgardens.org/sites/default/files/wysiwyg
/Discussion_And_Question_Guide_Braiding_Sweetgrass.pdf.

Lesson: Terminology

There are several terms that might provoke debate in an Indigenous foods course. For example, a key term used throughout a course on Indigenous foodways is "traditional" food. Does that refer to precontact times? Or does it mean more recently, because your grandparents used it? Restaurants such as the Smithsonian's Mitsitam Native Foods Café, cookbooks including Beverly Cox's *Spirit of the Harvest: North American Indian Cooking* (New York: Stewart, Tabori and Chang, 1991), and online recipe sites like those in *Indian Country Today* feature "traditional" dishes, but the majority of ingredients are not from this hemisphere. Some "traditional" foods are labeled thus because people like to eat them. This is important when considering tribal foodways, because many refer to popular nonindigenous foods, such as unhealthy frybread, as "traditional." Warning: discussions about frybread can become heated and personal. Discussions about the term "traditional" are found in case study 3.

Another multifaceted term is "Three Sisters" (chapter 7). Tribes across the country now claim that they traditionally grew the Three Sisters. This claiming of the Three Sisters farming method has ramifications for the current Indigenous food sovereignty movement because it blurs the line between distinct cultures, traditional Indigenous foodways knowledge, and revitalizing pride for one's tribal history and particular planting methods. Still, the Three Sisters planting system does make sense, and no one should be shamed for planting this way.

Many Indigenous peoples also say "Turtle Island," but like the Three Sisters, that is a northeastern concept as well. Many tribes had traditional thirteen-month calendars that correspond to the number of scutes on turtle shells. However, the story of a great turtle that carries the world on her back is traditional to Iroquois tribes. It is up to the teacher to moderate creative and useful classroom discussions about how terms can and should be used.

Often tribes are designated agricultural, hunter, gatherer, or hunter-gatherer. These labels are sometimes used incorrectly. Some tribes were mainly agriculturalists, like Choctaws and Cherokees, but they also hunted and gathered. Hunters mainly utilized game, but they also foraged and sometimes planted gardens. Comanches were hunters, but they also gathered wild foods and traded (and raided) for agricultural crops such as corn, squash, beans, and melons.

"New World" refers to the Western Hemisphere and the Americas. Old World refers to Europe, Africa, Asia. Some Natives disagree and assert that the cultures of the Western Hemisphere are just as old as those in the Old World and prefer that the Western Hemisphere be labeled the Old World.

"Cultural appropriation" is an interesting term. This means that one group takes the intellectual property (ideas, concepts), symbols (dress, images), or physical aspects (medicinal plants, headdresses, feathers) from another culture for their own. In regard to Indigenous foods, cultural appropriation refers to the using of precontact Indigenous foods for profit. An obvious concern is the use of Native wild foods, such as mushrooms, persimmons, pawpaws, camas bulbs and wild onions, plums, piñon nuts, and leafy greens for use in restaurants. Many do not reveal the location of their wild food patches for good reason: if those wanting to make a profit from these plants know where they are, they would soon be decimated. Another example is how non-Natives use Indigenous foods as a "trendy food" for profit. Many restaurateurs use gimmicks. Francis Ford Coppola's restaurant in Virginia Dare Winery in Geyserville, California, is called Werowocomoco. It is an Algonquin word, and the fare is supposed to be based on "culinary traditions of the earliest inhabitants of North America," although the frybread on his menu is not traditional, and no tribe prepared it. Still, he profits from the dish. Even Indigenous chefs borrow liberally from other tribal

Nations for profit. Tribal Nations were and are culturally distinct from each other. Their languages, religions, physiologies, housing, clothing, and foods were different. This brings up the awkward reality that some Native chefs create dishes utilizing ingredients that were not from their own tribe. Is this not also cultural appropriation? Lively class discussions might ensue. What follows is a list of other terms pertaining to Indigenous food studies. There are more, of course. When teaching about terminology, make sure that students stay within the context of the class.

activism
Affordable Care Act
agriculture
agroecology
allotments
ancestral health
arctic
bison
boarding schools
buffalo (African animal)
cancer
ceremony
chef
climate change
colonialism
colonization
commercial farming
commodities
community
cultural appropriation
cultural knowledge
cultural property rights
decolonization
desert

diabetes
dry farming
ecosystem
elders
endangered species
environmental racism
EPA
ethnobotany
ethnoecology
family gardens
farmers
farming community
First Nations
fishing
food celebration
food desert
food forest
food justice
food preservation
food security
food sustainability
food systems
foodways
foraging

fossil fuels
fracking
frybread
full-blood
gardens
gatherer
genetically modified
    organisms (GMOS)
grassroots movements
Great Lakes
greenhouses
harvest
haute cuisine
health
heart disease
heirloom seeds
high blood pressure
hunter
hunter-gatherer
Indian
Indian Health Service
Indigenous
intellectual property rights
interconnected
invasive species
irrigation
islanders
junk food
kitchen gardens
local
localvores (https://blog
    .oup.com/2007/11
    /locavore/)
maize
majority

milpas
minority
mixed-blood
multi-heritage
Native
natural resources
natural world
new world
obesity
oceans
oil
Old World
permaculture
pipelines
pollinators
pollution
postcontact foods
poverty
precontact foods
prediabetes
progressive
Promise Zone
racism
rematriation
restoration
security
seed saving
slow food
sovereignty
sugar
sustenance
toxins
traditional ecological
    knowledge
traditional foods

traditional Indigenous
   knowledge
treaties

treaty rights
wild game
wild plants

OBJECTIVES

Understand the cultural, social, and political aspects of using the terms "traditional," "sovereignty," "Indigenous food sovereignty," "civilization," "Native American," "American Indian," "Indigenous," "First Nations," and so on.

Consider why the "frybread myth" still persists. Is it because many consider it "traditional?"

Explore why it is that some people do not eat precontact foods.

RESOURCES

Case study 3, "Frybread," this volume.

Michael Yellow Bird, "What We Want to Be Called: Indigenous Peoples' Perspectives on Racial and Ethnic Identity Labels," *American Indian Quarterly* 23, no. 2 (Spring 1999): 1–21.

Elizabeth Hoover, "'You can't say you're sovereign if you can't feed yourself': Defining and Enacting Food Sovereignty in American Indian Community Gardening," in Mihesuah and Hoover, *Indigenous Food Sovereignty in the United States*, 57–93.

IFS Chart, in Mihesuah and Hoover, *Indigenous Food Sovereignty in the United States*, 14.

"Introduction," in Mihesuah and Hoover, *Indigenous Food Sovereignty in the United States*, 3–25.

ACTIVITIES

Explain your definitions of "traditional," "sovereignty," "Indigenous food sovereignty," "civilization," and so on, and why you do or do not use the terms "Native American," "American Indian," "Indigenous," and "First Nations."

Discuss the importance of traditional foods and how they connect to culture.

Write a paper discussing the pros and cons of preparing and eating frybread.

List the "traditional"—that is, precontact—foods your family uses.

Lesson: Indigenous Food Sovereignty and Food Sustainability

What tribes want is to recover is "food sovereignty," including sustainable agriculture and cultural educational programs, but there are significant challenges in creating a self-sufficient food system and reconnecting tribal members with their traditional foodways. Many Indigenous people cannot access fresh foods, much less culturally connected ones, because of federal policies, treaty abrogation, climate change, environmental degradation and pollution, racism, and poverty.

"Indigenous food sovereignty" is a common phrase we see today, but there is no agreed-upon meaning. This lesson requires analysis of the term "sovereignty" and discussion of the challenges to tribes producing and distributing their own food. Treaties are legally binding contracts between tribes and the federal government. They are declarations that promise self-determination, health care and educational services, religious freedom, and rights to hunt and fish. The federal government is required to protect tribal treaty rights, tribal lands, and resources. Treaties agreed upon and signed by the federal government and the tribes guaranteed—depending on the arrangement—food, shelter, clothing, lands, and/or education and farming monies. Any discussion about the challenges of food sovereignty and food justice for tribes necessarily includes an understanding of the relationship between tribal, federal and state jurisdiction and Indian self-determination. Discussions about food sovereignty should include tribal food initiatives, such as stores that stock culturally relevant foods, community and backyard gardens, large farms to feed the entire tribe, bison ranching, heirloom seed distribution, and economic development. *Merriam-Webster* online dictionary defines "sovereign" as autonomous, free from external control. The federal government declares that tribes are sovereign entities with the right to govern themselves, but also deems them "domestic dependent nations," and ultimately holds power over every tribe. As Jeff Corntassel and Cheryl Bryce wrote in 2012, "the indigenous rights discourse has limits and can only take struggles for land reclamation and justice so far"; see Jeff Corntassel and Cheryl Bryce, "Practicing Sustainable Self-Determination: Indigenous Approaches to Cultural Restoration and Revitalization," *Brown Journal of World Affairs* 18, no. 2 (Spring–Summer 2012): 152. Tribes can attempt revitalization of traditional foodways and will succeed in many endeavors, but until they have control over their lands and resources and are independent of neoliberal food policies, they cannot achieve food sovereignty. Mohawk activist Taiaiake Alfred reminds us that "sovereignty" is a European concept and does not adequately describe Indigenous peoples' traditional philosophies. Indeed, if the goal is to revert to traditionalism, then the quest for food sovereignty is further complicated, because not only are many tribal governments patterned after the U.S. government—many tribal members have vested interests in keeping them that way.

OBJECTIVES

Understand the cultural, social, and political aspects of using the terms "Indigenous food sovereignty," "sovereignty," and "food security."

RESOURCES

Chapter 3, "Challenges to Recovering Health," this volume.

For a discussion about the implications of using the term "sovereignty," see Taiaiake Alfred, "Sovereignty," in *A*

Companion to American Indian History, ed. Philip J. Deloria and Neal Salisbury (Malden MA: Blackwell, 2004), 460–74.

Jeff Corntassel and Cheryl Bryce, "Practicing Sustainable Self-Determination: Indigenous Approaches to Cultural Restoration and Revitalization," *Brown Journal of World Affairs* 18, no. 2 (2012): 152.

"Introduction" and Hoover, "'You can't say you're sovereign if you can't feed yourself,'" in Mihesuah and Hoover, *Indigenous Food Sovereignty in the United States,* 3–25, 57–93.

ACTIVITIES

Define the terms "Indigenous food sovereignty" and "sovereignty." (Students will explain their interpretations of these terms again at the end of the course.)

Create other terms that express similar meanings as "Indigenous food sovereignty."

Debate the usefulness of the term "Indigenous food sovereignty."

Lesson: Homeland, Food, and Connection to Culture

Homeland is where tribes believe they emerged, the site of ceremonies, resources, animal and plant foods, and medicinal plants. Where one's ancestors lived determine one's identity. The loss of those homelands, because the tribes were forcibly driven out or removed was and still is disastrous for tribes and is a major factor in mental and physical health problems today. Being removed from homeland means one has been taken away from site of worship, burial sites, and medicinal plants and foods. *Indigenous Knowledge* (IK) is the basis for local decision-making about fundamental aspects of day-to-day life, such as hunting, farming, gathering, seed saving, fishing, water, health, and adaptation to environmental change. IK includes codes of conduct of how to behave as a member of the group. A tribe's traditional ɪK defines that community's uniqueness and explains its relation to the world. This knowledge is maintained and developed by peoples with long histories of close interaction with the natural environment of their homeland. Tribes needed to understand the seasons and weather patterns in order to successfully hunt and farm. Tribes followed their own calendars—often thirteen months—that included ceremonies corresponding with the seasons (see chapter 1). Researching their own tribal calendars and learning months and foods in their languages is greatly empowering.

OBJECTIVES

Understand how food is a foundational element of culture.

Appreciate the role of females in tribal cosmological stories.

Learn strategies for decolonizing and empowering Indigenous Nations through recovering traditional foodways.

Compare and contrast traditional tribal calendars.

Understand the importance of connecting the seasons to when game animals are plentiful, as well as the cycles of planting, harvesting, gathering, preserving, and seed saving.

SAMPLE RESOURCES

Choctaw Calendar, https://mike-boucher.com/wordpress/
   ?page_id=139.
Index of Hopi Katsinam, http://www.nairiok.org
   /KatsinaIndex2.html.
Lakota Calendar, Akta Lakota Museum and Cultural
   Center, http://aktalakota.stjo.org/site/News2?page=
   NewsArticle&id=8991.
Ojibway, Cree, and Mohawk "Thirteen Moons" curriculum,
   https://onlc.ca/wp-content/uploads/2014/06/13-Moon
   -curriculum2.pdf.

RESOURCES

Traditional Choctaw foods and the seasons in chapter 1, this volume.

The connection of food and females in tribal cosmology stories in chapter 1, this volume.

"Best Practices on Indigenous Knowledge," a Joint Publication of the Management of Social Transformations Programme (MOST) and the Centre for International Research and Advisory Networks (CIRAN).

Kevin K. J. Chang et al., "Kua'āina Ulu 'Auamo: Grassroots Growing through Shared Responsibility," in Mihesuah and Hoover, *Indigenous Food Sovereignty in the United States*, 122–54.

Gerald Clarke, "Bringing the Past to the Present: Traditional Indigenous Farming in Southern California," in Mihesuah and Hoover, *Indigenous Food Sovereignty in the United States*, 253–75.

Mihesuah, "Nephi Craig," in Mihesuah and Hoover, *Indigenous Food Sovereignty in the United States*, 300–319.

Devon G. Peña, "On Intimacy with Soils: Indigenous Agroecology and Biodynamics," in Mihesuah and Hoover, *Indigenous Food Sovereignty in the United States*, 276–99.

Leanne R. Simpson, "Anticolonial Strategies for the Recovery and Maintenance of Indigenous Knowledge," *American Indian Quarterly* 28, nos. 3–4 (Summer and Fall, 2004): 373–84.

Explore these sections of my site about Western Hemisphere foods and health problems: http://www.aihd.ku.edu/foods/western hemisphere. html; http://www.aihd.ku.edu/health/index.html.

ACTIVITIES

Describe the importance of food in your culture.

What ceremonies does your tribe/cultural group perform in regard to food?

Research and document your tribe's calendar.

Lesson: Foraging

OBJECTIVES

List the tribes that gathered foods to supplement what they hunted and cultivated.

Identify plants that tribes foraged.

Explain why foraging today is difficult.

Understand the dangers of revealing precontact foods to outsiders who may want to use those foods for profit.

RESOURCES

Daniel E. Moerman, *Native American Ethnobotany* (Portland: Timber Press, 1998) is a compilation of multiple sources. Also available online: http://naeb.brit.org/.

————, *Native American Plant Foods: An Ethnobotanical Dictionary* (Portland: Timber Press, 2010).

Listen: https://www.kcur.org/post/seg-1-debate-kc-seg-2 -indigenous-eating?utm_source=KU+Today+Newsletter +List&utm_campaign=fec4be1ec2-EMAIL_CAMPAIGN _2019_05_09_02_52&utm_medium=email&utm _term=0_ec834ed00f-fec4be1ec2-278654713&fbclid =IwAR3TDtg0XYDH-toTF63Wh7w7ul-KlKQ3gQ7jS _tNfMA6Y89Ivwcs5AfYeA4#stream/0.

Harvesting pinons: https://www.youtube.com /watch?v=7UC3t7oVn6E&feature=youtu.be& fbclid=IwAR2nGZqZNQ6udrOk3vwJ6nigzuXc -x63a9ACHD9njnc5sOdLjovyjVm4k3E.

ACTIVITIES

Compile a list of plants you forage within walking distance from your home.

Research the plants your tribe foraged. Are any of those plants still available?

Identify plants that are endangered in your region.

Discussion: Is sharing tribal foraging plants with outsiders a threat to IFS?

Lesson: Challenges to Food Sovereignty

OBJECTIVES

Understand the complex elements involved in achieving Indigenous food sovereignty.

Research general examples of obstacles to IFS.

RESOURCES

Chapter 3, "Challenges to Recovering Health," this volume.

IFS Chart, in Mihesuah and Hoover, *Indigenous Food Sovereignty in the United States*, 14.

ACTIVITIES

List challenges to IFS mentioned in chapter 3.

List challenges to IFS in your tribe or another specific tribe.

Explain why the lack of a common definition of "traditional" food is a major obstacle to IFS.

Lesson: Tracing the Decline of Health

Colonization has affected tribal cultures in myriad ways. Some were positive. Colonizers brought new plants (oats, rye, barley, asparagus, garlic, etc.) and animals (cattle, sheep, goats, chickens, pigs) that altered the social construction of Indigenous culinary practices, beliefs, and traditions. However, colonization has been devastating to tribes from loss of tribal land and sacred sites. Intermarriage with non-Natives, pressure from missionaries, and the influence of boarding schools has resulted in a disconnection from their ties to land and the natural world, and cessation of a diet of unprocessed natural foods acquired by hunting, gathering, or cultivating. Food-related diseases developed after contact. People are also suffering from cancers not only because of their choice to smoke commercial tobacco products but also because of environmental influences. As discussed in chapter 2 and case studies 2 and 3, the trajectories different tribes traveled to their current states of health were different, but they ended up in much the same kinds of situations.

OBJECTIVES

Understand the health problems that tribes face today.
Chronicle the historical factors that accounted for the decline of tribes' health.

RESOURCES

Chapter 2, "The State of Indigenous Health," this volume.
Case study 2, "Changing Diets and Health in Indian Territory," this volume.
Case study 3, "Frybread," this volume.
Centers for Disease Control, "Native Americans with Diabetes," *Vitalsigns* (January 2017): https://www.cdc.gov/vitalsigns/aian-diabetes/.
"Culture of Diabetes: Native Americans and Futurelessness" (2:21), http://www.youtube.com/watch?v=RkpghPm7gyQ&feature=related.
"Diabetes and the Body" (8:44), https://www.youtube.com/watch?v=X9ivR4y03DE.
"Diabetes Mellitus: An Overview," https://my.clevelandclinic.org/health/diseases/7104-diabetes-mellitus-an-overview.
"Impact of Poverty and Stress on Diabetes among Native Americans" (3:21), http://www.youtube.com/watch?v=_3CJKtC8aCc.
Harriet V. Kuhnlein and Olivier Receveur, "Dietary Change and Traditional Food Systems of Indigenous Peoples," *Annual Review of Nutrition* 16 (1996): 417–42.

ACTIVITIES

Describe the health problems that Natives face today.
Chronicle the history of your tribe's health decline.
List the factors that contribute to food-related health maladies.
Have students keep a diary of what they eat for one week and determine how many calories and which nutrients each meal contained. In combination with a lack of exercise, diets of sugary, salty, and fatty foods have created tribal Nations of overweight and unhealthy Natives. Many of my students have been surprised to discover the unhealthiness of their daily routines. If you work with dieters, ask them these questions:

Do you eat when you are hungry, out of habit, because you are nervous, or are under pressure from friends or family?
Does your diet change while you travel?
Do you stop eating when you feel full?
What keeps you from purchasing healthy foods?

"My Favorite Foods" essay: What are your favorite precontact? Talk about nutrition, colors, taste, texture, smell, cultural connections, appearance, etc. Do not make this a "train of thought" essay. We all have our taste preferences. "Because crickets are yummy" is not an adequate response. Back it up with data and creative observations.

You are stuck on an island for six months and can choose ten precontact foods that will always be available to you. Which foods are the most nutritious and palatable? Use a nutrition guide. You will have to live with these foods for many months, so choose wisely.

Lesson: Pollinators

OBJECTIVES

Assess the importance of the pollinators to the world's food supply.

List the different types of pollinators.

Identify the challenges that pollinators face and why they are diminishing.

RESOURCES

"Ancient Totonac Vanilla Pods" (4:30), https://www.youtube.com/watch?v=vu6ILZ9luB8.

"Bee Conservation Project" (6:16), http://www.youtube.com/watch?v=-ZUx7xWpioM.

"Melipona Bee Defies Evolution" (3:43), http://www.youtube.com/watch?v=7DV7TS3XB94.

Monarch Watch, University of Kansas, https://biosurvey.ku.edu/monarch-watch.

Penn State Center for Pollinator Research, https://ento.psu.edu/pollinators/resources-and-outreach/what-are-pollinators-and-why-do-we-need-them.

"The Pollinator Crisis: What's Best for Bees," http://www.nature.com/news/2011/111109/full/479164a.html.

Xerces Society, https://xerces.org/pollinator-resource-center/.

Google "decline of insects" and "decline of bees" for a plethora of source material online.

ACTIVITIES

Make a list of pollinators. Younger students can draw pictures.

Write the importance of pollinators. What will happen to humans if the pollinators die?

Lesson: Environmental Issues

One of the most dangerous effects of our industrialized society is climate change and its detrimental impacts on the environment. This damage to the natural world is inexorably linked to humans' physical and mental well-being. Plants and animals have disappeared or are endangered, and many ecosystems have been destroyed or imperiled by pollution, damming, overgrazing, erosion, deforestation, invasive flora and fauna, and development. Genetically modified plants and animals are now commonplace, and tribal crops are endangered from pollen and pesticide drifts. Fracking in Oklahoma and pipelines such as the Dakota Access Pipeline and Diamond Pipeline potentially threaten multiple waterways, groundwater, and soils. The loss of pollinators such as bees, moths, butterflies, wasps, hummingbirds, and flies threatens the survival of fruits and vegetables.

OBJECTIVES

Identify the reasons for environmental degradation on tribal lands.

Investigate the various tribal lands that are being seriously impacted by pollution, climate change, and environmental damage.

Explain why tribes have difficulties in dealing with environmental problems.

RESOURCES

Brien Bienkowski, "Pollution, Poverty and People of Color: A Michigan Tribe Battles a Global Corporation," *Scientific American*, June 12, 2012, http://www.scientificamerican .com/article.cfm?id=pollution-michigan-tribe-battle -global-corp.

Rachel Carson, *Silent Spring* (Houghton-Mifflin, 1962).

"Engineering Salmon a Cause for Concern," https://www .adn.com/voices/article/engineering-salmon-cause -concern/2011/11/15/.

LaDuke, *All Our Relations.*

Winona LaDuke, "Salt, Water, Blood and Coal," "Klamath Land and Life," "Namewag," and "Recovering Power to Sow Climate Change," in LaDuke, *Recovering the Sacred*, 33–66, 227–54.

Deborah McGregor, "Coming Full Circle: Indigenous Knowledge, Environment, and Our Future," *American Indian Quarterly* 28, nos. 3–4 (Summer and Fall, 2004): 385–410.

M. Peterson, "The Lost Boys of Aamjiwnaang," https://www.menshealth.com/health/a19516489/industrial-pollution-health-hazards/.

Kyle Powys Whyte, "Indigenous Climate Justice and Food Sovereignty," in Mihesuah and Hoover, *Indigenous Food Sovereignty in the United States*, 320–54.

Linda Robyn, "Indigenous Knowledge and Technology Creating Environmental Justice in the Twenty-First Century," *American Indian Quarterly* 26, no. 2 (2002): 198–220.

ACTIVITIES

Study your readings and look on the web to find seven tribal reservations or lands in the United States that are being impacted by pollution, climate change, and environmental damage. Write a one-hundred-word summary for each place that you have investigated. Include one or two statements in each summary about why tribes have difficulty in combating environmental problems.

Read the book *Silent Spring* and any other online resource about the book you find helpful. Write about specific issues that Carson predicted and compare them with today's realities.

Lesson: Seed Saving

Seed Saving was crucial to tribes' survival. If they had nothing to plant, then there was nothing to cultivate. Saving seeds meant that those plants that had adapted to a particular environment would continue to procreate. Today there are 150 crop plant species, whereas there used to be at least 7,000. Without great diversity, food plants are much more susceptible to disease, insects, and climate changes.

Here are three seed saving curriculums that are appropriate for K–12, university, and more advanced.

Kohala Center, "Outline for a Basic Seed Saving Class," https://kohalacenter.org/docs/resources/hpsi/OutlineBasicSeedSavingClass.pdf.
Modern Steader, "Seed Saving Curriculum," http://ediblelearninglab.com/seed-saving-curriculum/.
Community Seed Network, "Seed Saving Class," https://www.communityseednetwork.org/assets/storage/Twelve-Seed-Saving-Presentation-English.pdf.

OBJECTIVES

Appreciate the importance of seed saving.
Understand the difference between heirloom, hybrid, and open-pollinated seeds.
Learn the effects of genetically modified seeds.
Learn how to save seeds from select plants.

RESOURCES

Pat Gwin, "What If the Seeds Do Not Sprout? The Cherokee Nation Seed Bank and Native Plant Site," in Mihesuah and Hoover, *Indigenous Food Sovereignty in the United States*, 198–208.
Rowen White, "Placing Sacred Seeds in a Modern World: Restoring Indigenous Seed Sovereignty," in Mihesuah and Hoover, *Indigenous Food Sovereignty in the United States*, 186–97.
Rowen White's essays at *SeedSongs Blog*, http://sierraseeds.org/blog/.
Seed Savers Exchange seed-saving guide, https://www.seedsavers.org/learn#seed-saving.

ACTIVITIES

Identify various fruit and vegetable seeds.

Save seeds from selected plants.
Discuss why it is important that tribes be able to save their seeds and keep them for future generations.
Describe how seeds are a connection to cultural identity.
(See the preceding linked curriculums for many ideas.)

Lesson: Tribal Initiatives: Stores, Gardens, Farms

OBJECTIVES

Identify tribal IFS initiatives.
Learn the importance of grassroots planning.
Learn how to conceptualize an IFS initiative.

RESOURCES

Academy of Culinary Nutrition, "The Top 50 Food Activists," https://www.culinarynutrition.com/top-50-food-activists/.

Garden Warriors, https://gardenwarriorsgoodseeds.com/.

"How to Be an Activist for Causes You Believe In," https://www.nbcnews.com/better/pop-culture/7-ways-be-better-activist-ncna791856.

Denisa Livingston, "Healthy Diné Nation Initiatives: Empowering Our Communities," in Mihesuah and Hoover, *Indigenous Food Sovereignty in the United States*, 173–85.

Michael P. Milburn, "Indigenous Nutrition: Using Traditional Food Knowledge to Solve Contemporary Health Problems," *American Indian Quarterly* 28, nos. 3–4 (Summer and Fall, 2004): 411–34.

Presentations at the Seeds of Native Health Second Annual Conference, https://seedsofnativehealth.org/resource-center-2017-presentations/.

Derrick Rhayn, "The Growth of the Native Food Sovereignty Movement," https://nonprofitquarterly.org/the-growth-of-the-native-food-sovereignty-movement/.

ACTIVITIES

Discuss three tribal food or environmental initiatives that interest you enough to get involved.

Present to your class your IFS project from conceptualization to implementation. Include what you predict might be potential drawbacks.

Lesson: Health Care and Tribal Medicine

Historically, tribal doctors (that is, medicine men and women) treated physical and emotional ailments. Ceremony was a part of the rituals, as were flora and fauna with medicinal properties. Many Indians still prefer the treatment of medicine men and women, although they also seek treatment from non-Indian physicians. Many Native students have experiences with Indian Health Service (IHS) hospitals and clinics, but what they do not know are overall health statistics within tribal nations. Food-related issues such as diabetes, obesity, and tooth decay require medical treatment, but so do other maladies tribes face—alcoholism, drug abuse, and emotional problems. The section on Indigenous health care meshes with the question of whether tribes can achieve food sovereignty. Repeal of the Affordable Care Act (ACA), as debated in Congress in summer 2017, could potentially affect tribal nations because the Indian Healthcare Improvement Act (IHCIA) is part of the ACA. Indian health centers can bill third party insurers—Medicare and Medicaid. The Indian Health Service could lose at least $800 million in funding from Medicaid programs and that might impact over two million Natives. This topic offers an opportunity to debate the question "Are foods medicine or are they preventatives?" Can eating right, being physically active, and caring for the environment reduce your risk of diabetes, obesity, and cancers? Because of the costs of health care, this is an important question. Also, there is a need for more Native health care professionals, and discussions can spur students to explore careers in the fields of health and nutrition.

OBJECTIVES

List plants that were and are used as medicine by tribes.
Understand the complexity of the U.S. health care system.
Understand the function of the Indian Health Service.
Discuss the importance of medicine men and women to tribal health.

RESOURCES

Chapter 1, "Traditional Diets and Activities," this volume.
"Medicinal Plants Used by the Five Tribes in Indian Territory," http://www.aihd.ku.edu/health/MedicinalPlantsoftheFiveTribes.html.
Native American Ethnobotany Database: A Database of Foods, Drugs, Dyes and Fibers of Native American Peoples, Derived from Plants, http://naeb.brit.org/.

ACTIVITIES

List by tribes the plants that were and are used as medicine.
Debate the complexity of the U.S. health care system.
Outline the hierarchy and functions of the Indian Health Service.
Discuss the importance of medicine men and women to tribal health.

General Class Activities

Food tastings. I bring food samples for students most class periods, including cacao nibs and dark (90 percent) and milk chocolate; boiled flint, flour, and sweet corn and blue corn tortillas; venison (white tailed deer and elk); chile pepper slices; grilled nopales (prickly pear cactus paddles); wild and domestic turkey; crickets and mealworms (farm-raised from Educational

Innovations); and a variety of Indigenous and introduced Latin American fruits (grilled plantain, mango, papaya, and bread-fruit). Students have shared nettle tea, dandelion honey, and cattails. In my "Latin American Foodways" course I have many more foods from which to choose. Warning: Check with your school about distributing food products.

Projects give students an opportunity to focus on a topic of import to them. Examples of a term project include:

History of your culture's foodways, from precontact to present (including how diets were altered because of colonization)

Trace the history of a tribe's health to present

The roles of Indigenous women in food economies

Environmental issues on tribal lands and how these issues impact food production, foraging, hunting, and fishing

Slow Food movement and how it impacts tribes

Challenges to achieving food sovereignty among tribes

Indigenous protests of pipelines, including repercussions for activists

Controversies over genetically modified plants

Successful tribal health initiatives

How to challenge the food industry

Create a school food or health curriculum

Problems with the Indian Health Service

Strategies for health recovery of a certain tribe (recovery of agricultural techniques, tribal health efforts, etc.)

Indigenous foods in fiction, film, and art

Traditional foods cookbooks with photographs

Students can focus on a specific group or issue: "What contributed to the health decline of Pima women?"; "NW salmon farms as contributors to oceanic pollution"; "The benefits of chia seeds to distance athletes and diabetics"; and so on.

University connections. Many students who enroll in my Indigenous foodways courses are interested in agriculture, nutrition, and cooking. Any related initiatives, organizations, clubs, and projects on university campuses related to foodways, environmental and plant protection, and food sustainability reinforce what they learn in class and can inspire them to complete their degree. At the University of Kansas, for example, there are opportunities for students to connect with the Center for Sustainability, the Native Medicinal Plant Research Garden, the School of Pharmacy Medicinal Plant Garden, Monarch Watch, Kansas Biological Survey, the student-led environmental advocacy group Environs, KU Farm Hands, and the American Indian Health and Diet Project.

Recipes

Indigenous peoples of the Americas had a cornucopia of foods available. Nothing much can beat the connection to culture and the pride one feels by preparing food in the "old way," such as gathering wild onions, cultivating crops, hunting wild game, and grinding corn.

Eating precontact foods is greatly empowering, and knowledge of those foods is crucial to our cultural identity. There are, however, too many nutritious foods from the Old World that complement this hemisphere's offerings, and we must take advantage of them. Many of my favorite foods are from the Old World: I cannot imagine grilling squash without sprinkling garlic on it or making *banaha* without adding sweet peas. The point is that "eating simply"—that is, consuming fruits, vegetables, and lean meats and avoiding sugar—can make a tremendous difference in our physical and mental health.

Because we do have choices and because many of us have limited time to spend in the kitchen and at the grinder, you will read here that some of these dishes feature some Old World foods, mainly spices such as garlic and onions, and preparation tactics are different from historical methods. Foods not indigenous to this hemisphere are marked with an asterisk. Regardless of what you choose, try to buy non-GMO ingredients. See the Non-GMO Shopping Guide site, http://www.nongmoshoppingguide.com/.

Experiment with Foods

One way to start on the road to better health is to learn as much as you can about what your ancestors ate on a regular basis. Here is a list of some healthy, vitamin- and mineral-rich foods. Make a star by the foods you like and cross out the ones you know you probably will never eat, either because you have no access to them (such as mink and wolves, perhaps) or because you have an allergy or you simply cannot stomach it. For more information about specific foods in these recipes, browse these websites:

http://www.nutritiondata.com/index.html
http://www.formulaforlife.com.au/asp/vegetables.asp

Try out foods you are not familiar with, or try cooking familiar foods in different ways: baked, boiled, braised, in casseroles, as chips, fried, grilled, mashed, microwaved, as pancakes, pickled, in relish, with chutney or jam, roasted in salad (cooked), in salad (raw), on sandwiches, steamed, in soups, stir fried, steamed, stewed, stuffed, or as a filler.

Because many people must watch their calorie intake, it is important to find substitutes for those fattening foods that are off limits. Try spices to make your dishes tastier. You don't have to buy an entire bottle of a spice; see if your neighbors have an herb you want to try before buying it. Some to consider: achiote, avocado leaf, powdered peppers, coconut, epazote, hoja santa, Mexican five spice, onion powder, popcorn flower, vanilla, tomato powder (my favorite), dark cacao powder (you won't need much), and Old World powders such as carrot, cumin, cinnamon, clove, paprika, mustard, and so on. If you have a chance to visit a spice shop, you should try as many spices as you can.

Note that these dishes use only ingredients from the Americas, and none are complicated.

Some recipes are as simple as mixing together raw ingredients that you like, such as pecans, walnuts, pumpkin seeds, dried cranberries, and fresh blueberries.

For this snack and other recipes, add Old World spices and ingredients, such as garlic, olive oil, cumin, whole grains, cheese, and so on. Many people want to use game meats, but if you are not a hunter, then ask friends who are if you could

6. Pecans, walnuts, pumpkin seeds, blueberries, and dried cranberries.
Author's collection.

contribute something to their next hunting trip (food, or
perhaps loan camping gear or an ATV), so that they can repay
you with meat.

Kitchen Equipment

Equipment for these recipes is for the most part inexpensive,
although you may not want to skimp on the food processor and
blender. I have a variety of cooking gadgets, but the ones I use
repeatedly are my blender, outdoor grill, crock pot, food pro-

cessor, knives, garlic press, tea kettle, kabob skewers, and large spaghetti pot (with a colander that fits into it). Crock pots are very affordable. If you have a large family, or if you do most of your cooking on the weekends and freeze food for the week, consider buying two crock pots so you can cook more than one dish at a time.

Appetizers

Guacamole Dip

Avocados probably originated in south-central Mexico. The fruits are rich and highly nutritious and can be mixed into a dip, milkshakes, sauces, or sliced for salads or on sandwiches. Avocadoes also are high in fat, and 1 cup contains approximately 230 calories. This recipe is the basic guacamole dip and can have many other items added to it, such as Old World garlic and lime juice.

INGREDIENTS

2–3 ripe avocadoes
  1 cup diced ripe tomato
  ¼ cup finely chopped sweet onion
  ½ cup chopped roasted and peeled green chilies
    (optional)
    Salt to taste
    Pepper to taste

Halve and pit the avocadoes and scoop insides into a bowl. Add remaining ingredients and mash with a fork or potato masher. Serve with homemade baked tortilla chips.

7. Lima bean hummus. Author's collection.

Lima Bean Hummus

Lima beans are indigenous to South America. Also known as butter beans, lima beans are high in fiber and protein and are low in fat. The dish succotash is a base of lima beans and sweet corn mixed with tomatoes, bell peppers, or okra. This dish does not use traditional hummus ingredients, that is, chickpeas, olive oil, tahini, lemon juice, paprika, or cumin.

INGREDIENTS

2 cups cooked lima beans
2 T walnut oil
1 t ancho chile powder
2 T piñon nuts to sprinkle on top
  Salt to taste

Blend cooked lima beans, walnut oil, and chile powder in a food processor until smooth. You might need to add beans a half cup at a time into the processor, depending on the strength of your machine. Add a few tablespoons of water if the mix is very thick. Taste as you blend and add salt to taste. Pour into bowl, top with piñons, and use as a dip or sandwich spread.

Summer Salsa

I call this Summer Salsa because I can make it from almost everything I grow in my garden. My family eats gallons of salsa. Like the green chilies, salsa goes on almost everything and is a staple in our home. I strain the salsa and use the liquid for soups, stews, and crock pot dishes such as pinto beans. The liquid is already spiced and adds much flavor to any dish.

INGREDIENTS

6 cups tomatoes (we like the small cherry tomatoes, but the larger ones work well too, as long as they're sweet)
1 cup sweet corn
1 chopped sweet onion
1 green bell pepper
1 cup green chilies (roasted is best)

8. Summer salsa and baked tortilla chips. Author's collection.

   1 T vegetable or olive oil
     Salt to taste
  ½ cup cooked and drained black beans (optional)
  ¼ cup yellow pepper (optional)

Sauté the corn, onion, chilies, and green bell peppers until soft. In a food processor, add sliced tomatoes, chilies, black pepper and sea salt to taste, sweet corn, and black beans. Experiment with how smooth or chunky you like your salsa. Add and subtract ingredients according to the size of your processor and what ingredients you like best.

9. Dandelion salad. Author's collection.

Salads, Soups, and Stews

Dandelion Salad

You know it's springtime when dandelions, lamb's quarters (goosefoot), poke weed, wild amaranth (pigweed), and other greens pop up. Many people consider them weeds, but these plants are just as nutritious as spinach and collard greens. I harvest all of these in my yard. Morel mushrooms hide around my neighborhood, and I gather walnuts and pecans in the fall.

INGREDIENTS

5 cups washed young dandelion leaves (can also add lamb's quarters and wild amaranth leaves)
½ cup tomatoes
¼ cup foraged morel mushrooms
¼ cup blueberries
¼ cup sunflower seeds, pinons, pecans, or walnuts
¼ cup dried cranberries
Sliced avocado

Add all ingredients to a large bowl. Ingredients can be changed depending on what you like. We prefer salsa as the dressing.

Poke Salat

One of my father's favorite dishes was poke salat, although he'd also be happy with any kind of deep green, leafy vegetable such as collard or turnip greens. Ham is a common addition.

INGREDIENTS

Young poke weed leaves (with tender shoots)
Black pepper
Vinegar

I prepare the very young leaves by placing them in the top part of a spaghetti pot and steaming them. You can also tear leaves and shoots into small pieces and place in water in a pot, then boil for 5 minutes. Some cooks recommend that you rinse and then cover with cool water and boil again for another 5 minutes in order to clean the vegetable thoroughly. Drain the poke salat and place it in the pot with desired seasonings. You also can finish the greens in a skillet with grape oil. Dad was happy with just black pepper, vinegar, and a small amount of butter.

Vegetable, Turkey, and Game Stocks

Stock can serve as the liquid for any recipe that requires water, such as soup or stews, and also as a substitute for butter or cream in recipes such as mashed potatoes. The first recipe is very basic and is not as flavorful as the second, which incorporates common Old World ingredients. Game stock is used mainly in sauces.

A purely traditional vegetable stock from the Americas might consist of the following:

6 quarts water
3 (or more) large onions, chopped (or 7–8 chopped bunches of spring onions)
½ cup sage
1–2 cups chopped tomatoes
1 cup chopped peppers (red, green, orange, yellow)

   1 cup chopped roasted chilies of your choice
   1 cup lamb's quarters leaves
1–2 T black pepper
   2 T sea salt

In a large pot (I use a spaghetti pot with a colander inside for
easy straining), bring ingredients to a boil, then simmer for
1 hour, adding water if needed. Strain before adding liquid
to soup, stew, etc. If you have small pieces in the liquid, use a
pointed sieve.

OLD WORLD VEGETABLE STOCK

Start with the preceding ingredients but also add Old World
ingredients:

3–4 celery stalks (including leaves), chopped
3–4 large carrots, chopped
   1 leek including washed stems
   1 bouquet garni:
      1 bay leaf
      2 parsley stalks
      1 thyme stalk

Tie the bouquet garni with cooking twine and drop the
bunch into the pot. Bring ingredients to a boil and simmer
for 2 hours. Strain before adding liquid to soup, stew, etc. If
you have small pieces in the liquid, use a pointed sieve.

TURKEY STOCK

   Ingredients chosen from the preceding recipe
   Leftover turkey carcass and giblets

Bring to a boil and simmer for 4 hours. Continually skim
impurities off the top. The carcass will start to collapse after

a time; just continue to stir it all together. After simmering, remove and discard the carcass, strain out the vegetables, and run the liquid through a sieve to remove particles. Note that this stock is very strong in flavor.

GAME STOCK

    6 lb. game b ones (elk, deer, bison)
      Ingredients from vegetable stocks in addition to:
    ½ cup tomato paste
    1 additional large tomato
    1½ cups red wine (the alcohol completely burns off—this is for flavor)
    1 T crushed juniper berries
      Some recipes call for 1 bar of bittersweet chocolate to add more flavor

Heat oven to 425 degrees. Place bones in roasting pan. Cook until bones become colored. Add the vegetables and make sure the tomato paste lightly covers the bones. Cook until everything is dark brown.

Place all ingredients into large cooking pan (I use a spaghetti pot). Add 6 quarts of turkey stock. Add the red wine. Simmer for 8–10 hours and consistently skim off the fat. When done, remove the large pieces and strain out the small particles.

Butternut Squash Soup

INGREDIENTS

    1 peeled and cubed butternut squash
    1 large yellow onion (or any other onion you prefer)
    1 red bell pepper
    4 cups of vegetable, turkey or game broth

10. Butternut squash soup. Author's collection.

     Black pepper to taste
  1 red bell pepper
     Salt to taste

If you have access to a newly harvested butternut squash, the skin should be tender and you won't have to peel it. If you make this soup in winter, then the squash you find may have tougher skin and needs to be peeled. Tip: Invest in a good potato peeler—it will make your cooking life much easier; but be very careful with your peeler, since it is easy to slice off some of your hand. As an option, you can roast the squash after cutting it in half lengthwise and then scoop out the meat.

Peel and cut the squash into medium to small squares (and don't forget to take out the core of seeds; it's similar to a pumpkin). Chop the onion (rough cut is okay). Put ingredients into skillet or saucepan and cook until squash is tender.

Place all hot ingredients into food processor or blender, mix with water or broth, and blend it to the desired consistency. In the meantime, put the sliced red pepper into the pan to sauté and cook until tender. Pour blender contents into a bowl, then top with the pepper and it's ready to eat.

Dakota *Waskuya* (Dakota Dried Sweet Corn Soup)

By Waziyatawin Angela Wilson, Upper Sioux Community

INGREDIENTS

Dried sweet corn
Meat (venison, buffalo, elk, beef)

Waskuya is a traditional Dakota soup, still eaten today at many of our gatherings. To dry the sweet corn: Boil corn on the cob and place on large platters. Place a towel over the corn and let it drain and slightly dry for at least 10 hours. Then shell the corn from the cobs. Do not slice the corn from the cob with a knife, as you want the kernels to be intact. Use a butter knife or spoon to lift the kernels from the cob.

When all the corn is shelled spread it out on a sheet or tablecloth to dry in the sun. In Minnesota this process usually takes 3–4 days, but this will vary depending on the climate and amount of sunshine. Bring the corn in each evening and return it to the sunshine in the morning. Keep it in the sun just long enough for it to dry thoroughly (it will make a rattling sound in your hand when you shake it), but don't let it stay too long in the sun because it can burn. Then place it in breathable storage containers. I often store the corn in pillowcases for the winter. Because this is such a labor-intensive process, it is good to dry the corn in large quantities. I usually do my entire crop of sweet corn from my garden at one time. A word about drying the corn—some insects will get into the corn as it is drying, but they leave as soon as the corn gets hard from the drying process. This is nothing to worry about. However, to prevent determined ants from climbing up to the platform and infesting the corn, it helps to provide them a handful of corn on the ground as an offering.

Cooking the corn: Rinse the dried sweet corn briefly before cooking and then place it in a pot of fresh water. Add the meat and cook for a few hours until corn and meat are tender. You may also add *tipsinna* (wild turnips) or *taniga* (tripe) for added flavor and nutrition.

Gazpacho

There are a variety of ways to prepare gazpacho, and it all depends on the types of vegetables you prefer. Common Old World ingredients include lime juice, cucumber, dill, garlic, parsley, basil, and plain nonfat yogurt.

INGREDIENTS

   3 cups pureed tomatoes (some prefer vegetable juice cocktail)

  ½ cup chopped green onions

  1 small green bell pepper, diced

  1 small zucchini, diced

1–3 small banana peppers

     Salt and pepper to taste

Put all ingredients into food processor or blender and blend until mixed but still "dicey" (or chunky). Chill. Many like it topped with yogurt.

Elk Stew

This is a family favorite. We take it to potlucks and parties. Deer or moose can be substituted. Other ingredients include Old World garlic and celery with leaves.

INGREDIENTS

   1 lb. elk meat (the "jerky" cut works best, although roast is fine) cut into small cubes or slices

   1 chopped green bell pepper

   1 chopped bunch little onions

11. Elk stew. Author's collection.

5 cups cooked pinto beans
1 cup cooked hominy (optional)
1 jalapeño (optional)
3 cups water, although broth is tastier
Salt and pepper to taste

Sauté elk, bell pepper, onions, jalapeño, and spices with
3 tablespoons of vegetable oil. After meat is browned and
vegetables are soft, place in crock pot with beans and broth.
Slow cook on high for 6 hours. Then switch to low cook for 2
hours.

Choctaw Stew

Every Sunday in winter my dad announced that he was making
Choctaw Stew. His Choctaw mother made it at least once a week.
The base of the stew is rather boring to my taste; the asterisked
ingredients are my additions.

INGREDIENTS

3 peeled potatoes
1 large chopped white onion
Cooked corn from 5 cobs
3 cups cooked green beans
*6 large peeled carrots
*1 cup sweet peas (if you don't grow sweet peas, use 1
drained can)
*5 cups broth of your choice
Salt to taste
Black pepper to taste
*Garlic to taste (optional)
Jalapeños to taste (optional)
1 cup chopped roasted green chilies (optional)

You can turn this into turkey stew with the addition of 1 turkey breast. We use wild turkey, which is drier than store-bought or farmed turkey.

Dad put all ingredients into a large pot until it boiled. Then he allowed it to simmer for at least 1 hour, adding more broth when needed. I prefer to add all the ingredients to a large crock pot and let them cook on high for at least 6 hours—put it together in the morning when you leave for work, and it's ready for dinner.

Osage Strip Meat Soup (*Ta-ni'*)

By Andrea Hunter, director and tribal historic preservation officer for the Osage Nation

INGREDIENTS

3 or 4 lb. buffalo meat, preferably from rump

Take the buffalo meat and, following the grain, cut into strips about as thick as one's thumb and about 1½ to 2 inches long. Wash meat. Put in kettle and cover with cold water, no more than 1 inch over the meat. Take a ladle and mash the meat. Put on fire to boil. Boil about 45 minutes to 1 hour with no lid. Serves 12 or so.

Posole

Posole (hominy) is a Mexican dish made with hominy, meat, chile peppers and avocado, in addition to a various other non-indigenous ingredients, such as radishes, lime juice, cumin, and cabbage. I make a purely precontact-ingredient posole, usually from leftover Thanksgiving turkey, so the meat is already cooked. I always have tomato broth on hand as well as roasted

12. Posole. Author's collection.

chilies and hominy. But you can add anything you prefer. Making posole, like creating mole, is an art, and this is the quick version. Consult *Food and Wine* and the Food Network for more complicated and time-intensive recipes.

INGREDIENTS

  1 lb. cooked and shredded turkey
  1 cup roasted and peeled chile peppers
 16 oz. cooked hominy
1½ cups water
1½ cups tomato broth (this is the liquid strained from the
    Summer Salsa)
  1 large onion, chopped
   Salt and pepper to taste
*½ t cumin
*½ t chipotle powder

These instructions assume your meat and hominy are cooked and the chilies are already roasted. Simmer all ingredients in a large pot for 2 hours. That's it.

Main Dishes

Meat and Vegetable Kabobs

This is a dish your kids can help make, although teach them that skewers can be sharp!

INGREDIENTS

> Long metal skewers
> Meat of your choice (elk, deer, buffalo, turkey, etc.; salmon works nicely, too), cut into cubes
> 2 red, yellow, and/or green bell peppers, seeded and cut into squares
> 2 cups large whole mushrooms
> 2 zucchinis cut into chunks
> 2 yellow crooked-neck squash, cut into chunks

Marinate meat in either a baggie or covered bowl with marinade of your choice for at least 4 hours. Pre-heat the grill by allowing coals to burn for 15–20 minutes. Use a cooking brush to oil the skewers with vegetable oil then thread meat and vegetables onto skewers, "paint" on a thin layer of olive oil, and sprinkle with pepper and other spices. Place the kabobs onto the rack and turn every 8 minutes until meat is done. Be sure to wear oven mitts when handling hot skewers.

If you use fish, the cooking time is less, around 2–3 minutes depending on the thickness of the meat.

Venison Steaks

My husband, Josh, hunts the family allotment in southern Oklahoma several times a year and brings home enough venison and turkeys to keep our freezer stocked. Game meat is lower in fat than cow meat and does not contain the additives that cattle receive.

13. Venison steaks with whipped purple potatoes, grilled peppers, and mushrooms. Author's collection.

INGREDIENTS

Venison steaks (deer, elk, moose, antelope)
1 onion, sliced (optional)
5–6 large roasted and peeled green chilies of your choice of heat (optional)
2 cups of sliced mushrooms (optional)
Pepper to taste
Marinade (optional):
  *1 clove crushed garlic
  ½ minced white onion
  *½ cup low salt soy sauce

Put the meat into a plastic container and cover with marinade for at least 4 hours. You can either cook the meat in a frying pan, with 1 tablespoon of oil and the other ingredients piled on top, or on the grill with the vegetables grilled separately. Turn after 5–10 minutes.

Good for Your Heart Fried Moose Meat

By Brad Young

Many meats are prepared by frying in lard, Crisco, or other unhealthy oils. Use grape or *olive oil instead. And for this one, Brad suggests using the natural meat juices instead of soy sauce.

INGREDIENTS

2 lb. moose meat
*½ cup olive oil (extra light)
Seasoning salt

Cut moose meat into thin strips approximately 3–4 inches in length. Pour olive oil into large deep-walled frying pan (not

heated up yet). Place moose meat into frying pan. Cover
frying pan so juices cannot escape. Turn heat to medium
high and keep there until meat is boiling in juices and oil.
Reduce heat to maintain high simmer. Stir meat occasionally.
Add seasoning salt to taste. This is best served over mixed
brown and wild rice with vegetables and bannock.

Venison Burgers

There are many ways to make burgers, but one thing should
always be the main ingredient: lean meat with no additives. I
don't eat burgers with bread, but I can add enough other items
to make this filling.

INGREDIENTS

    1 lb. lean, ground venison
    ½ cup chopped onions
      Pepper to taste
      Whole peeled and roasted green chilies
    1 cup summer salsa (optional)

Mix the meat and other ingredients then form into balls
slightly smaller than tennis balls (we prefer larger burgers,
and they do "shrink" down a bit while cooking). Flatten for
cooking. I cook burgers in a pan, although you can also cook
them on a grill. I prefer tomatoes, pickles, onions, salsa and
greens on top.

   You also can add ½ cup of nonindigenous seasoned
(Italian) bread crumbs. Not only does this make more
burgers, it also "plumps" them up. If you have kids or picky
adults in the house, you can add very finely chopped greens
such as lamb's quarters to the mixture as a way of sneaking
the vegetable into their diet.

Salmon

Salmon is a staple for many Native households, and there are various ways to prepare it. Check with tribes in the Northeast and Northwest, however, for dozens of cooking suggestions. Choose wild salmon. Farm salmon is cheaper, gray in color (until they are dyed pink, that is), and not as nutritious. Farmed salmon are concentrated in small areas, are exposed to contaminants, and eat only what is fed to them, including GMOs and antibiotics. In addition, farmed fish deposit enormous amounts of waste into the water, thereby destroying ecosystems.

INGREDIENTS

Salmon fillet (how big depends on how many people will be at your table)
Salt (optional)
Pepper (optional)

Bake in a glass baking dish for 20–30 minutes, depending on the thickness of the fillet.

Also try baking salmon in a glaze of agave nectar, marinated in white wine, and cooked on the grill.

To grill:

Cut fillets into 4 manageable pieces. Leave the skins on.
Coat the fillets with grape or *olive oil
Sprinkle with a mix of spices you like, such as salt, pepper, onion powder, or nothing at all.
The grill should be set to medium. Grill the fish for about 5 minutes each side; it is done when the flesh flakes.

Venison Meatloaf

INGREDIENTS

1½ lb. ground venison, bison, moose, or antelope
¾ cup cornmeal (instead of bread crumbs)
1 chopped onion
1½ cups salsa (to plump the cornmeal)
2 T agave nectar (instead of brown sugar)
2 T chopped pecans
⅓ cup zucchini
   Salt, pepper, and chile powder to taste

Mix all ingredients together, pour into baking pan or loaf dish and bake in preheated oven at 350 degrees for 1 hour.

Osage Pounded Meat (*Ta'-pshe*)

By Andrea Hunter, director and tribal historic preservation officer for the Osage Nation

INGREDIENTS

Roasted buffalo meat
Chopped pecans
Honey

Pound the dried buffalo meat strips until as fine as meat that has been run through a grinder. Add pecan nuts and honey, forming mixture into small balls.

Corn Crust Pizza

While it would be ideal to have a crust made exclusively from corn meal, the problem is that corn meal does not possess gluten and will not rise like a regular flour crust. This is why most recipes for "corn meal crust" have flour as the prominent ingredient. You can use a pure polenta crust without adding flour. Prepare grits and add *cheese to the mix, then spread evenly onto a pizza pan or stone and allow to cool for 1 hour. Add toppings and bake. This recipe uses flour and gluten in the crust mixture. The less flour you use, the crispier and more delicate the crust. You may need to eat the pizza with a fork instead of holding it.

CRUST

        1 cup corn flour or meal
    *1½ cups all-purpose flour
        1 t garlic salt
        1 T yeast
        ¾ cup warm water
        1 t honey

Mix warm water (110–115 degrees) with yeast and honey and wait until it foams, about 5 minutes.

Add flour and cornmeal and garlic salt, and knead for 10 minutes on a floured board until smooth. Place in a greased bowl in a warm place for 1 hour (or less if very warm).

Put on your toppings, adding the tomato base first. Sample toppings for a 12-inch pizza:

    ½ cup roasted or sautéed sweet corn
    ½ cup roasted or sautéed jalapeños
    ½ cup roasted or sautéed red bell pepper
    ½ cup roasted or sautéed onion
    ½ cup roasted or pan-seared tomatoes

½ cup cooked black beans
½ cup ground and cooked venison
   *Mozzarella cheese

Bake in 350-degree oven for about 20 minutes *or* 400 degrees for 12–15 minutes (or until the crust is browned). Remove from oven and add other ingredients such as more peppers, parmesan cheese sprinkles, dried pepper sprinkles, and so on.

Enchiladas

The precursor to what we know as enchiladas were the Aztec dishes of corn tortillas wrapped around various ingredients such as chilies, snails, tadpoles, turkey, fish, axolotls (salamanders), and so on.

14. Enchiladas. Author's collection.

INGREDIENTS

Blue or yellow corn tortillas
Sautéed vegetables:
    Chopped yellow squash
    Zucchini
    Onions
    Carrots
    Sweet red and orange peppers
Cumin, chile powder, garlic, and black pepper to taste

There are plenty of Indigenous ingredients to include, although the most common are black or pinto beans, onions, meat, and cheese. We prefer vegetables and plenty of chilies.

Mix vegetables in a large bowl with black beans and green chilies. Layer a large glass dish with corn tortillas, then spread the mix on top, another layer of tortillas, and more mix. Top with some *cheese and green chile sauce. Bake at 350 degrees for about 20 minutes, then let set for 15 minutes. Serve topped with avocado, tomato, and onion.

Vegetables and Side Dishes

Pumpkins

Pumpkins can serve as interesting containers for other ingredients, and you can eat it. Roasted pumpkin has a rich and delicious flavor. Options are numerous, and you can experiment to see which dishes are most appealing to your family.

Pick pumpkins that weigh approximately 1 lb. Pie and sugar pumpkins are a good size.

15. Roasted and stuffed pumpkins. Author's collection.

Cut the tops off so that you have "covers" or "lids" that can be replaced. Scoop out the seeds and the stringy portions. Use a paper towel and lightly coat the insides with vegetable oil.

Preheat oven to 325 degrees and cook on cookie sheet until outer skin is tender. This takes about 30–50 minutes. Remove pumpkins from oven and set aside.

Fill with mixtures such as vegetable sauté or wild rice.

You can also eat the meat of the pumpkin along with the inside ingredients. It is especially tasty with additional sprinkles of garlic, onion, and chile powder. Try chopped sweet tomatoes or a small amount of brown sugar or maple syrup.

Tepary Bean–Prickly Pear Casserole

By Gary Nabhan, co-founder, Native Seeds SEARCH,
ethnobotanist, award-winning scholar and writer

Tepary beans and prickly pear pads (called "nopalitos" in Mexican grocery sections) are among the best "slow release" foods that reduce blood sugar and increase insulin levels in diabetic Native Americans. Both were regularly used by Native American communities in the Desert Southwest and adjacent Mexico, including the O'odhams, Yoemems, Ndes, and Cucupas. These desert-adapted plants are rich in soluble fibers that slow water loss from their tissues during drought; these same mucilages slow down blood sugar changes in our bodies. This recipe also includes two Native American spices that are among the best anti-oxidants in the world, therefore providing additional protection against diabetes; if sumac berries and wild oregano are unavailable, substitute cinnamon in their stead.

INGREDIENTS

    2 lb. white tepary beans, cleaned, soaked, and boiled
      until tender
    1 lb. tender prickly pear pads (*nopalitos tiernitos*), already
      in strips or diced, with spines removed
    4 wild green onions (scallions, shallots, or chives), with
      shoots minced
    4 t ground sumac berries (called "simmac" in Middle
      Eastern groceries)
    4 t crushed dried "Mexican" wild oregano leaves
   *6 t extra virgin oil
   *4 cloves garlic, minced
    2 t salt

Boil the tepary beans or cook in a crock pot until very
tender—often an hour longer than what pinto or navy beans

require in a crock pot. Remove from heat and drain. In a skillet or wok, heat 1 teaspoon of olive oil, then toss in the diced prickly pear, sauté for 3–5 minutes, then add onions, garlic, and oregano. Keep on low heat for another 3 minutes. Pour beans into an oven-worthy (or microwaveable) casserole dish a quarter larger in volume than the bean volume, and then stir into them the prickly pear, onions, garlic, and spices. Preheat oven to 300 degrees (or prepare microwave for a 5-minute low heat program). Pour the remaining olive oil into the beans and sprinkle ground sumac berries over the top. Cover with a lid and bake for half an hour, or microwave for 5 minutes. Serve hot.

Comanche *Ata-Kwasa*

By Wallace Coffey, former chairman, Comanche Nation

INGREDIENTS

Two bushels of corn (Indian corn with the red and blue kernels, or you can get sweet corn and it will work just as well)

Prepare two small fires, about three feet in diameter, with a lot of wood. Make sure you are not anywhere that carries a risk of starting a forest fire. A charcoal burner will work but will not make the quantity desired.

Shuck the corn until just a few layers of husks remain. When the coals have dropped, place the ears of corn on the coals and let them roast. Allow the corn to roast but make sure it does don't burn. Periodically turn the ears over so they are thoroughly cooked. This is the hardest part of the task, because the fire is hot and it doesn't take long for the coals to roast them. If it takes a long time, it's because the fire was not hot enough.

After the corn is all roasted, take off the husks and let the corn dry and cool down. It's amazing to see the kernels on the cob swell up because of the roasting process. When they are cooled down, pop off the kernels or take a sharp knife and cut the kernels off close to the cob. Place them on an oilskin tablecloth or canvas to let them dry. Even out the corn on the tablecloth to let the kernels absorb the sun. Let them dry in the hot sun for several days until they have dehydrated and are shriveled up.

When they are completely dry and hardened, place them in canning jars or some type of container that will not allow moisture to get in.

During the wintertime boil a couple of cups of the corn with some beef. The kernels will expand to their normal size, and you will taste the sweetness of the corn coupled with the beef—mmmmm!

Baked New Potatoes

Instead of French fries, try these along with your burgers. My kids would eat them every night.

INGREDIENTS

10–30 red new potatoes
   3 T grape or *olive oil
      Salt (optional)
      Pepper (optional)
      Sage (optional)
      *Garlic (optional)
      *Oregano (optional)
      *Rosemary (optional)

Scrub new potatoes and cut them into fourths with the skins on. Place in a large baggie and add a few tablespoons of

16. Vegetable sauté and quinoa. Author's collection.

olive oil (just enough so the spices will stick), and sprinkle in
pepper, oregano, rosemary, and whatever spice you like, but
go easy on salt. Shake them up well. Place on cookie sheet
and bake until done.

Vegetable Sauté

This is a quick and easy way to eat your vegetables. Take any
combination of vegetables (or just one vegetable) you like.

  2–3 yellow squash sliced lengthwise
  2–3 zucchini sliced lengthwise
  1–2 cups sliced mushrooms
    3 large sliced tomatoes
  3 T grape oil

Place grape or vegetable oil in skillet. Cover the pan with a layer of vegetables, sprinkle with a favored condiment such as pepper, tomato powder, or sage, then cook over medium heat and turn after 2 minutes. Turn to low, cover, and simmer until vegetables are tender.

Sweet Potatoes

My daughter loves sweet potatoes, and this is the way she eats them. Although she insists on using a sprinkle of brown sugar, I refuse to argue with a kid who loves a food so full of vitamins A and C plus niacin and potassium.

    1 sweet potato
    1 T brown sugar

Scrub the skin of the potato (no need to peel it) and poke a few holes in it with a fork. Wrap in foil and bake at 350 for 30 minutes. Or microwave (without foil) for 7–10 minutes or until soft. Cut open and sprinkle with brown sugar. I think the potato is sweet enough by itself.

Mamaw Helton's Creamed Corn

By Pamela Jean Owens

INGREDIENTS

Essential: Very fresh sweet corn on the cob, shucked
Optional: A little butter, salt and pepper to taste, something to sweeten if really needed. But if it's needed, then the corn probably isn't fresh enough in the first place.

Tools needed: Skillet, very sharp knife, cutting surface, spoon (wooden is best)

Pick enough corn for the crowd you are having and the time you have to prepare it. It isn't possible to have too much. Shuck and wash, removing as many threads as you possibly can. They get stuck in the elders' teeth, and the point of this dish is to make corn for the old people, who don't have many or very good teeth any more, and for the littlest people who don't have many teeth yet. The problem is that it is so delicious, everyone else will want some too. Stand an ear of corn on end on your cutting surface, biggest end flat on the surface and small end up. Take a real sharp knife and start cutting down the kernels, starting at the smaller end, but cut off just the tops, not the insides of the kernels.

As you go, you'll have to scrape the corn off the knife and stop to scrape it into your skillet so that you keep still have room to work. Be really careful, because it is easy to cut yourself. Give the children something else to do so they don't come and stick a finger in to taste while you are cutting. Sending them to pick something else from the garden or shuck peas are good ways to keep them out of the way of the knife.

When you have gone all the way around the ear, go back to the top and scrape the inside of the kernels out, going all the way down and as deep as you can get; but scrape, don't cut. Again go all the way around doing this until you can't get any more corn out.

Put it all in the skillet and stir it up. Cook it very slowly, stirring a lot. You may need to add a little bit of water to keep it from sticking as you cook, and to keep it from drying out, but don't let it get runny. You want to cook it down so it comes out creamy.

Cook it down well, then season to taste with salt and
pepper and butter. Remember, fresh is very important in the
corn. That's it. Now eat it while it's hot.

Osage *Yonkopin (Tse'-wa-the)*, Water Chinkapin Roots and Seeds

By Andrea Hunter, director and tribal historic
preservation officer for the Osage Nation

INGREDIENTS

Chinkapin

The roots look like long sweet potatoes and the seeds like
small round chestnuts. Large quantities of *yonkopin* roots
are pulled up in the fall and eaten raw or boiled if they have
been dried. The yonkopin seeds are collected and eaten raw
or dried and stored for later use. To process the roots for
storage, scrape the outer skin off the long root. The bare root
is then cut into 1- or 2-inch pieces, which are strung together
by thongs in 30-piece strands. The strands of yonkopin roots
are then hung up outside to dry on wooden frames like those
used for jerking meat. To prepare the dried root, boil until
tender and add salt.

Chahta Tanfula

Tanfula is another Choctaw dish that can be prepared the "long
way" (that is, grind and soak the corn and filter it with wood ash,
then boil all day) or can be simplified for our fast-paced lifestyles. I make enough in a crock pot to last for 3–4 days and eat
it alongside vegetables, in soup, and by itself with salsa on top.

INGREDIENTS

   3 cups ground corn
*6 cups water or meat broth, depending on taste
   preference
   (If you use a smaller pot, then use 1 cup of corn and
   3 cups of water)

Place ingredients in cooking pot and boil for 3 hours or until the mixture is soft. Traditionally, the dish was boiled for hours, sometimes all day. But if you cannot stand in front of a stove that long, then use a crock pot instead. Set on high and cook for 4 hours. You will need to stir it often during the first hour and check every half hour to make sure it does not dry out. Add water or broth when needed.

There are a variety of items you can add to your dish:

   Cooked pinto beans
   Roasted chilies
   Diced hickory nuts, pecans, or sunflower seeds
   Diced turkey breast
   Chopped squashes
   Sautéed cactus paddles
   Pepper to taste
   *Garlic to taste

This dish can also be used for breakfast. Swap the chilies, cacti, and squashes for berries. Add agave nectar on top.

Pashofa

By Matt DeSpain, professor of history and director, Native American Studies Program, Rose State College

(Also called *pishofa, picofa, tunchie pashofa, ta sh pishofa,* or *tansh-pa-shoo-phah,* depending on the reference.) This is a traditional Chickasaw dish that has been a part of the Chickasaw diet for generations and essential to Chickasaw culture, ceremony, and identity. Though its meaning, traditions, and uses among the Chickasaws have changed over time, the dish remains a part of Chickasaw identity today. It is *the* traditional dish of the tribe. The first historical mention of it came from James Adair in 1775, but certainly the dish (or a type of it) was part of Chickasaw diet and ceremony long before then. Note the similarity between this and the Choctaw dish *banaha*.

INGREDIENTS

- 1 lb. cracked corn (pearl hominy)
- 1 lb. fresh pork (meaty backbone; today's pashofa uses pork, but James Adair mentions venison in 1775— using elk, venison, or bison would be fine)
- 2 quarts water (add more if needed)

Wash and clean the corn. Bring the water to a boil and add corn. Cook slowly, stirring often. When the corn is about half cooked, add the meat to the mix. Cook until the meat and corn are tender and soft. The mixture should be thick and soupy. Cooking time is about 4 hours. Do not add salt while cooking. Individuals salt to their own taste.

17. Pinto beans. Author's collection.

Pinto Beans

A crock pot of pinto beans is a staple of Flagstaff winters. If you make too much, you can always freeze the leftovers in small plastic containers for individual servings. Beans are a wonderful all-around food that has no cholesterol and is high in fiber, folate, protein, vitamins, and minerals but low in fat and sodium.

4 cups dried pinto beans
8 cups unsalted vegetable or meat broth or water
1 large chopped white onion
  Black pepper to taste
  Salt to taste
  Chile powder to taste
  *3 large sliced carrots (optional)
  *Garlic (optional)

Soak dried pinto beans in a large pot overnight (placing beans in a spaghetti colander then putting them in the pot of water makes them easier to drain). In the morning rinse and drain, then place ingredients in crock pot along with broth and spices. The longer you can cook this, the better the beans taste. Serve over corn bread and top with salsa and *shredded cheddar cheese.

Avocados

Avocados are an ingredient for a variety of foods in Latin America: relish, soup, sliced as a garnish, and *crema de abacate* (dessert). Avocados contain 20 vitamins, plus monounsaturated and polyunsaturated fat, and are a healthy substitute for foods rich in saturated fat. You can top ripe avocado halves with anything you like. These ingredients are what we use, either alone or mixed.

> Ground bison or venison
> Shredded turkey
> Roasted green chilies
> Dried and diced tomatoes
> Shrimp
> Diced roasted red bell pepper
> Black pepper
> Salt
> Tomato powder
> Chile powder
> Sage
> *Cumin
> *Lime juice

18. Avocado halves. Author's collection.

19. Prickly pear paddles. Author's collection.

Prickly Pear Paddles

Prickly pear cactus paddles are the stems of the cactus. These cacti are high in fiber, vitamins A and C, and calcium. The cooked pads (or paddles) have been used in Mexican cooking for hundreds of years. There are several ways to prepare the pads: boiling, sautéing, pickling, grilled, or chopped up and mixed raw into salads. I think they taste like a combination of okra and green pepper. The brightly colored "pears" at the top of the paddles can be peeled and eaten raw or made into jelly. This is a very easy recipe.

INGREDIENTS

3–4 prickly pear paddles
2 T vegetable oil
Salt, pepper, garlic, onion powder to taste

You can buy these at many grocery stores, but be careful of spines when you pick them up. You also can pick them in the wild, but don't take too many. Choose the greenest, most unblemished pads. Watch out for the long spines; grocery stores often get rid of those, but the smaller, almost fuzzy spines will remain. If you manage to get a spine in your finger, tweezers are helpful. But if the spines are too small, spread some Elmer's glue over the area and peel it off after it dries. You also can try tape.

Use a fork to keep one end of the pad still while you use a knife or potato peeler to scrape off the spines and "eyes." I usually trim off the rough edges.

After peeling, chop or slice the pads into stripes or into small chunks. If you don't like the slimy texture, cover the cactus in salt for about 15 minutes. Rinse thoroughly with cold water.

Put in a sauté pan with the oil, and then add spices you like. Sauté at medium low heat for about 5 minutes or until tender.

You can serve this as a side dish, or mix with scrambled eggs, blend into salsas, add to tacos, or use as a topping on a baked potato or garnish on fish.

Grilled Corn on the Cob

Grilled corn on the cob is also a staple in many homes, and it tastes great when grilled outdoors along with other vegetables, like zucchini and mushrooms, and perhaps an elk steak.

INGREDIENTS

6–12 ears of corn, husks on
Vegetable or grape oil
Salt to taste
Pepper to taste

Preheat your outdoor grill and "paint" the grill with oil. Peel back the corn husks and remove the silk. It is optional to add spices and oil (most like butter) on the corn before closing the husks. Wrap each piece of corn in aluminum foil and put on the grill for about 30 minutes. Turn occasionally.

Also try soaking the corn with husks before cooking to make the corn tender. Some like to add a few tablespoons of sugar to the water to make the corn sweeter. Others do not wrap the corn in foil, but they turn the corn often so that it won't burn.

Be careful with butter and flavor sprinkles (like the ones you see at carnivals and at farmer's markets), as you can add hundreds of unwanted calories and many milligrams of sodium in just a few seconds.

Luiseño *Weewish*

By Joely Proudfit (Luiseño), chair of American Indian studies and director of the California Indian Culture and Sovereignty Center at California State University, San Marcos

This recipe has been passed down through generations. The elders enjoy talking about gathering and preparing *weewish* and long to do it more frequently, but preparation is laborious. This particular recipe is from 1975 from Pechanga elders, who at the time were aged 96 and 84. Most important, preparing weewish is important for family bonding and a time to share stories and songs, the elders in their discussion of preparation also encouraging the young people to continue the tradition.

GATHERING

Gather acorns during the summer months until the rainy season begin (late summer or early fall). Luiseño people gather their acorns from the Palomar Mountains.
Meat of the acorn must be firm and dry (once they are wet they are no good). Centers of acorn should not be black or dark brown; this is usually a sign of being harvested too late in the season. The nut should be a yellowish color. Gather both small and medium-sized acorns. Small acorns, called *gunite*, are considered by some to have a better taste. Large acorns, called *weeowkt*, are dry in taste.

CLEANING

Remove the shell from the acorn. To do this take the flat end of the acorn and hammer it with a hammer stone. The acorn should be split in thirds or in half but not into small pieces. A good-sized hammer stone would be about 2 inches wide and 6 inches long, weighing about 2 lb., and should be smooth and rounded. Place acorns on cookie sheets out in the sun to dry. This process can take several days. You may use the oven, but using the oven turns the acorns black, which changes the taste.

To test the acorns for dryness, insert your finger into the center of the acorn meat. Once dry, place the acorns on a large flat basket and begin tossing them in the air and blowing off any skin, hide, or what is referred to as *quedo*. Pick up a few acorns in your hands and rub them together, so as to take off the dry outer skins. About 60 percent of the skin is removed by this method. Take a paring knife and remove what skin is left.

GRINDINGS

Put the cleaned acorn through the meat grinder; you will get half the amount of acorn you started with. Sift until you have a fine grain. Use a large oval rock with a hollow middle and grind the meat with a smaller stone in your hand until the acorn meal is very fine. Place this in the sifter one last time. Now you will have the amount you started with. Pound the meal to remove air from the acorn.

LEACHING AND WASHING PROCESS

Use a frame of a small window and set it on two boxes over a large pot. Use fine cheesecloth and put this over the screen that is on the frame, and then begin pouring the acorn flour onto the cheesecloth that strains into the pot. Now pour water over the acorn flour that is in the cheesecloth. Once all the meal is covered by a layer of water, stop pouring until all the water soaks through the meal, and repeat the process at least 20 times. With a water dipper, now add cold water. Let the water run through your fingers slowly so as not to splash the flour off the cheesecloth. The water will soak through the meal, and this too should be done at least 20 times, until the meal looks clear and clean of all foreign specks. Taste it to be sure that the bitter tannic acid taste has been removed by this leaching process. If so, let stand until all the water has drained completely out.

COOKING PROCESS

You can use a wood stove or cook outdoors over a campfire, or use a gas stove to control the heat better. Set the pot of meal on the gas burner and cook over a low flame for an hour. Stir frequently so as not to burn it. As it thickens, add water. In the last 15 minutes of cooking, add three times as much water as meal. To taste to see if it is done, drop a little meal in a glass of cold water: if it stays together and drops to the bottom, it is done. If it falls apart in this water, it needs more cooking. Now you have weewish. You can add various berries and nuts to your weewish for taste. Acorn meal can be substituted for corn meal in most recipes. Acorns can also be used in place of chickpeas, nuts, peanuts, and olives in a variety of dishes. Acorn meal is excellent in soups and stews.

Wild Onions

Each spring Choctaws head out to look for the 6- to 12-inch stems of wild onions that feature 1-inch wide clusters of small white blossoms. Wild onions go into a variety of dishes, and you can decide what you like best. I prefer them on top of baked potatoes, with scrambled eggs and mixed with squash.

INGREDIENTS

> 1 cup of chopped wild onions (cultivated from an area away from cows and pollution)
> 1 T meat broth
> 1 cup of water

Cook the onions in the water until the water is almost gone, then spray with PAM or butter and add desired seasonings (pepper and garlic are what we use). Then either add stirred eggs and cook until done or add onions to your other dish.

Zucchini Canoes

This is a good recipe for those giant zucchinis many of us often miss in our gardens. It's hard to believe, but sometimes these squashes manage to hide under the wide leaves and grow to be more than a foot long. Many people use these giant squashes to make bread, but you also can make a side dish that kids will like, especially if you call them "canoes."

INGREDIENTS

2–4 large zucchinis
½ lb. ground lean meat (we like turkey)
1 cup cooked wild rice
1 cup chopped onions
4 large tomatoes, pureed
2 T vegetable oil
  *Garlic (optional)
  *Dill (optional)
  *Parsley (optional)
  *Parmesan cheese (optional)

Cut the squash lengthwise and take out the flesh (a melon ball scooper works well for this). Place the emptied zucchini skins in a baking pan (I use a glass pan). Sauté the ground meat, squash, spices, and oil until meat is done. Remove from heat and add the cooked rice and beaten egg and beat well. Fill each emptied zucchini skin with the mixture, cover with foil (or glass top) and bake at 350 degrees for approximately 45 minutes—or until squash is firm and tender.

Stuffed Bell Peppers

This is another good recipe to ensure your family get their vitamin A and C.

INGREDIENTS

4–6 bell peppers
½ lb. ground meat
1 cup mushrooms

20. Stuffed bell peppers. Author's collection.

    1 cup cooked wild rice
    1 cup onions
    1 cup garden salsa
      Pepper to taste
      Chopped jalapeños
      *Garlic (optional)
      *Cheddar cheese (optional)

Place peppers in a pan deep enough to cover them. Fill the container with water until the peppers are covered. Put on the stove to bring the water to a boil, then simmer for about 20 minutes, or until the peppers are softened (but not soft enough to split). While the peppers are softening, sauté the meat, mushrooms, rice, onions, and salsa in a pan until meat is brown. Open the peppers at the top, place peppers in a baking dish, and add stuffing mixture to the empty peppers. Add some of the mix around the base of the peppers to make sure they stay soft. Bake at 350 degrees for 30 minutes. Depending on your caloric intake for the day, you can add some grated cheddar cheese over the top.

Poblano Peppers Stuffed with Wild Rice, Cranberries, or Vegetables

Few things smell better to me than roasting chilies—and among my favorites are poblanos. You can fill the peppers with a variety of vegetables, plus rice, beans, and avocado and top them with Old World cheese. Peppers filled with wild rice and covered with salsa are the kind my kids tend to like best. This recipe takes a bit of preparation but smells so good that I particularly like to work on it.

PREPARING YOUR PEPPERS

Here are four different ways to roast your 6 large poblano peppers.

1. For those with no access to a flame, place the peppers on a cookie sheet in one layer and put into your preheated 450-degree oven for about 10–15 minutes (sometimes less), or until you see the skin has blistered. Watch closely to make sure they don't burn. When blistered, remove from oven.

2. If you have a gas stove in your kitchen, lay the chilies on a small grill that stands over your stovetop and roast them that way.

3. Lay chilies over the grate on your backyard grill and let the flames roast them—turn often to make sure they don't burn too much (some people like them roasted until they turn black).

4. Use a small blow torch to blister the skin—just be sure you don't blister your own. Wear gloves, and do this outdoors.

Mashed Potatoes with Corn Gravy

We love potatoes. Gravy adds so much flavor and texture, but it does not need to include wheat flour, butter, or animal fat to taste good. This gravy is made from corn meal, water, nuts, and spices.

INGREDIENTS

2 lb. quartered potatoes (we like red-skinned ones, but you also can use purple or white potatoes; I leave the skins on)
Vegetable broth
Gravy:
1½ cups corn meal
3 cups water or broth (at least)
½ cup pecans
Red pepper flakes to taste
Black pepper and salt to taste
Venison sausage (optional)

Boil potatoes in a large pot for about 15 minutes. When tender, drain well. In a large bowl, add broth and mash or use hand processor to make potatoes the desired texture.

21. Mashed potatoes with corn gravy. Author's collection.

The gravy is similar to *tanfula*. Stir corn meal with vegetable or meat broth in crock pot. Add pecans and spices. Cook for 3 hours, consistently checking to make sure it does not clump or become too dry. The pecans will fall apart and add fat to the gravy. The longer it cooks, the creamier it becomes.

Grits

Grits are ground from hominy, which is made from the varieties of corn with hard kernels. The kernels are dried on the cob, then removed and soaked in a solution of wood ash (although baking soda and lime can be used), which causes the kernels to swell and soften. Then the kernels are hulled and dried; afterward the hominy is ground, and the result is grits. This process causes the protein value to be decreased, but lysine and tryptophan are increased. Without this process of using wood ash, however, pellagra can occur because the food becomes deficient in tryptophan and niacin. Obviously tribes learned that to use wood ash would increase the nutritional value of the corn. Grits are popular in southern states; there are hundreds of recipes featuring grits, and many southern towns host grits festivals. It is interesting to me that many people I know have never heard of grits.

FOR BREAKFAST

    1 cup stone-ground or other good quality grits
 3½ cups boiling water
      Salt to taste (optional)
      Pepper to taste (optional)
      Stevia for sweetness (optional)
      Raisins or dried cranberries, amount depends on how
      much you like them (optional)
  ½ banana (optional)

The basic way to eat grits is not from store-bought packages (like the oatmeal packs). You need to buy freshly milled grits, usually obtained from a health food store.

Add grits, water, and seasonings to pot. Stir well, cover tightly and cook over low heat from 45 minutes to an hour and a half, or more, depending on the coarseness of the grits. You will need to check them often to make sure they don't scorch. Add more water if they become dry. When the grits are soft, add the fruit and serve.

GRITS SIDE DISHES

The options for preparing grits are endless; you can add all kinds of sautéed chopped vegetables and meats to the cooked grits.

GRITS AS APPETIZERS

While other families were eating cookies and sweet rolls on Christmas mornings, my Aunt Billie Mills made cheese jalapeño grits. She used pickled peppers, so I don't recall them being too hot for me. Put cooked grits into a bowl and add chopped jalapeños (you could substitute green chilies, or raisins, or whatever you are in the mood for) and ½ cup of low-fat cheese to hold the mix together. Stir, then put the grits into a square cookie pan and refrigerate until set. Slice and serve as you would serve brownies.

Spaghetti Squash

This is a perfect dish for anyone who cannot digest gluten or wheat, or for anyone counting calories. Although it does not taste exactly like pasta, the texture and appearance are close. Add spices and you'll have a meal more nutritious than a plate of spaghetti.

INGREDIENTS

    1 spaghetti squash (about 3 lb.)
    3 T olive oil
       Marinara sauce (tomato based, not cream based, like alfredo sauce)

Slice squash in half, remove seeds, and bake at 350 degrees for 45 minutes to 1 hour or until tender. Using a fork in a scraping motion, remove squash from shell (it will come out in spaghetti-like strands). Top with sauce.

Breads

Banaha

Corn and most of the dishes we can create with corn are at the top of my list of food favorites. What I like the best about tamales is the corn, not the filling. *Banaha* is similar to tamales but with no filling.

FOR PURISTS

 2 cups cornmeal
1½ cups boiling water
 1 t baking soda
 1 t salt
  Corn shucks

22. Choctaw *banaha*. Author's collection.

Boil corn shucks for 10 minutes. In a large bowl mix together the cornmeal, water, soda, and salt until it is doughy. Roll into long shape that will fit into the corn shucks. Wrap the shucks around the dough and tie each with a shuck string (a strip from the corn shuck), then boil in pot of water for 30–40 minutes. We eat it with salsa on top.

To make banaha more interesting, I add a variety of things to the cornmeal mixture: chopped onions, spinach, garlic, pepper. For added flavor I prefer to boil the banaha in unsalted chicken broth instead of water.

Osage Persimmon Cakes (*Wah-zha'-zhe wa-dsiu'-e çta-in'-ge*)

By Andrea Hunter, director and tribal historic preservation officer for the Osage Nation

Persimmons are under-exposed and under-appreciated. Besides presenting a very special traditional flavor, this recipe offers a unique experience in the practice of traditional foodways. (Lard may be substituted for buffalo grease.)

INGREDIENTS

Persimmons
Buffalo grease

Go to the woods and collect as many persimmons as you can. Build a fire. Using a small woven screen made from saplings, separate the seeds from the pulp. Do this by grating the persimmons against the screen, so that the seeds fall through the screen, leaving the pulp behind. Mold the persimmon pulp into small cakes. Take a wooden drying board, about 9 inches wide and 18 inches long with a handle, and apply buffalo grease. Layer three or four persimmon cakes on the drying board and hold over an open fire until the first persimmon cake layer is about cooked. Then remove the cakes and cool. When the cakes are completely cooled they can be stored. These cakes will last until the next season.

Corn, Bean, and Turkey Bread

INGREDIENTS

4 cups corn meal
1 lb. ground turkey
2 cups hot water
2 cups cooked and drained pinto beans
½ t baking soda
½ cup chopped sweet onions
   Salt, pepper, and garlic to taste

Sauté the turkey along with spices. Mix together the turkey with the other ingredients and form into desired shape (balls work best) and gently drop into boiling water. Cook approximately 30–40 minutes. Using a spaghetti pot with a colander that fits into the pot makes it easy to drain—just lift the colander out after cooking and hold over the sink to drain.

Blue Corn Pancakes

I make pancakes every Sunday morning. These are dense, nutritious, and earthy. The foundational ingredient is blue corn meal, and you can add your favorite flours, nuts, and fruits.

INGREDIENTS

1 cup blue corn meal
¼ cup mesquite flour

23. Blue corn pancakes. Author's collection.

   2 T chia seeds
2½ cups warm water
  ⅓ cup strawberry mash
  3 T chopped walnuts
  1 t pure vanilla
  ¼ cup agave nectar (that is, the "syrup" is baked in)
    Blackberries, blueberries, or other toppings

Mix the corn meal, mesquite flour, and chia seeds with warm water. Let set for 4 minutes, then add more water or corn meal until the mix is similar to pancake batter made with wheat flour. The chia seeds will expand, so you may have to add even more water after you use part of the batter.

Pour pancake-sized portions onto hot griddle and cook until you see bubbles. Before you turn the entire cake, lift a bit to make sure the bottom is cooked. Turn the cake. You may have to cut into a corner to make certain the cake is cooked through.

Top with berries, nuts, agave nectar, or other ingredients of your choice.

Drinks and Desserts

Abuske

By Susan A. Miller, Seminole Nation

Although we need trace minerals in tiny quantities and usually give them little thought, they are important for our health, and this drink delivers some of them. (Any dry spot safe from small animals will serve for drying the corn.)

Boil young corn on the cob a few minutes. Cut the kernels from the cob, and spread them evenly on an old window screen (do not use screens made of copper or aluminum, or galvanized with cadmium or zinc), leaving space between kernels. Cover with several layers of cheesecloth, and place in an abandoned car to dry. When the corn has dried, heat clean wood ash in a cast-iron skillet until it is nearly hot enough to smoke, add the corn to the ash, and stir constantly until the kernels turn brown. Sift away the ash, but do not wash the corn. The ash adds calcium and trace minerals, helps free the corn's niacin for absorption by the body, and is believed to have a positive effect on the balance of the corn's amino acids. Grind the corn to a fine flour. (A coarser meal may be cooked and eaten as a side dish.) Stir the corn flour into cold water. Flavor with honey, if desired. This refreshing drink has a comforting taste and provides a pleasant burst of energy.

Pawpaw Sorbet

Pawpaws are fine just as they are, but you also can make sorbet and bake the fruit into breads, pancakes, or cookies. Some say it's not sorbet without at least 1 cup of sugar per 2 lb. fruit, but I never use sugar. The fruit is sweet and needs nothing added to it. Pawpaws have a very short shelf life. The best ones have just fallen to the ground and look rather rugged.

INGREDIENTS

- 2 cups pawpaw pulp (be patient—the pulp is hard to separate from the seeds)
- 1 cup blueberries

Put blueberries in pan with 2 tablespoons water. Use a potato masher to crush the berries. Bring to boil, then simmer until berries thicken. The longer you simmer, the more the water evaporates, and the fruit becomes sweeter. Mash again. Mix blueberries and pawpaws with a hand mixer until smooth. Put in small containers and freeze.

24. (*opposite top*) Pawpaw half. Author's collection.

25. (*opposite bottom*) Pawpaw sorbet. Author's collection.

26. Grape dumplings. Author's collection.

Grape Dumplings

Truly traditional grape dumplings were made with corn meal and possum grapes. If you look up "Traditional Grape Dumplings" online, you will see the same recipe no matter the tribe: flour, sugar, sugared grape juice, and sometimes eggs. Not one of those ingredients was used traditionally. Of course, the term "traditional" is wielded in several ways today. If you have no possum grapes, you can substitute organic grapes from the store.

INGREDIENTS

   1 cup corn meal
   2 cups possum grapes (or other type of grape)

Crush the grapes and simmer in a pot until thick. The more the water evaporates, the sweeter the mix. Run the mix through a strainer to remove the seeds. Skins can remain. Mix the corn meal with water until you can form balls. Simmer the corn balls and grape mix in a pot for 30 minutes. The finished product will be deep purple and doughy.

No Wheat, Butter, Eggs, or Sugar Cookies

There are many foods you can use to make cookies without Old World ingredients. Here are the ingredients we like:

   1 cup corn meal
   2 cups water (to start—you might need to add more)
   ⅓ cup mesquite flour

Be mindful of the ratio of the following ingredients to the corn meal. Use 2–3 tablespoons, depending on how many you choose.

   Chia seeds
   Dried blueberries
   Pecans
   Sunflower seeds
   Walnuts
   Hickory nuts
   Cranberries (dried or fresh)
   Agave nectar (optional)

The first step is to create thick corn mush—I put organic ground corn in a crock pot with water and cook until very tender (you'll know by the taste). Check periodically and add water if needed.

27. Cookies. Author's collection.

Then mix in whatever ingredients you like: I add agave nectar to make them sweet, although dried cranberries really help with that too. The mix has to be pretty thick or else it will just run all over the cookie sheet. Place dollops on a cookie sheet and bake at 350 until firm. These are not like regular cookies—they do not rise and might be a tad soft in the middle. Don't expect a sugar cookie—it's corn and therefore might fall apart.

Mamaw Helton's Stewed Fruit

By Pamela Jean Owens

This is a wintertime dessert using dried fruits, but it can also be made with the fresh fruit of summer or with a mix of dried and fresh fruit.

Take absolutely any kind of fruit. Reconstitute the dried fruit with water. Or, if using fresh fruit, wash it, peel it, and cut it up, as needed. A combination of dried fruit and fresh berries is wonderful.

Put all the fruit in a saucepan with water (not too much) and bring to a boil. Use the same water you used to reconstitute the dried fruit and add some more, as needed.

Simmer until tender, but don't let it get mushy. Stir often and don't let it stick.

If you use berries, add them right at the end so they don't cook too long. If you use fresh pears, they shouldn't go in right at the start either, unless they are the very firm kind. If you are using dried fruits, then they all cook together.

Good fruits are apples, plums, pears, peaches and their relatives, and apricots. All kinds of berries are great, but mixing kinds of berries isn't a good idea. Generally only one red or purple fruit is best—so plums or berries, but not both, and not multiple kinds of berries. But you can experiment. There isn't any wrong combination if you like it. Of course fresh fruit before modern times would have depended on where you lived, , but dried fruit might have been obtained by trade even if it didn't grow locally.

Depending on how sweet or tart the fruits are, you can sweeten or not. Mamaw always thought a little real butter made everything better. Aunt Jean thinks the same about white sugar. My mother always adds cinnamon. My seasoning of choice is brown sugar. But only the fruit itself is essential. Serve in small bowls as dessert. You can also pour some cream over the top.

Wojapi

Wojapi is a thick berry dish, sometimes the consistency of pudding. Traditionally it was not made with flour or sugar, but today it often is, rendering it only a marginally nutritious dish (even less so if the berries used are frozen "with sugar added"). If the berries you find are ripe and tasty, there is no need for additional sweeteners.

INGREDIENTS

4–5 cups berries of your choice that are fresh and preferably growing wild (blueberries, grapes, and chokecherries were used historically but can be bitter and must be pitted)
½ cup water
Honey
Cornstarch (Cornstarch possesses double the thickening power of flour; if you use this ingredient, don't add to hot liquids. First add the cornstarch to cold water and mix, then add to your hot mixture.)

Clean the fruit. Place in bowl and mash using potato masher (or a fork, but that takes longer). Add fruit and liquid to large saucepan and bring to boil—be careful not to scorch the fruit. Lower heat to a simmer and cook for about an hour, constantly checking.

Taste and see if you need to add honey for sweetness—only add a little at a time.

If you want the mixture to be thicker, either continue to simmer and "reduce" the mix (that is, the liquid evaporates, rendering the taste more intense and the mix thicker) or add a small amount of cornstarch. If you go with the latter option, place 1 tablespoon of cornstarch into small bowl and add cold water to that. Stir until you have a desired consistency (add more water or starch if needed). Then slowly add to hot pot of berries and stir.

Cranberry Pie with Cornmeal Crust

INGREDIENTS

Fresh cranberries
Walnuts
Cornmeal
Rice flour
Chia seeds
Agave nectar

Mix cornmeal, rice flour, chia, and agave with hot water, then let set until water is absorbed. The chia really expands. Press the mix into a pie pan.

Simmer cranberries and walnuts in a saucepan with a 4 tablespoons of water. Cook until the berries fall apart and the mix thickens. Pour mix over the crust mix. Bake until the crust turns a bit darker. I tend to bake things by estimating amounts and times, but this was about 25 minutes. Let stand until it cools.

28. Cranberry pie with corn meal crust. Author's collection.

Preserving Food

Roasted Pumpkin Seeds

These seeds can be used in a variety of ways—sprinkled on salads, added to breads, or eaten alone as a snack. Old World garlic and a few squeezes of lime juice (after cooking) can be added into the spicier version.

SWEET VERSION INGREDIENTS

    1 cup pumpkin seeds
    1 t sugar
      Dash (¼ t) sea salt

SPICY VERSION INGREDIENTS

    1 cup pumpkin seeds
    1 T dried red chile peppers, crushed
      Dash salt

29. Roasted pumpkin seeds. Author's collection.

Add seeds to a heated frying pan. Stir seeds continually until they swell. Add other ingredients and stir.

You also can dry them in the oven. After washing to remove all the stringy parts, spread seeds on a baking sheet and drizzle with vegetable oil. Or try grapeseed oil. Roast for 10 minutes at 325. Check a few seeds at the 7-minute mark. The insides will burn first, so make sure they don't overcook.

Pemmican

Pemmican was traditionally made by Northern Plains tribes with game meat and fat, and with berries such as chokecherries. It was a long-lasting, high-calorie traveling food. If you want your version of pemmican to last for months, the key is to make sure meats, nuts, and berries are completely dry before grinding them. If you plan to eat your creation within a week, the ingredients do not have to be completely dry.

INGREDIENTS

1 lb. dried and salted meat; venison, moose, and bison work well

1 cup dried berries such as huckleberries, chokecherries, blueberries, mulberries

½ cup nuts or seeds such as pecans, walnuts, sunflower seeds, pumpkin seeds, chia seeds

6 T coconut oil or rendered fat from the meat you chose

For long-lasting pemmican, thoroughly dry the meat, berries, and nuts. Use a mortar and pestle or food processor to crush the ingredients. Mix in a bowl with the liquefied oil. Either roll into balls, or spread on a cookie sheet and cool. Then cut into strips. Coconut oil is good for up to two years, but we eat our pemmican long before that.

Preserving Foods

By Joyce Ann Kievit (Eastern Cherokee)

When I was young I spent summers with my Cherokee grandparents in a really remote area of the Great Smoky Mountains not far from Qualla Boundary, North Carolina. They raised their own vegetables and preserved their meat without benefit of electricity. The major reason I stayed with my grandparents was to help them lay in food for the winter and to go for help if either of them needed medical care.

Green beans: One of the foods I used to help with was green beans. My grandma called them Leather Breeches Beans. We'd pick buckets of green beans and wash them. Then the beans would be strung together using a stout needle filled with a long, strong thread. After stringing, the beans would be hung in warm air out of the sun until they were dry. Once dry the beans would be stored in cloth sacks until the time came to use them. (The cloth sacks were made from scraps of cloth from old clothing or from recycled flour bags.) To rehydrate the beans she simply poured boiling water over them and simmered then on low heat until they were plump and tender, about 45 minutes.

Peas: I enjoyed helping with the preservation of peas the most. First the peas were put in the sun to dry and, when thoroughly dry, put away until there was a windy day. On the first good windy day the peas would be put outside on a bed sheet, and the peas would be beaten with a stick—the wind would blow the chaff away and leave just the peas behind. The peas would then be stored in a sack until needed and rehydrated by pouring boiling water over them and simmering until tender.

Pumpkins: In the fall of the year they would dry pumpkins. My grandmother would take the seeds out of the pumpkin and then slice the flesh into really thin rings, slicing or scraping off the peel as she went along. Then the circles would be hung on a stick to dry. Once dry, the pumpkin was stored in sacks. She used dried pumpkin in soup and pudding recipes in the winter.

Peaches and apples: Peaches and apples were dried in a similar manner. The fruit was sliced thin and put on the tin roof of the house to dry. Sometimes, depending on the weather, fruit rings would be strung on a stick and placed in front of the fireplace. Once dry, they would be stored in sacks for use during the winter.

Animals: My grandparents raised chickens for food and eggs. They also ate wild animals they killed. They prepared possum by bleeding the animal immediately after it was caught and then scalding it in boiling water containing a handful of ashes. Then the animal was gutted and the head and musk glands were removed. The remains were then soaked overnight. The following day the possum would be boiled in salty water or baked in a pan lined with sassafras sticks until tender.

A favorite of my grandmother was [ra]coon. Like the possum, the coon would be bled as soon as it was killed to prevent spoilage. The head, tail, and feet were cut off and the musk glands removed. They skinned the coon and soaked it in salty water overnight. The following day my grandmother would either boil it in water with broken spicewood twigs or the coon would be salted and smoked for later use.

In the winter my grandparents ate meat they cured themselves. They had a small smokehouse made out of logs chinked with mud. It kept out most insects, kept the meat cool in the summer and kept it from freezing in the winter. They would begin the curing process by covering each piece of meat with salt until it was totally white. Then the meat would be put on a shelf in the smokehouse to "take the salt." When they needed meat in the winter they would simply cut off the amount they wanted and wash the salt off and soak the meat overnight in water. The following day the meat could be boiled or baked. They also smoked deer and bear. Holes were poked in the meat and it was hung from the joists of the smokehouse. Then a fire was built on the dirt floor, using hickory or oak chips or sometimes dried corncobs. The fire was kept burning for several days until the meat developed a thick brown crust. The food remained in the smokehouse until needed.

Appendix A *Precontact Foods of the Western Hemisphere*

FRUIT

Agave
American plum
Atemoya
Avocado
Beach plum
Black cherry
Black raspberry
Blueberry
Buffaloberry
Cacao
Cactus pear
Calabash
Cape gooseberry
Cassabanana
Catawba grape
Cayenne pepper
Ceriman
Chayote
Cherimoya
Chiltepin pepper
Chokecherry
Cranberry
Custard apple
Feijoa
Giant granadilla
Guanábana

Guava
Habanero pepper
Hackberry
Huckleberry
Jalapeño pepper
Mamey sapote
Naranjilla
Papaya (not the same fruit
    as a pawpaw)
Passion fruit
Pawpaw (not the same
    fruit as a papaya)
Pepino
Persimmon
Pimento pepper
Pin cherry
Pineapple
Prickly pear cactus
Raspberry
Rose hip
Rum cherry
Saguaro fruit
Sapodilla
Serviceberry
Silverberry
Soapberry

Squawberry   Sumac
Strawberry   Tamarillo
Sugar apple   Vanilla

BEANS

Black bean   Screwbean
Green bean   Snap bean
Haricot bean   String bean
Kidney bean   Tarwi
Lima bean   Tepary bean
Mesquite bean   Yellow wax bean
Scarlet runner bean

MONOCOTS

Arrowhead
Arrowroot
Blue camas

ALGAE

Giant kelp
Spirulina

ASTERACEAE

Jerusalem artichoke
Sunflower

VEGETABLES

Bell pepper   Cholla
Butternut   Corn
Ceriman   Hopniss
Chayote   Huitlacoche

Jicama
Manioc (cassava)
Milkweed
Oca
Onion
Poke weed
Potato
Prairie turnip
Pumpkin
Ramp
Sassafras
Spicebush

Spring beauty
Squash
Sunflower
Sweet potato
Tomatillo
Tomato
White sapote
Winter squash
Wild mustard
Prickly pear cactus
Zucchini

NUTS

Acorn
Black walnut
Brazil nut
Hickory nut
Macadamia nut
Malanga

Peanut
Pecan nut
Pine nut
Piñon nut
Piñon root

GRASSES AND GRAINS

Amaranth
Indian ricegrass
Quinoa

Rice (brown)
Wild rice

WETLAND PLANTS

Bulrush
Cattail

Pickerelweed
Water plantain

DRINKS

Pulque (fermented maguey sap)

MEATS

Alligator	Mink
Antelope	Moose
Axolotl (salamander)	Muskrat
Bass	Mussel
Bear	Newt
Beaver	Opossum
Bison	Otter
Caribou	Oyster
Carp	Panther
Catfish	Pike
Clam	Porcupine
Crane	Prairie chicken
Crayfish	Prairie dog
Deer	Ptarmigan
Duck	Quail
Eel	Rabbit
Elk	Raccoon
Fox	Rattlesnake
Frog	Salamander
Goose	Salmon
Grasshopper	Scallop
Grouse	Seal
Guanaco	Shad
Guinea pig	Skunk
Hare	Smelt
Heron	Snail
Herring	Sturgeon
Iguana	Tadpole
Lark	Trout
Llama	Turkey
Lynx	Turtle
Maguey slug	Walrus
Marten	Whale

Wildcat   Wolf

SWEETS

Black birch   Maple syrup
Camas   Melipona honey

SPICES

Achiote   Popcorn flower
Avocado leaf   Sassaparilla
Epazote   Spicebush
Hoja santa   Vanilla

Appendix B *Diet Chart for One Week*

Monday

Food	Calories	Protein	Carbohydrates	Sodium	Fat	Cholesterol	Fiber
BREAKFAST							
LUNCH							
DINNER							
SNACKS							

Totals

CALORIES
EXPENDED

Tuesday

Food	Calories	Protein	Carbohydrates	Sodium	Fat	Cholesterol	Fiber
BREAKFAST							

LUNCH

DINNER

SNACKS

Totals

CALORIES
EXPENDED

Wednesday

Food	Calories	Protein	Carbohydrates	Sodium	Fat	Cholesterol	Fiber

BREAKFAST

LUNCH

DINNER

SNACKS

Totals

CALORIES
EXPENDED

Thursday

Food	Calories	Protein	Carbohydrates	Sodium	Fat	Cholesterol	Fiber

BREAKFAST

LUNCH

DINNER

SNACKS

Totals

CALORIES
EXPENDED

Friday

Food	Calories	Protein	Carbohydrates	Sodium	Fat	Cholesterol	Fiber

BREAKFAST

LUNCH

DINNER

SNACKS

Totals

CALORIES
EXPENDED

Saturday

Food	Calories	Protein	Carbohydrates	Sodium	Fat	Cholesterol	Fiber

BREAKFAST

LUNCH

DINNER

SNACKS

Totals

CALORIES
EXPENDED

Sunday

Food	Calories	Protein	Carbohydrates	Sodium	Fat	Cholesterol	Fiber

BREAKFAST

LUNCH

DINNER

SNACKS

Totals

CALORIES
EXPENDED

Notes

Abbreviations

ARCIA   *Annual Report of the Commissioner of Indian Affairs*
BAE   Bureau of American Ethnology
CHN   Cherokee Nation records (microfilm), Archives and
          Manuscripts Division, Oklahoma Historical Society, Oklahoma
          City
GPO   U.S. Government Printing Office
IPH   *Indian and Pioneer Histories*, Archives and Manuscripts
          Division, Oklahoma Historical Society, Oklahoma City
IPP   *Indian and Pioneer Papers*, Western History Collections,
          University of Oklahoma, Norman

1. Traditional Diets and Activities

Information about flora and fauna available in the geographic regions was compiled from a variety of sources, including Lowell Bean and Thomas Blackburn, *Native Californians* (Socorro NM: Ballena Press, 1976); Vincent Brown, *Native Americans of the Pacific Coast* (Happy Camp CA: Naturegraph, 1985); Alfred W. Crosby Jr., *The Columbian Exchange* (Westport CT: Greenwood Publishing, 1972); Philip Drucker, *Cultures of the North Pacific Coast* (San Francisco: Chandler Publishing, 1965) and *Indians of the Northwest Coast* (New York: McGraw-Hill, 1955); R. Heizer and M. Whipple, *California Indians* (Berkeley: University of California Press, 1951); George Hyde, *Indians of the Woodlands* (Norman: University of Oklahoma Press, 1962); Peter Kalm, *The America of 1750: Travels in North America by Peter Kalm*, vol. 2 (1770; repr., English version of 1770 revised from the original Swedish and edited by Adolph B. Benson, New York: Dover Publications, 1966), 561; A. L. Kroeber, *Handbook of the Indians of California* (Washington DC: Government Printing Office, 1925); Paul E. Minnis, *People and Plants in Ancient Western North America* (Tucson: University of Arizona Press, 2010) and *People and Plants in Ancient Eastern North America* (Tucson: University of Arizona Press, 2010); William Wilmon Newcomb, *The Indians of Texas from Prehistoric to Modern Times* (Austin: University of Texas Press, 1961); Marla N. Powers, *Oglala Women: Myth Ritual and Reality* (Chicago: University of Chicago Press, 1986), 83–84; Sylvester K. Stevens, Donald H. Kent, and Emma Edith Woods, eds., *Travels in New France by J.C.B.* (Harrisburg: Pennsylvania Historical Commission, 1941), 138–39; Emory Strong, *Stone Age in the Great Basin* (Portland: Bimfords and Mort, 1969); Thomas Vennum Jr., *Wild Rice and the Ojibway People* (St. Paul: Minnesota Historical Press, 1988); and Jack McIver Weatherford, *Indian Givers: How the Indians of the Americas Transformed the World* (New York: Fawcett Columbine, 1988; repr., New York: Ballantine Books, 1990). See also http://www.kstrom.net /isk/food/wildrice.html and http://www.kstrom.net/isk/food/maple .html for information about wild rice and maple sugar cultivation and production by Anishinaabe and other tribes in Wisconsin and Minnesota and around the Great Lakes.

1. See appendix A for a list of precontact foods of this hemisphere.
2. For a brief history of corn, see Lance Gibson and Garren Benson, Iowa State University, Department of Agronomy, "Origin, History, and Uses of Corn (*Zea mays*)," revised January 2002, http://www.agron.iastate.edu/courses/agron212/Readings /Corn_history.htm.
3. Sally Fallon and Mary G. Enig, "Guts and Grease: The Diet of Native Americans," http://www.westonaprice.org/traditional _diets/native_americans.html.
4. See Moerman's Native American ethnobotany database: http:// naeb.brit.org/.
5. Compiled from Berndt Bergland and Clare E. Bolsby, *The Edible Wild: A Complete Cookbook and Guide to Edible Wild Plants in Canada and North America* (New York: Charles Scribner's Sons, 1971); Michael A. Weiner, *Earth Medicine, Earth Food: Plant Remedies, Drugs and Natural Foods of the North American Indians* (New York: Collier Books, 1980).
6. Richard Irving Dodge, *The Plains of North America and Their Inhabitants*, ed. Wayne R. Kime (Newark: University of Delaware Press, 1989).
7. Reay Tannahill, *Food in History* (New York: Crown Publishers, 1989), 214–16.
8. Tannahill, *Food in History*, 203.
9. Tannahill, *Food in History*, 213–14.
10. "Lost Foods of the Incas Crop up as Study Digs into the Past," *Arizona Republic*, November 5, 1989, AA18.

11. This first calendar was used precontact, corresponded to thirteen moons, started in March, and does not correspond with the twelve-month English calendar we use today. One can also see the difference between this traditional calendar and the one documented by H. B. Cushman in his *History of the Choctaw, Chickasaw and Natchez Indians* (1899; repr., Norman: University of Oklahoma Press, 1999), 249–50. That later calendar uses introduced plants such as African watermelon, and the foods used in February, according to Cushman, were walnuts, chestnuts, and "other nuts." Nuts are harvested in the fall, ending in October.

12. Polingaysi Qoyawayma, as told to Vada F. Carlson, *No Turning Back* (Albuquerque: University of New Mexico Press, 1964), 5.

13. Bernard Romans, *A Concise Natural History of East and West Florida* (1775; repr., Gainesville: University Press of Florida, 1962), 42–43, https://ufdc.ufl.edu/UF00095971/00001/1x.

14. James Adair, *History of the American Indians, Particularly Those Nations Adjoining to the Mississippi, East and West Florida, Georgia, South and North Carolina, and Virginia* (London: Edward and Charles Dilly, 1775), 5.

15. Edward Kimber, *A Relation or Journal of a Late Expedition, &c.: The Oglethorpe Expedition of 1744 into Florida* (1744; repr., Gainesville: University Press of Florida, 1976), 16.

16. Peter Kalm, *The America of 1750: Travels in North America by Peter Kalm*, vol. 2 (1770; repr., English version of 1770 revised from the original Swedish and edited by Adolph B. Benson, New York: Dover Publications, 1966), 561.

17. Indian agency correspondence, National Archives, microfilm series M234, Letters Received by the Office of Indian Affairs, 1824–80, roll no. 186, Choctaw Agency 1846–49.

18. George Catlin, Letter no. 7, *Letters and Notes on the Manners, Customs and Conditions of North American Indians* (London, 1844), Library of Western Fur Trade Historical Source Documents, New York, http://www.xmission.com/~drudy/mtman/html/catlin /letter7.html.

19. William Wood, *New England's Prospect*, ed. Alden T. Vaughan (Amherst: University of Massachusetts Press, 1977), 81–82.

20. Christopher Columbus, *Diary of Christopher Columbus's First Voyage to America, 1492–1493*, transcribed and translated by Oliver C.

Dunn and James E. Kelley Jr. (Norman: University of Oklahoma Press, 1989), 65–73.

21. Adair, *History of the American Indians*, 2.

22. Kalm, *The America of 1750*, 462.

23. Nicholas Cresswell, *The Journal of Nicholas Cresswell, 1774–1777* (New York: Dial Press, 1928), 49, 120.

24. James M. Hadden, *A Journal Kept in Canada and upon Burgoyne's Campaign in 1776 and 1777* (Albany: Joel Munsell's Sons, 1884), 12.

25. Sherry Smith, *A View from Officer's Row: Army Perceptions of Western Indians* (Tucson: University of Arizona Press, 1990), 59.

26. Smith, *View from Officer's Row*, 89.

27. Smith, *View from Officer's Row*, 64.

28. Sylvester K. Stevens, Donald H. Kent, and Emma Edith Woods, eds., *Travels in New France by J.C.B.* (Harrisburg: Pennsylvania Historical Commission, 1941), 138.

29. Patrick M'Robert, *A Tour through Part of the North Provinces of America: Being a Series of Letters wrote on the Spot, in the Years 1774 & 1775* (Edinburgh, 1776; repr., edited by Carl Bridenbaugh, New York: New York Times, 1968), 39.

30. Jonathan Carver Esq., *Travels, through the Interior Parts of North America, in the Years 1766, 1767, and 1768* (Minneapolis: Ross and Haines, 1956), 279. Note that "s" at that time was printed as "⦚."

31. M. D. Eaton, S. Boyd, Marjorie Shostak, and Melvin Konner, *The Paleolithic Prescription: A Program of Diet & Exercise and a Design for Living* (New York: Harper Collins, 1989), 32–33.

32. Eaton et al., *Paleolithic Prescription*, 177.

33. Eaton et al., *Paleolithic Prescription*, 31–32.

34. Rev. John Heckewelder, *History, Manners and Customs of the Indian Nations Who Once Inhabited Pennsylvania and the Neighbouring States* (Philadelphia: Historical Society of Pennsylvania, 1876), 220.

35. Eaton et al., *Paleolithic Prescription*, 35.

36. Eaton et al., *Paleolithic Prescription*, 45.

37. See Joseph B. Oxendine, *American Indian Sports Heritage* (Champaign: Human Kinetics Books, 1988) for discussions about various traditional sports and games.

38. Catlin, Letter no. 49, *Letters and Notes*, http://www.xmission.com/~drudy/mtman/html/catlin/letter49.html.

39. Jeff Corntassel, personal communication, June 2004.

40. Peter Nabokov, *Indian Running* (Santa Fe: Ancient City Press, 1981), 19–20.

41. Garnered from Alfred W. Crosby Jr., *The Columbian Exchange* (Westport CT: Greenwood Publishing, 1972) and Russell Thornton, *American Indian Holocaust and Survival: A Population History Since 1492* (Norman: University of Oklahoma Press, 1990).

Case Study 1

1. "Indian Removal Act," Library of Congress Research Guides, https://guides.loc.gov/indian-removal-act.

2. Romans, *Concise Natural History*; John R. Swanton, "Social and Religious Beliefs and Usages of the Chickasaw," in *Forty-Fourth Annual Report of the Bureau of American Ethnology* (Washington DC: GPO, 1928), 240–42; John R. Swanton, "Social Organization and the Social Usages of the Indians of the Creek Confederacy," in *Forty-Second Annual Report of the Bureau of American Ethnology* (Washington DC: GPO, 1924–25), 279–325; John R. Swanton, "Aboriginal Culture of the Southeast," in *Forty-Second Annual Report of the Bureau of American Ethnology* (Washington DC: GPO, 1924–25), 673–726; John R. Swanton, *Early History of the Creek Indians and Their Neighbors*, BAE, Bulletin 73 (Washington DC: GPO, 1922); Adair, *History of the American Indians*, 330–31, 387; Margaret Zehmer Searcy, "Choctaw Subsistence, 1540–1830: Hunting, Fishing, Farming, and Gathering," in *The Choctaw before Removal*, ed. Carolyn Keller Reeves (Jackson: University Press of Mississippi, 1985), 32–54; T. N. Campbell, "Choctaw Subsistence: Ethnographic Notes from the Lincecum Manuscript," *Florida Anthropologist* 12, no. 1 (1959): 9–24. Gideon Lincecum (1793–1874), a nineteenth-century physician and "naturalist," wrote his observations and information gleaned from Choctaw informers from 1823 to 1825. The Lincecum Manuscript is housed at the Center for American History, University of Texas, Austin.

3. *Annual Report of the Commissioner of Indian Affairs for the Year 1840*, 313 (hereafter cited as *ARCIA* with year; digitized annual reports can be accessed online, http:// digital.library.wisc.edu/1711.dl /History); Elapotubee interview, in Grant Foreman, ed., *Indian and Pioneer Histories*, Oklahoma Historical Society, Oklahoma City, Archives and Manuscripts Division, microfilm versions (hereafter cited as *IPH*), 3:354. The 115 volumes of the *IPH* com-

prise a series of interviews of residents of Oklahoma conducted by Works Progress Administration workers in the 1930s. Citations include the interviewees' last names. Also used in this volume are the digital versions of these papers, which are known as the *Indian and Pioneer Papers* collection (*IPP*) from the Western History Collections at the University of Oklahoma. The volume and page numbers are not the same in the two collections. Interviews for *IPH* are from the Oklahoma Historical Society unless indicated from the University of Oklahoma Western History Collections as *IPP*. See https://digital.libraries.ou.edu/cdm/search /collection/indianpp.

4. *ARCIA* 1840, 313; Commissioner of Indian Affairs, 25th Cong., 3d sess., S. Docs. 1, Serial 338; *ARCIA* 1838, 511.

5. *ARCIA* 1842, 448.

6. Burk, *IPH* 17:373

7. Muriel H. Wright, "Notes and Documents: Sugar Loaf Mountain Resort," *Chronicles of Oklahoma* 38, no. 2 (1960): 202–3; *South McAlester Capital,* July 12, 1894; Conger, *IPH* 2:196–97; Palmer, *IPH* 69:58.

8. Catlin, Letter no. 39, *Letters and Notes,* user.xmission.com/~drudy /mtman/html/catlin/letter39.html; *ARCIA* 1840, 311, 314.

9. *ARCIA* 1840, 314; *ARCIA* 1842, 448.

10. Elapotubee, *IPH* 3:354; Cole, *IPH* 8:200; *ARCIA* 1872, 364. Early Indian agents lauded the new tribal lands in glowing terms, perhaps attempts to justify or rationalize the tribes' removals. Agents around the time of the Civil War, however, had different assessments, reporting that a good portion of those lands were unfit for cultivation, perhaps because later officials were more aware that some Native families did not have access to the best lands, but white intruders or intermarried whites did.

11. On timber and shellbark hickory nuts, see John R. Swanton, *Source Material for the Social and Ceremonial Life of the Choctaw Indians,* BAE, Bulletin 104 (Washington DC: GPO, 1931; repr., Tuscaloosa: University of Alabama Press, 2001), 48; David I. Bushnell Jr., *The Choctaw of Bayou Lacombe, St. Tammany Parish, Louisiana,* BAE, Bulletin 48 (Washington DC: GPO, 1909), 8; on the use of acorn flour, see Swanton, *Source Material,* 38, 48; on *okshash,* see Cyrus Byington, *Dictionary of the Choctaw Language,* BAE, Bulletin 46 (Washington DC: GPO, 1915), 301.

12. *IPH* 108:24–25.

13. "Journal of the Fourth Annual Session of the General Council of the Territory Held at Okmulgee, I. T. from the 5th to the 15th of May, 1873," Inter-national Council file, Indian Archives Division, Oklahoma Historical Society, Oklahoma City.

14. Mulkey, *IPH* 65:368; Bird Doublehead, *IPH* 25:239; Flint, *IPH* 3:527; Cartarby, *IPH* 19:195, 203; Monroe, *IPH* 37:10; Cherry, *IPH* 79:159; *IPH* 95:534–35; McCoy, *IPH* 102:82–83; Ludlow, *IPH* 106:394–95. The turnips in question may be Indian breadroot (*Pediomelum hypogaeum*) or the prairie turnip (*Psoralea esculenta*), indigenous to this hemisphere.

15. Catlin, Letter no. 39.

16. Lamar, *IPH* 31:23; Pusley, *IPH* 4:18; Sharp, *IPH* 44:237–38; Cherry, *IPH* 79:159; Culbertson, *IPH* 2:432; Czarina, *IPH* 21:432; Harkins, *IPH* 27:443–44; Lattimer, *IPH* 33:84.

17. *ARCIA* 1843, 409; *ARCIA* 1845, 526; *ARCIA* 1845, 522.

18. Harris, *IPH* 63:413; McKee, *IPH* 102:182.

19. Benson, *IPH* 14:422; Harkins, *IPH* 27:444.

20. Crawford, *IPH* 104:467; Culberson, *IPH* 21:291. On stockpiling in the larder, see Hurst, *IPH* 46:123.

21. Fleming, *IPH* 24:340.

22. Flint, *IPH* 3:527; Frazier, *IPH* 3:589.

23. Jack, *IPH* 30:473; Bohanan, *IPH* 1:211–12; Gardner, *IPH* 25:354; on bear meat, see Johns, *IPH* 48:164, and Taaffe, *IPH* 46:155; on small game, see Mulkey, *IPH* 65:368; Hayes, *IPH* 28:316; *IPH* 38:264; Edwards, *IPH* 51:404.

24. Cherry, *IPH* 79:168.

25. Kelley, *IPH* 32:122; Norwood, *IPH* 7:537–38; Hayes, *IPH* 28:318; Johnson, *IPH* 106:195–96.

26. Frazier, *IPH* 3:589.

27. Camp, *IPH* 11:190–91; Culbertson, *IPH* 21:301; Putnam, *IPH* 41:26; Fleming, *IPH* 52:342; Harris, *IPH* 63:414; Folsom, *IPH* 91:347. That practice is illegal today in Oklahoma, as are dynamiting and using a crank phone to electrocute the fish.

28. Ludlow, *IPH* 106:394–95; Netherton, *IPH* 37:517; *IPH* 106:432.

29. Bohanan, *IPH* 1:226; Cline, *IPH* 2:149–50; Thomas, *IPH* 10:382.

30. Ludlow, *IPH* 106:395; Noah, *IPH* 7:518

31. Billy, *IPH* 38:130.

32. Ward, *IPH* 11:194; Culberson, *IPH* 21:291; Graham, *IPH* 26:255; Turnbull, *IPH* 47:384.

33. Bohanan, *IPH* 1:225.

34. Cole, *IPH* 20:229; Culbertson, *IPH* 21:298; Hornbeck, *IPH* 29:444; Lewis, *IPH* 106:242.

35. *ARCIA* 1838, 508; *ARCIA* 1839, 469; *ARCIA* 1840, 313; *ARCIA* 1841, 334, 335, 337, 340, 342; *ARCIA* 1842, 445, 449; *ARCIA* 1844, 418, 425.

36. For information and pictures of the Three Sisters planting technique, see "Three Sisters Garden," American Indian Health and Diet Project, www.aihd.ku.edu/gardens/ThreeSistersGarden.html.

37. "Beating," Wesley, *IPH* 49:187; "pounding," Carnes, *IPH* 54:433. See also Dennis, *IPH* 78:332; Ross, *IPH* 109:21–22; Kelley, *IPH* 79:35.

38. Andrews, *IPH* 12:379; Lattimer, *IPH* 33:83–48; Wesley, *IPH* 49:187; Pierce, *IPH* 70:286–87; *IPH* 13:127.

39. Kelley, *IPH* 79:35.

40. For a *tanfula* recipe, see "Recipes" section, this volume.

41. James, *IPH* 31:125; Pulsey, *IPH* 41:17.

42. Neighbors, *IPH* 37:474–75; Elliott, *IPH* 64:31. For traditional and modern riffs on Choctaw *banaha*, see "Traditional Indigenous Recipes: American Indian Dishes," American Indian Health and Diet Project, www.aihd.ku.edu /recipes/chahta_banaha.html; Peter J. Hudson, "Choctaw Indian Dishes," *Chronicles of Oklahoma* 17, no. 3 (1939): 333–35; Muriel Wright, "American Corn Dishes," *Chronicles of Oklahoma* 36 (1958): 155–66.

43. Bates, *IPH* 6:38.

44. Robert E. Trevathan, "School Days at Emahaka Academy," *Chronicles of Oklahoma* 38 (1960): 272.

45. Harjo, *IPH* 27:407.

46. Cross, *IPH* 22:77.

47. Bushnell, *Choctaw of Bayou Lacombe*, 8; John R. Swanton, "Early Account of the Choctaw Indians," *American Anthropologist* 5 (1918): 58; Romans, *Concise Natural History*, 57.

48. John R. Swanton, *The Indians of the Southeastern United States*, BAE, Bulletin 137 (Washington DC: GPO, 1946), 291.

49. Turnbull, *IPH* 47:385; Bushnell, *Choctaw of Bayou Lacombe*, 8.

50. Cora Bremer, *The Chata Indians of Pearl River* (New Orleans: Picayune Job Print, 1907), 7–8.

51. Romans, *Concise Natural History*, 42; Edwards, *IPH* 23:245–46; Noah, *IPH* 7:518; Fleming, *IPH* 24:342.

2. The State of Indigenous Health

1. Neal D. Barnard MD and Derek M. Brown, "Commentary: U.S. Dietary Guidelines Unfit for Native Americans," https://dontgotmilk.com/articles/10-u-s-dietary-guidelines-unfit-for-native-americans. These 1995 dietary guidelines were reviewed in mid-2000. Note that the theory of smallpox-infected blankets is controversial. See, for example, Thomas Brown, *Did the U.S. Army Distribute Smallpox Blankets to Indians? Fabrication and Falsification in Ward Churchill's Genocide Rhetoric* (Ann Arbor: MPublishing, University of Michigan Library, 2006), http://hdl.handle.net/2027/spo.5240451.0001.009.

2. President's Council on Sports, Fitness and Nutrition, https://www.hhs.gov/fitness/eat-healthy/dietary-guidelines-for-americans/index.html.

3. "Lactose Intolerance," https://ghr.nlm.nih.gov/condition/lactose-intolerance.

4. See http://www.celiac.com/ for detailed information.

5. National Center for Chronic Disease Prevention and Health Promotion, *National Diabetes Statistics Report, 2017*, 3, https://www.cdc.gov/diabetes/pdfs/data/statistics/national-diabetes-statistics-report.pdf.

6. Centers for Disease Control and Prevention, "Native Americans with Diabetes," https://www.cdc.gov/vitalsigns/aian-diabetes/index.html.

7. Centers for Disease Control and Prevention, "Age-adjusted percent distribution (with standard errors) of body mass index among adults aged 18 and over," Summary Health Statistics: National Health Interview Survey, 2017, Table A-15, https://ftp.cdc.gov/pub/Health_Statistics/NCHS/NHIS/SHS/2017_SHS_Table_A-15.pdf.

8. Yessenia Funes, "Native Tribe Fights Diabetes by Educating Schools on Traditional Foods," *New York Times*, May 27, 2015, http://tucson15.nytimes-institute.com/2015/05/27/native-tribe-fights-diabetes-by-educating-schools-on-traditional-foods/.

9. Leslie O. Schulz and Lisa S. Chaudhari. "High-Risk Populations: The Pimas of Arizona and Mexico." *Current Obesity Reports* 4, no. 1 (2015): 92–98, doi:10.1007/s13679-014-0132-9.

10. Benny Polacca, "Health Survey: Reservation Osages Report 'Poorer Health' than Osages Living Elsewhere," *Osage News*, August 30, 2010, http://www.osagenews.org/en/article/2010/08/30/health-survey-reservation-osages-report-poorer-health-osages-living-elsewhere/.

11. "IHS Awards $138 Million for Diabetes Prevention and Treatment for American Indians and Alaska Natives," Indian Health Service, March 16, 2016, https://www.ihs.gov/newsroom/pressreleases/2016pressreleases/ihs-awards-138-million-for-diabetes-prevention-and-treatment-for-american-indians-and-alaska-natives/.

12. Anne Gordon and Vanessa Oddo, *Addressing Child Hunger and Obesity in Indian Country: Report to Congress* (Princeton NJ: Mathematica Policy Research, January 12, 2012), 5–7.

13. Oklahoma State Department of Health, *2014 State of the State's Health*, 13, 15, 24, 26, 28, 30, 35, 36, https://ok.gov/health2/documents/SOSH 2014.pdf.

14. Sarah McColl, "With Heirloom Seeds, Cherokee Nurture Cultural History and Future Health," takepart, January 29, 2016, http://www.takepart.com/article/2016/01/29/cherokee-seeds/.

15. Polacca, "Health Survey: Reservation Osages."

16. *BISKINIK* archive, https://www.choctawnation.com/biskinik-newspaper-archive.

17. *BISKINIK*, February 2002.

18. *BISKINIK*, September 2002.

19. Choctaw Nation Diabetes Wellness Center, https://www.choctawnation.com/DiabetesWellnessCenter.

20. National Center for Chronic Disease Prevention and Health Promotion, https://www.cdc.gov/obesity/index.html. An adult is "overweight" when above a healthy weight, which varies according to height and physical fitness. People are overweight when their "body mass index" (BMI) is between 25 and 29.9. A person with a BMI of 30 or more is obese. For example, for a 5'4" woman, this means that she is 30 or more pounds over her healthy weight. This can be confusing, however, because some people are quite muscular, and because muscle weighs more

than fat, they weigh more than the healthy value in height-weight charts that are geared toward the "normal" population. Calculate your BMI and read more about the difference between overweight and obese at http://www.halls.md/body-mass-index/bmi.htm. Men can calculate their BMI by dividing their weight in pounds by their height in inches, squared. Then multiply by 705. If your BMI is over 25, you're supposedly overweight; over 30 and you're obese. There is an obvious problem with this, just as there is a problem with muscular women who apply to be airline attendants but are considered to be "overweight": muscle weighs more than fat, so many fit people would be considered overweight or obese.

A way for men to check their body fat content (although the underwater method is the most accurate) is to measure your waist around your belly button; if it's more than 40 inches then you have too much fat. Women have too much fat if their waist is over 35 inches. You can check the fat on your thigh by sitting in a chair with your feet on the floor. Pinch the skin on the top of a thigh, and if the width of that pinch is more than an inch, you have too much fat. Barnard and Brown, "Commentary: U.S. Dietary Guidelines Unfit for Native Americans."

21. *Outside*, December 2003, 142.
22. Craig M. Hales, Margaret D. Carroll, Cheryl D. Fryar, and Cynthia L. Ogden, "Prevalence of Obesity among Adults and Youth: United States, 2015–2016," NCHS Data Brief #288 (October 2017), https://www.cdc.gov/nchs/data/databriefs/db288.pdf.
23. For information about research on Pimas, see Schulz and Chaudhari. "High-Risk Populations."
24. For an overview of the tobacco issue, see Vernellia R. Randall, "Lesson 03: Tobacco and Native Americans," http://academic.udayton.edu/health/syllabi/tobacco/lesson03.htm. See also Christina M. Pego et al., "Tobacco, Culture, and Health among American Indians: A Historical Review," *American Indian Culture and Research Journal* 19, no. 2 (1995): 143–64.
25. Indigenous SeedKeepers Network, https://nativefoodalliance.org/indigenous-seedkeepers-network/.
26. See Devon Mihesuah, "Comanche Traditional Foodways and the Decline of Health," in *Indigenous Food Sovereignty in the United*

States: Restoring Cultural Knowledge, Protecting Environments, and Regaining Health, ed. Devon A. Mihesuah and Elizabeth Hoover (Norman: University of Oklahoma Press, 2019), 223–52.

27. *Comanche Nation News*, http://www.comanchenation .com/index.php?option=com_k2&vie w=itemlist&layout=category&task=category&id=109&Itemid=171.

28. "Oklahoma Academy of Science Statement on Global Climate Change," November 8, 2013, https://www .oklahomaacademyofscience.org/uploads/4/6/0/5/46053599 /oas_statement_of_global_climate_change__2013_.pdf.

29. Alexander Kent, "20 Grocery Items that Are Driving Up Your Food Bill," *USA Today*, February 22, 2016.

30. Ken Roseboro, "The GMO Seed Monopoly: Fewer Choices, Higher Prices," *Food Democracy Now*, October 4, 2013.

31. Kate Taylor, "These Ten Companies Control Everything You Buy," *Business Insider*, September 28, 2016.

32. Wendell Berry, *The Unsettling of America: Culture and Agriculture* (San Francisco: Sierra Club Books, 1977), 218.

33. "What America Eats," *Parade*, November 16, 2003, 4; *U.S. News and World Report*, February 9, 2004, 52.

34. Devon Mihesuah, *American Indians: Stereotypes and Realities* (Atlanta: Clarity International, 1996; rev. 2009), 54–55.

Case Study 2

1. Kelly M. West, "Diabetes in American Indians and Other Native Populations of the New World," *Diabetes* 23, no. 10 (October 1974): 841–55, https://doi.org/10.2337/diab.23.10.841. He reiterates this information in "Diabetes in American Indians," *Advances in Metabolic Disorders* 9 (1978): 29–48, https://doi.org /10.1016/B978-0-12-027309-6.50008-2.

2. Wilburn Hill interview, March 28, 1938, *IPP* 42:403.

3. Peter Mancall, *Deadly Medicine: Indians and Alcohol Abuse in Early America* (Ithaca NY: Cornell University Press, 1997).

4. Romans, *Concise Natural History*, 230–32.

5. See Paul Kelton, *Epidemics and Enslavement: Biological Catastrophe in the Native Southeast, 1492–1715* (Lincoln: University of Nebraska Press, 2009).

6. For information on agricultural pursuits of the tribes, see Laura Baum Graebner, "Agriculture among the Five Civilized Tribes, 1840–1906," *Red River Valley Historical Review* 3 (1978): 45–60.

7. Grant Foreman, *The Five Civilized Tribes* (Norman: University of Oklahoma Press, 1934), 81.

8. ARCIA 1837, 541.

9. Southern, *IPH* 68:2. See also Fox, *IPH* 25:28; Agnew, *IPP* 1:290.

10. ARCIA 1838, 508; ARCIA 1841, 340.

11. ARCIA 1845, 470.

12. ARCIA 1845, 514.

13. Devon Mihesuah, *Indigenous American Women: Decolonization, Empowerment, Activism* (Lincoln: University of Nebraska Press, 2003), xi–xii.

14. Bohanan, *IPH* 1:225.

15. Grant Foreman, ed., *A Traveler in Indian Territory: The Journal of Ethan Allen Hitchcock* (Norman: University of Oklahoma Press, 1930), 23.

16. ARCIA 1860, 353.

17. Frazier, *IPP* 25:76–78; Jefferson, *IPP* 48:30; Christie, *IPH* 20:19.

18. Edward E. Dale, "Additional Letters of Stand Watie," *Chronicles of Oklahoma* 1, no. 2 (1921): 136.

19. Holden, *IPH* 29:291.

20. Harlan, *IPH* 28:70, 73; Miller, *IPH* 7:214.

21. *IPP* 7:178–79; Edwards, *IPH* 23:250; Cartarby, *IPH* 19:196; Miashintubbee, *IPH* 63:6; Culberson, *IPH* 21:292.

22. Cross, *IPH* 2:341.

23. Ward, *IPH* 11:191. See also Hampton, *IPH* 3:343.

24. Burk, *IPP* 17:374.

25. Fullen, *IPP* 32:414.

26. Turnbull, *IPH* 47:385.

27. See Devon A. Mihesuah, *Choctaw Crime and Punishment* (Norman: University of Oklahoma Press, 2009) for discussions about whiskey, Indian Territory violence, and tribal laws dealing with crime.

28. ARCIA 1889, 210.

29. Harvey Wickes Felter, *The Eclectic Materia Medica, Pharmacology and Therapeutics* (Cincinnati: John K. Scudder, 1922), 112–13; Steven L. Sewell, "Choctaw Beer: Tonic or Devil's Brew?" *Journal of Cultural Geography* 23 (2006): 105–16; ARCIA 1894, 143. See also

Weston LaBarre, "Native American Beers," *American Anthropologist* 40 (1938): 224–34.

30. See Devon Mihesuah, *Cultivating the Rosebuds: The Education of Women at the Cherokee Female Seminary, 1851–1909* (Urbana: University of Illinois Press, 1993) and Mihesuah, "Out of the 'Graves of the Polluted Debauches': The Boys of the Cherokee Male Seminary," *American Indian Quarterly* 15, no. 4 (1991): 503–21, https://doi.org/10.2307/1185367.

31. On federal schools, see David Wallace Adams, *Education for Extinction: American Indians and the Boarding School Experience, 1875–1928* (Lawrence: University Press of Kansas, 1995); Michael C. Coleman, *American Indian Children at School, 1850–1930* (Jackson: University Press of Mississippi, 1993).

32. The schools' populations were microcosms of the larger Cherokee Nation both physiologically and socioeconomically, with students in a range from mixed-blood to full-blood and from upper to lower class. Graduates of the Cherokee Female and Male Seminaries in the late nineteenth and early twentieth centuries often became attorneys, dentists, physicians, and teachers. Those Cherokee parents who disagreed with the schools' "white" pedagogy refused to send their children to the seminaries, and in contrast, the youth from these families tended to become farmers, metal smiths, or laborers. See Mihesuah, *Cultivating the Rosebuds*, 95–112.

33. For detailed information on the health care at the seminaries, see Devon Irene Abbott [Mihesuah], "Medicine for the Rosebuds: Health Care at the Cherokee Female Seminary, 1876–1909," *American Indian Culture and Research Journal* 12, no. 1 (1988): 59–71.

34. See CHN 99: Cherokee (Tahlequah)-Schools: Female Seminary, n.d. and December 5, 1874–January 16, 1909, Microfilm Publications, Archives and Manuscripts Division, Oklahoma Historical Society, Oklahoma City. All subsequent source citations with the prefix CHN similarly indicate Cherokee Nation records on microfilm rolls held at the Oklahoma Historical Society; see https://www.okhistory.org/research/forms/CherokeeMG.pdf.

35. CHN 97: Cherokee-Schools: Female Seminary, Documents 2735–2777, May 11, 1887–December 1902.

36. CHN 98: Cherokee-Schools: Female Seminary, Documents, December 31, 1902–June 29, 1905; CHN 100: Cherokee-Schools: Male Seminary, Documents 2925–2984, January 1, 1904–July 3, 1905.

37. Annual Report, Medical Superintendent of Male and Female Seminaries, November 7, 1879, Cherokee Nation Papers, M 943-1-10, box 4, folder 876, Western History Collections, University of Oklahoma Library, Norman; Abbott [Mihesuah], "Medicine for the Rosebuds"; CHN 100: Cherokee (Tahlequah)-Schools: Male Seminary, n.d. and December 10, 1875–February 1, 1911; CHN 100: Cherokee (Tahlequah)-Schools: Medical Superintendent, n.d. and November 22, 1876–January 12, 1901.

38. Annual Report of the Medical Superintendent of the Male and Female Seminaries, November 7, 1899, Cherokee Nation Papers, M 943-1-10, box 4, folder 876, Western History Collections, University of Oklahoma Library, Norman.

39. Lulu Hair interview, September 20, 1969, Doris Duke Oral History Collection, T-514, Western History Collections, University of Oklahoma, Norman (hereafter cited as Doris Duke Oral History Collection).

40. Carolyn Thomas Foreman, "The Choctaw Academy," *Chronicles of Oklahoma* 6, no. 4 (1928): 463–64.

41. Kentucky Historical Society, *Dick Johnson's Indian School at White Sulphur, Scott County, Ky.* (Scott County and White Sulphur: Kentucky Historical Society, 1909), 5, http://kyhistory.com/cdm/ref/collection/RB/id/89.

42. *ARCIA* 1848, 503.

43. *Indian Advocate,* July 1947; Grant Foreman, "Notes from the Indian Advocate," *Chronicles of Oklahoma* 14, no. 1 (March 1936): 67.

44. Edna Hunt Osborne, "How a Little White Girl Grew up among the Choctaw Indians," September 3, 1937, *IPP* 38:309.

45. Billie Fullen, September 25, 1937, *IPP* 32:414.

46. Ethel Brotherton, March 24, 1938, *IPP* 11:432, 434, 435.

47. Edward J. McClain, May 14, 1937, *IPP* 50:160–62.

48. Katie Wacachee, June 6, 1970, Doris Duke Oral History Collection, T-590.

49. John W. Lane, "Choctaw Nation," in *The Five Civilized Tribes in Indian Territory: The Cherokee, Chickasaw, Choctaw, Creek, and Sem-*

inole Nations (Washington DC: Department of Interior, Census Office, 1894; repr., CreateSpace, 2012), 58.

50. Romans, *Concise Natural History*, 64, 77.

51. Hall, *IPP* 92:255.

52. Christie, *IPP* 18:9.

53. For example, walnut and other trees were cut (often clandestinely) by the banks of the Arkansas, Grand, and Verdigris Rivers and quickly floated downstream out of the Cherokee Nation. CHN (Cherokee) vol. 119, July 6, 1881, ledger book, 68. National Records of the General Council, Senate, and House of Representatives, and census and mercantile records of the Five Tribes— Choctaw (CTN), Cherokee (CHN), Chickasaw (CKN), Creek (CRN), and Seminole (SMN)—are found on microfilm and in ledgers at the Oklahoma Historical Society, Oklahoma City, and Western History Collections, University of Oklahoma, Norman. Some are written in the tribal languages. For discussions of tribal timber and resource issues, see Craig H. Miner, *The Corporation and the Indian* (Norman: University of Oklahoma Press, 1976) and Sandra Faiman-Silva, *Choctaws at the Crossroads* (Lincoln: University of Nebraska Press, 1997).

54. For discussion about changes to the landscapes, see Charles F. Meserve, *The Dawes Commission and the Five Civilized Tribes of Indian Territory* (Philadelphia: Indian Rights Association, 1896).

55. See National Records of the General Council, Senate, and House of Representatives, census and mercantile records of the Five Tribes. Also see *Constitutions and Laws of the American Indian Tribes*, 20 vols. (Wilmington: Rowman and Littlefield, 1975).

56. Camp, *IPH* 18:190.

57. James, *IPH* 31:124; Culberson, *IPH* 21:291.

58. W. B. Morrison, "Biographical Sketch of Wn. N. Jones," typescript in Wilson N. Jones Collection, box 1, folder 42, Western History Collections, University of Oklahoma, Norman.

59. Brown, *IPH* 17:80.

60. *Indian Citizen*, January 31, 1901.

61. J. Cole, *IPH* 19:175.

62. West, "Diabetes in American Indians," 841.

63. Dozens of articles published in the *Chronicles of Oklahoma* recount biographies of Indian Territory and Oklahoma physicians that contain plenty of personal information but little about how they

treated patients. For examples, see Basil A. Hayes, "Leroy Long: Teacher of Medicine," *Chronicles of Oklahoma* 20, no. 2 (June 1942): 107–19 and Robert L. Williams, "Dr. Daniel Morris Hailey, 1841–1919," *Chronicles of Oklahoma* 18, no. 3 (September 1940): 170–77.

64. Extra Census Bulletin, *The Five Civilized Tribes in Indian Territory: The Cherokee, Chickasaw, Choctaw, Creek and Seminole Nations* (Washington DC: Department of the Interior, U.S. Census Office, 1894), 57; see also the National Records of the Five Tribes, Oklahoma Historical Society.

65. *The Problem of Indian Administration Report of a Survey Made at the Request of Honorable Hubert Work, Secretary of the Interior, and Submitted to Him, February 21, 1928* (Baltimore: Johns Hopkins Press, 1928), 191, 234.

66. Muriel H. Wright, "A Brief Review of the Life of Doctor Eliphalet Nott Wright," *Chronicles of Oklahoma* 10, no. 2 (June 1932): 270.

67. ARCIA 1872, 242.

68. Mollie Beaver, December 9, 1937, IPP 6:293.

69. Dr. E. O. Barker, September 17, 1937, IPP 5:216.

70. Grady F. Mathews, "History of the Oklahoma State Department of Health, 1890–1907," *Chronicles of Oklahoma* 28, no. 2 (1950): 134. The exam administered in the Choctaw Nation was not particularly arduous. My great-grandfather worked as "physician" for numerous mining towns in the Choctaw Nation. He attended medical school at Paducah, Kentucky, for one year, then "apprenticed" with two German doctors. He passed the modest tribal medical test and then served as physician for hundreds of miners who worked for the Bolen-Dornell, Dan Edwards, McEvers, and Galveston coal companies around what is today McAlester. Many of those miners were tribal members. See *Pittsburg County, Oklahoma: People and Places* (McAlester OK: Pittsburg County Genealogical and Historical Society, n.d.), 1–2; Clyde Wooldridge, *McAlester, The Capital of Little Dixie: A History of McAlester, Krebs and South McAlester* (Krebs OK: Bell Books, 2001), 35, 48, 63, 65, 204; "Dr. William Elliott Abbott," typewritten MS at the Pittsburg County Genealogical and Historical Society; Fred S. Clinton, "The First Hospital and Training School for Nurses in the Indian Territory," *Chronicles of Oklahoma* 25, no. 3 (1947): 223.

71. "An Act in Regard to Physicians and Mechanics Obtaining Permits," March 17, 1879, in *General and Special Laws of the Chickasaw Nation, Passed During the Sessions of the Legislature from the Years from 1878 to 1884, Inclusive* (Muskogee: Indian Journal Steam Job Print, 1884), 9–10.

72. Article 32, "Relating to Physicians," in *Complied Laws of the Cherokee Nation* (Tahlequah, Indian Territory: National Advocate Print, 1881), 305–6.

73. Section 4, section 1, "The Practice of Medicine," approved October 29, 1884, in *Acts and Resolutions of the Creek National Council of the Extra Session of April, 1894, and the Regular Session of October, 1894* (Muskogee, Indian Territory: F. C. Hubbard, 1893), 180–81; Chapter 26, "Act Regulating the Practice of Medicine in the Muskogee Nation," in *Constitution and Laws of the Muskogee Nation* (Muskogee, Indian Territory: F. C. Hubbard, 1893), 110–11.

74. Wright, "A Brief Review of the Life of Doctor Eliphalet Nott Wright," 270, 273.

75. R. L. Owen, Indian Agent, Union Agency, to J. D. C. Atkins, Commissioner of Indian Affairs, May 17, 1888, in *The Executive Documents of the Senate of the United States for the First Session of the Fifty-First Congress, 1889–90*, U.S. Congressional serial set, Issue 2689, Ex. Doc. 219, 102.

76. "An Act Regulating the Practice of Medicine and Surgery in the Indian Territory," April 23, 1904, HR 11963, Public, No. 157, 33 Stat., 299, in Charles J. Kappler, *Indian Affairs: Laws and Treaties*, vol. 3 (Washington DC: GPO, 1913), 76–79.

77. ARCIA 1853, 142.

78. ARCIA 1884, 83.

79. ARCIA 1889, 83; also see numerous comments about medicine men from individual agents that year.

80. *Oklahoma Champion* (Oklahoma City), October 16, 1896.

81. ARCIA 1924, 25; 1899, 284; 1902, 208, 381, 519.

82. Ada Adair interview, April 16, 1969, Doris Duke Oral History Collection, T-481.

83. American Diabetes Association, "Statistics about Diabetes: Overall Numbers, Diabetes and Prediabetes," http://www.diabetes.org /diabetes-basics/statistics/?referrer=https://www.google.com/.

84. West, "Diabetes in American Indians," 841–42. Institutional Review Boards were not established until July 12, 1974—the year

West's paper was published. Normally medical researchers do not mention the names of their subjects to protect their privacy, and this could be why West did not identify them. Regardless, in this case he still did not have enough subjects to demonstrate a convincing conclusion about no diabetes presenting in Indigenous populations prior to 1940.

85. Fannie Saswanokee Gann, November 8, 1969, Doris Duke Oral History Collection, T-538.

86. Lena Carey, October 5, 1969, Doris Duke Oral History Collection, T-514.

87. West, "Diabetes in American Indians," 847.

88. See Dennis W. Weidman, "Diabetes Mellitus and Oklahoma Native Americans: A Case Study of Culture Change in Oklahoma Cherokee," PhD diss., University of Oklahoma, 1979, 221–23.

89. Martin Blackwood, June 22, 1937, *IPP* 8:335. This claim is repeated multiple times. See, for example, Joseph Ammons, July 22, 1937, *IPP* 2:255; Richard Young Audd, October 11, 1937, *IPP* 3:296; Isaac Batt, May 24, 1937, *IPP* 6:50; Jane Battiest, September 21, 1937, *IPP* 6:69; Susie Blackwood, July 12, 1937, *IPP* 8:343; V. A. Camp, May 11, 1937, *IPP* 15:177–78; Eliza Elapotubee, April 27, 1937, *IPP* 27:308; B. M. Palmer, February 15, 1937, *IPP* 69:58.

90. See 1880 Cherokee Census and Index, schedules 1–6, 7RA-07, rolls 1–4; 1890 Cherokee Census (no index), schedules 1–4, 7RA-08, rolls 1–4; Index to the Five Civilized Tribes, the Final Dawes Roll, M1186, roll 1; and Enrollment Cards for the Five Civilized Tribes, 1898–1914, M1186, rolls 2–15, cards 1–11132, all at the Federal Archives, Fort Worth branch. Blood quantums of thousands of Cherokees are in Mihesuah, *Cultivating the Rosebuds*, 117, 170n1.

91. Thomas Donaldson, *Eleventh Census of the United States, Extra Census Bulletin. Indians. The Five Civilized Tribes of Indian Territory: Cherokee Nation, Creek Nation, Seminole Nation, Choctaw Nation, and Chickasaw Nation* (Washington DC: GPO, 1893), 10.

92. *ARCIA* 1838, 508; 1839, 469; 1840, 313; 1841, 334, 335, 337, 340, 342; 1842, 445, 449; 1844, 418, 425. See also Pete W. Cole, September 29, 1937, *IPP* 104:144.

93. Deborah L. Duvall, *The Cherokee Nation and Tahlequah* (Chicago: Arcadia Publishing, 1999), 70; Lucinda Sanders Wilhite, April 24, 1969, Doris Duke Oral History Collection, T-422–23, 427.

94. Bertha Provost interview, July 19, 1968, Doris Duke Oral History Collection, T-686. A freedman reported that his Choctaw "master" liked to pour grease over his meats. Jefferson L. Cole, March 17, 1938, *IPP* 19:173. Note that he still called him master after he was freed.

95. The topic of food on the reservation is discussed in detail in Devon Mihesuah, "Comanche Traditional Foodways and the Decline of Health," in *Indigenous Food Sovereignty in the United States: Restoring Cultural Knowledge, Protecting Environments, and Regaining Health*, ed. Devon A. Mihesuah and Elizabeth Hoover (Norman: University of Oklahoma Press, 2019), 223–52. See also Benjamin Kracht, "Diabetes among the Kiowa: An Ethnohistorical Perspective," in *Diabetes as a Disease of Civilization*, ed. Jennie R. Joe and Robert S. Young (New York: De Gruyter Mouton, 1994), 147–67; B. Randolph Keim, *Sheridan's Troopers on the Borders: A Winter Campaign on the Plains* (Philadelphia: David McKay, 1885), 295; Eugene E. White, *Service on the Indian Reservations: Being the Experiences of a Special Indian Agent while Inspecting Agencies and Serving as Agent for Various Tribes* (Little Rock AR: Diploma Press, 1893), 246–47; Tatum to CIA, July 24, 1869, Record Group 62: Letters Received by the Office of Indian Affairs, 1824–81, M234, roll 376, 291, National Archives. My full-blood Comanche father-in-law often spoke about his father, Joshaway (1874–1962), who farmed and raised a few dairy cows after being forced to boarding school at Fort Sill. Joshaway and his wife, Carrie (1882–1932), churned their own butter and gave away or sold milk to other Comanches. Henry Mihesuah, *First to Fight*, ed. Devon Abbott Mihesuah (Lincoln: University of Nebraska Press, 2002), 17–18. The Mihesuahs have been hunting on the family allotment since 1901.

96. In addition to the works about Comanche history listed in subsequent notes, see Albert S. Gilles Sr., *Comanche Days* (Dallas: Southern Methodist University Press, 1974); T. R. Fehrenbach, *The Comanches: The Destruction of a People* (New York: Alfred A. Knopf, 1974); William T. Hagan, *United States–Comanche Relations: The Reservation Years* (New Haven: Yale University Press, 1976); Elizabeth A. H. John, *Storms Brewed in Other Men's Worlds: The Confrontation of Indians, Spanish, and French in the Southwest, 1540–1795* (College Station: Texas A&M University Press, 1975); *Comanche Ethnography:*

Field Notes of E. Adamson Hoebel, Waldo R. Wedel, Gustav G. Carlson, and Robert H. Lowie, ed. Thomas A. Kavanagh (Lincoln: University of Nebraska Press, 2008); Thomas A. Kavanagh, *The Comanches: A History, 1706–1875* (Lincoln: University of Nebraska Press, 1999); Stanley Noyes, *Los Comanches: The Horse People, 1751–1845* (Albuquerque: University of New Mexico Press, 1993).

97. Elizabeth A. H. John, "Portrait of a Wichita Village, 1808," *Chronicles of Oklahoma* 60, no. 4 (1982): 416, 417, 418, 421–22; Pekka Hämäläinen, "The Western Comanche Trade Center: Rethinking the Plains Indian Trade System," *Western Historical Quarterly* 29 (1998): 485–513, https://doi.org/10.2307/970405.

98. Gustav G. Carlson and Volney H. Jones, "Some Notes on Uses of Plants by the Comanche Indians," *Papers of the Michigan Academy of Science* 25 (1940): 526–27; David E. Jones, "Comanche Plant Medicine," *Papers in Anthropology* 9 (1968): 3; Nelson Lee, *Three Years among the Comanches: The Narrative of Nelson Lee, the Texas Ranger* (Albany NY: Baker Taylor Company, 1859), 114–15; Thomas C. Battey, *The Life and Adventures of a Quaker among the Indians* (Boston: Lee and Shepard, 1876), 283.

99. This is discussed in Mihesuah, "Comanche Traditional Foodways and the Decline of Health."

100. See Craig H. Miner, *The Corporation and the Indian: Tribal Sovereignty and Industrial Civilization in Indian Territory, 1865–1907* (Columbia: University of Missouri Press, 1976). See also Mihesuah, "Sustenance and Health among the Five Tribes in Indian Territory," 276–78, and Charles F. Meserve, *The Dawes Commission and the Five Civilized tribes of Indian Territory* (Philadelphia: Office of the Indian Rights Association, 1896) about the changing environment of Indian Territory.

3. Challenges to Recovering Health

1. *Indigenous Food and Agriculture Initiative, a National Intertribal Survey and Report: Intertribal Food Systems* (Fayetteville AR: Indigenous Food and Agriculture Initiative, 2015), funded by W. K. Kellogg Foundation.

2. For a discussion of the history of the term "food sovereignty," see Raj Patel, "What Does Food Sovereignty Look Like?" *Journal of Peasant Studies* 36, no. 3 (July 2009): 663, https://doi. org/10.1080/03066150903143079.

3. "Declaration of Nyéléni: Declaration of the Forum for Food Sovereignty," February 27, 2007, https://nyeleni.org/spip.php?article290.

4. See, for example, "Winning the Future: Navajo-Hopi Land Commission Leverages DOE Grant to Advance Solar Ranch Project," October 22, 2015, https://www.energy.gov/indianenergy/articles/winning-future-navajo-hopi-land-commission-leverages-doe-grant-advance-solar; Katherine Saltzstein, "Hopi Woman Brings Power of the Sun to the People," *Native Sun News*, October 9, 2014.

5. See Devon Mihesuah, "Comanche Traditional Foodways and the Decline of Health," in *Indigenous Food Sovereignty in the United States: Restoring Cultural Knowledge, Protecting Environments, and Regaining Health*, ed. Devon A. Mihesuah and Elizabeth Hoover (Norman: University of Oklahoma Press, 2019), 223–52.

6. See *National Service Blog*, http://www.nationalservice.gov/blogs/2014–03–07/gardening-osage.

7. See Mark Shepard, *Restoration Agriculture* (Austin TX: Acres USA, 2013); Akihiko Michimi and Michael C. Winmerly, "Associations of Supermarket Availability with Obesity and Fruit and Vegetable Consumption in the Conterminous United States," *International Journal of Health Geographics* 9, no. 1 (2010): 49, https://doi.org/10.1186/1476-072X-9-49.

8. Food Distribution Program on Indian Reservations (FDPIR), https://www.fns.usda.gov/fdpir/eligibility-how-apply.

9. Choctaw Nation, "When Catastrophe Strikes: Responses to Natural Disasters in Indian Country," https://www.indian.senate.gov/sites/default/files/upload/files/7.30.14%20SCIA%20Witness%20Testimony%20-%20Matt%20Gregory%20-%20Choctaw.pdf.

10. Choctaw Nation, "Food," https://www.choctawnation.com/history-culture/choctaw-traditions/food.

11. Chickasaw Nation, "Foods," https://www.chickasaw.net/our-nation/culture/foods.aspx. Chickasaws did not grow corn, squash, and beans together in the manner of the "Three Sisters."

12. Shannon Shaw Duty, "Osage Cooking Classes Begin with Young Crop of Students," *Osage News* (Pawhuska OK), August 20, 2010.

13. Delaware Tribal Council member Nicky Michael, personal communication. See also C. A. Weslager, *The Delaware Indians: A History* (New Brunswick NJ: Rutgers University Press, 1990).

14. Barbara Harper, "Quapaw Traditional Lifeways Scenario," Superfund Research, Oregon State University (2008), https://superfund.oregonstate.edu/sites/superfund.oregonstate.edu/files/harper_2008_quapaw_scenario_final.pdf.

15. W. David Baird, *The Quapaw Indians: A History of the Downstream People* (Norman: University of Oklahoma Press, 1980).

16. Quapaw Cattle Company Store, http://www.quapawcattlecompanystore.com/about.html; Missouri State News, "An Enriching Agriculture Collaboration with Native Americans: Learning and Sharing with the Quapaw Nation," November 7, 2019, https://news.missouristate.edu/2019/11/07/quapaw/; Kimberly Barker, "Quapaw Tribe Opens New Meat Distribution Center," *Miami News-Record*, June 7, 2016; "Bumpers College, School of Law Help Quapaw Tribe with Processing Plant," *University of Arkansas News*, December 7, 2016, http://news.uark.edu/articles/37330/bumpers-college-school-of-law-help-quapaw-tribe-with-processing-plant. Pima and Maricopa tribal members in Arizona are also attempting to revitalize their food traditions by cultivating as many traditional foods as they can. They face challenges from federal food safety laws that restrict their food production and processing, so now they are writing their own laws, which will still ensure that foods will be properly refrigerated and free of contaminants such as salmonella and *E. coli.* One challenge is that bison are considered "exotic," so each animal must be inspected (for a fee), and the animals have to be processed in facilities approved by the Food and Drug Administration.

17. Food and Agriculture Organization of the United Nations (FAO), World Food Summit, "Rome Declaration on World Food Security," November 13–17, 1996, http://www.fao.org/docrep/003/w3613e/w3613e00.htm.

18. Eric Holt-Giménez, "Food Security, Food Justice, or Food Sovereignty?" in *Cultivating Food Justice: Race, Class, and Sustainability*, ed. Alison Hope Alkon and Julian Agyeman (Cambridge MA: MIT Press, 2011), 319.

19. Choctaw Nation of Oklahoma, *State of the Nation, 2018*, 27, https://www.choctawnation.com/sites/default/files/StateoftheNationDigital.pdf.

20. Amy Pereira and Trymaine Lee, "Hope on the Horizon for Choctaw Nation," MSNBC, March 19, 2014, http://www.msnbc.com /msnbc/choctaw-nation-hope-on-horizon#slide1.

21. Choctaw Nation Small Business Development Services, https:// www.choctawnation.com/business/division-commerce/small -business-development-services.

22. American Presidency Project, "Fact Sheet: President Obama's Promise Zones Initiative," January 9, 2014, http://www .presidency.ucsb.edu/ws/index.php?pid=108123.

23. See BISKINIK archive, https://www.choctawnation.com/biskinik -newspaper-archive.

24. Jessica McBride, "The Cost of Education," MvskokeMedia.com, June 13, 2017.

25. American Presidency Project, "Fact Sheet," 3.

26. Program director Peggy Carlton, personal communication; Choctaw Nation of Oklahoma, *State of the Nation, 2018*, 17, https://www.choctawnation.com/tribal-services/elder-services /eyeglasses-dentures-hearing-aids/senior-farmers-market -nutrition.

27. Dana Hertneky, "Oklahoma Native Americans Concerned about Future of Indian Healthcare," Newson6.com, January 31, 2017, http://www.newson6.com/story/34394277/oklahoma-native -americans-concerned-about-future-of-indian-healthcare.

28. Amanda Michelle Gomez, "Native Americans and Alaska Natives Will Disproportionately Suffer under the GOP Health Care Plan," *ThinkProgress*, June 7, 2017, https://thinkprogress.org/native -americans-and-alaska-natives-will-disproportionately-suffer-under -the-gop-health-care-plan-d695283153c2/.

29. Ronni Pierce, "A Healthy Outlook: New Regional Clinic to Open Its Doors," BISKINIK (Talihina OK), February 2017.

30. Mark Trahant, "How Bad Could It Be? Don't Get Sick If Senate (or House) Bill Becomes Law," TrahantReports.com, June 23, 2017, https://trahantreports.com/.

31. See, in particular, Angie Debo, *And Still the Waters Run: The Betrayal of the Five Civilized Tribes* (Princeton NJ: Princeton University Press, 1940).

32. Terry Wilson, *The Underground Reservation: Osage Oil* (Norman: University of Oklahoma Press, 1985); David Grann, *Killers of the*

Flower Moon: The Osage Murders and the Birth of the FBI (New York: Doubleday, 2017).

33. Ralph Keen II, "Tribal Hunting and Fishing Regulatory Authority within Oklahoma," *Oklahoma Bar Journal* 86, no. 24 (September 12, 2015).

34. Choctaw Nation of Oklahoma, *State of the Nation, 2016,* 21.

35. Muriel H. Wright, "Notes and Documents: Sugar Loaf Mountain Resort," *Chronicles of Oklahoma* 36 (1960): 202–3; *South McAlester Capital,* July 12, 1894; Elijah Conger interview, *IPP* 2:196–97.

36. Limon Pusley interview, December 28, 1937, *IPP* 73:346; J. T. Poston, September 16, 1937, *IPP* 72:286; Elijah W. Culberson, November 4, 1937, *IPP* 72:215–16; Sarah Noah and Robert Noah, April 12, 1937, *IPP* 67:254; Jim Spaniard, June 25, 1937, *IPP* 86:7.

37. Oklahoma Department of Wildlife Conservation, *Fishing in the Schools Manual* (Oklahoma City: Oklahoma Department of Wildlife Conservation, 2014), 4.

38. Nancy J. Turner, Fikret Berkes, Janet Stephenson, and Jonathan Dick, "Blundering Intruders: Extraneous Impacts on Two Indigenous Food Systems," *Human Ecology* 41, no. 4 (2013): 563–74, https://doi.org/10.1007/s10745-013-9591-y.

39. Darryl Fears, "This Mystery Was Solved: Scientists Say Chemicals from Fracking Wastewater Can Taint Freshwater Nearby," *Washington Post,* May 11, 2016; Jim Kelly, "On Oklahoma, Earthquakes, and Contaminated Water: The Fracking Connection," *A New Domain,* December 8, 2015, http://anewdomain.net/oklahoma-earthquakes-contaminated-water-fracking-connection/.

40. See "Recent Earthquakes Near Oklahoma," *Earthquake Track,* https://earthquaketrack.com/p/united-states/oklahoma/recent; Katie M. Keranen, Matthew Weingarten, Geoffrey A. Abers, Barbara A. Bekins, and Shemin Ge, "Sharp Increase in Central Oklahoma Seismicity since 2008 Induced by Massive Wastewater Injection," *Science* 345, no. 6195 (July 25, 2014): 448–51. See also "Oklahoma and Fracking," https://earthjustice.org/features/oklahoma-and-fracking; and Jessica Fitzpatrick, "Induced Earthquakes Raise Chances of Damaging Shaking in 2016," *USGS Science Features,* March 28, 2016, https://www.usgs.gov/news/induced-earthquakes-raise-chances-damaging-shaking-2016.

41. Matthew L. M. Fletcher, "Pawnee Nation and Walter Echo-Hawk Sue over Fracking," *Turtle Talk,* November 21, 2016. See

also Liz Blood, "Fracking in Bad Faith," *Tulsa Voice,* January 20, 2017, https://www.tulsapeople.com/the-voice/writers/liz -blood/fracking-in-bad-faith/article_56b42f9f-4cff-5261-b018 -8cf2c2a1cdc5.html.

42. "14 More Oklahoma Lakes Have Elevated Mercury Levels in Fish," Oklahoma's News 4, June 22, 2017, http://kfor.com/2017/06/22 /14-more-oklahoma-lakes-have-elevated-mercury-levels-in-fish/.

43. "Battling Pollution on Our Lands: Mekasi Horinek," *Cultural Survival Quarterly Magazine,* September 2016.

44. Movement Rights, "Ponca Nation of Oklahoma to Recognize the Rights of Nature to Stop Fracking," *Intercontinental Cry,* October 31, 2017, https://intercontinentalcry.org/ponca-nation -oklahoma-recognize-rights-nature-stop-fracking/.

45. Chalene Toehay-Tartsah, "Osage County Landowners Speak Out against Bad Drilling Practices," *Osage News,* August 18, 2014.

46. Inter-Tribal Environmental Council, http://itec.cherokee .org/; "Cherokee Nation Files, Is Granted Emergency Restraining Order," *Anadisgoi,* February 9, 2017, http://www.anadisgoi .com/archive/1519-cherokee-nation-files-is-granted-emergency -restraining-order-halting-disposal-ofradioactive-waste-near-the -arkansas-and-illinois-rivers.

47. Kristin Hugo, "Native Americans Brace for Impact as EPA Undergoes Changes," *PBS Newshour: The Rundown,* February 17, 2017, https://www.pbs.org/newshour/science/native-americans-brace -impact-epa-undergoes-changes.

48. See Bill Information for HB 1123, State of Oklahoma, 1st Session of the 56th Legislature (2017), http://www.oklegislature.gov /BillInfo.aspx?Bill=hb1123; Alleen Brown, "Oklahoma Governor Signs Anti-Protest Law Imposing Huge Fines on 'Conspirator' Organizations," *Intercept,* May 6, 2017, https://theintercept.com /2017/05/06/oklahoma-governor-signs-anti-protest-law-imposing -huge-fines-on-conspirator-organizations/.

49. Casey Smith, "The Diamond Pipeline," *Tulsa World,* February 3, 2017; Mark Hefflinger, "Fight Against Diamond Pipeline Spans Three States," *Bold Oklahoma,* January 30, 2017; Oka Lawa Camp Facebook page, https://www.facebook.com/OkaLawaCamp/.

50. Oklahoma Invasive Plant Council, "The Dirty Dozen Poster," https://okipc.wordpress.com/the-dirty-dozen/; Brianna Bailey,

"The Bradford Pear: Oklahoma's Worst Tree or Just Misunderstood?" *NewsOK*, March 5, 2017.

51. Chip Taylor, personal communication.

52. Oklahoma Department of Wildlife Conservation, "Feral Hogs in Oklahoma," https://www.wildlifedepartment.com/feral-hogs-in -oklahoma; "There Was Nothing I Could Do: Feral Hogs Wreaking Havoc on Oklahoma Watermelon Farmers," Oklahoma's News 4, September 5, 2017, http://kfor.com/2017/09/05/there -was-nothing-i-could-do-feral-hogs-wreaking-havoc-on-oklahoma -watermelon-farmers/.

53. For an overview of pollinators in Oklahoma in 1917, see Sister M. Agnes, "Biological Field Work," *Oklahoma Academy of Science* 1 (1917): 35–38, file:///C:/Users/mihesuah/Downloads/7100- 13445-1-PB.pdf.

54. Logan Layden, "Why Oklahoma Had the Nation's Highest Percentage of Bee Deaths Last Year," National Public Radio, StateImpact-Oklahoma, June 25, 2015, https://stateimpact.npr .org/oklahoma/2015/06/25/why-oklahoma-had-the-nations -highest-percentage-of-bee-deaths-last-year/.

55. Edmund Flint interview, April 23, 1937, *IPP* 3:527; Ben Cartarby, June 29, 1937, *IPP* 19:203; Josephine Usray Lattimer, September 23, 1937, *IPP* 33:84; T. P. Wilson, n.d., *IPP* 11:498; Elijah W. Culberson, November 4, 1937, *IPP* 22:216; W. C. Mead interview, January 17, 1938, *IPP* 62:17; Johnnie Gipson interview, April 21, 1927, *IPP* 34:175.

56. Chip Taylor, personal communication. See also Tribal Environmental Action for Monarchs, http://www.nativebutterflies.org /saving-the-monarch; Trilateral Committee for Wildlife and Ecosystem Conservation and Management, "Native American Tribes Pledge to Save the Monarch," http://www.trilat.org/index.php ?option=com_content&view=article&id=1197:native-american -tribes-pledge-to-save-the-monarch&catid=17&Itemid=256.

57. Kyle Powys Whyte, "Indigenous Food Sovereignty, Renewal, and US Settler Colonialism," in *The Routledge Handbook of Food Ethics*, ed. Mary Rawlinson and Caleb Ward (London: Routledge, 2016), 354–65.

58. Bhat, "Food Sustainability Challenges in the Developing World," 3–4.

59. Pat Gwin, personal communication. See also Pat Gwin, "What If the Seeds Do Not Sprout? The Cherokee Nation SeedBank

and Native Plant Site," in *Indigenous Food Sovereignty in the United States: Restoring Cultural Knowledge, Protecting Environments, and Regaining Health,* ed. Devon A. Mihesuah and Elizabeth Hoover (Norman: University of Oklahoma Press, 2019), 198–208.

60. Hope Radford, "Native American Food Sovereignty in Montana," August 2016, 6, http://aeromt.org/wp-content/uploads/2016/10/Native-American-Food-Sovereignty-in-Montana-2016-1-1.pdf.

61. See Intertribal Agriculture Council, https://www.indianag.org/programs; Native Food Systems Resource Center, http://www.nativefoodsystems.org/about; Seeds of Native Health, http://seedsofnativehealth.org/partners/; "Smokehouses, Farmers' Markets and More," *Indian Country Today,* June 20, 2017, https://newsmaven.io/indiancountrytoday/archive/smokehouses-farmers-markets-and-more-growing-food-sovereignty-_Kx8qz4fb0y8KPWRq2IqWw/; University of Arkansas School of Law Indigenous Food and Agriculture Initiative, https://www.facebook.com/IndigenousFoodandAg/. The initiative offers strategic planning and technical support for tribal governance infrastructure in the areas of business and economic development, financial markets and asset management, health and nutrition polities, and intellectual property rights. It also supports increased admission of students into land grant universities and creation of academic programs in food and agriculture.

62. Food sovereignty construction is discussed in Christina M. Schiavoni, "The Contested Terrain of Food Sovereignty Construction: Toward a Historical, Relational and Interactive Approach," *Journal of Peasant Studies* 44, no. 1 (2017): 1–32.

Case Study 3

Thanks to Joely Proudfit, Robb Redsteer, Martin Reinhardt, and Elizabeth Hoover. It is preferable to refer to Indigenous people by their specific tribal names. For generalities I normally use the term "Indigenous" or "Native," but in this case study I also use the more recognizable "Indian."

1. Anonymous comment on Navajofrybread.com, September 24, 2012.

2. Joely Proudfit, Pechanga Band of Luiseño Indians, personal communication.

3. "The 50 Fattiest Foods in the States," Health.com, http://www.health.com/health/gallery/0,,20393387_42,00.html.

4. Devon Mihesuah, "Decolonizing Our Diets by Recovering Our Ancestors' Gardens," *American Indian Quarterly* 27, nos. 3–4 (2003): 807–39. That commentary appeared in expanded form in *Recovering Our Ancestors' Gardens: Indigenous Recipes and Guide to Diet and Fitness* (Lincoln: University of Nebraska Press, 2005).

5. Suzan Shown Harjo, "My New Year's Resolution: No More Fat 'Indian' Food," *Indian Country Today*, January 20, 2005.

6. South Dakota Legislature, https://sdlegislature.gov/Statutes /Codified_Laws/DisplayStatute.aspx?Type=Statute&Statute=1-6-16.9.

7. Ron Jackson, "Fat's in the Fire: Activist Calls for Boycott of Eating Indian Frybread," *NewsOK*, August 21, 2005, http://newsok .com/fats-in-the-firebractivist-calls-for-boycott-of-eating-indian-fry -bread/article/2908445.

8. Angie Wagner, "Cultural Icon or High-Calorie Curse," *Dispatch*, August 22, 2005.

9. Erin Hobday, "Live Blogging Losing It with Jillian Michaels: Frybread Is Making You Fat," *SELF Magazine*, July 7, 2010.

10. Jen Miller, "Frybread," July 2008, http://www.smithsonianmag .com/arts-culture/frybread-79191/#F0g6s2ZpXwkSsMzt.99.

11. *Navajo Stories of the Long Walk Period* (Tsaile: Navajo Community College Press, 1973).

12. Fernando Divina and Marlene Divina, *Foods of the Americas* (Berkeley: Ten Speed Press, 2004), 98–99. See also the American Indian Health and Diet Project's (AIHD) list of foods of this hemisphere, http://aihd.ku.edu/.

13. ARCIA 1864, 186 for 38th Cong., H. Ex doc. 1, serial 1220; ARCIA 1865, 160–62 for 39th Cong., H. Ex doc. 1, serial 1248; ARCIA 1866, 149–50 for 39th Cong., H. Ex doc. 1, serial 1284.

14. Clifford Trafzer, *The Kit Carson Campaign* (Norman: University of Oklahoma Press, 1982), 173–75; Gerald Thompson, *The Army and the Navajo* (Tucson: University of Arizona Press, 1976), 35, 38; *Navajo Stories*, 113, 125.

15. Miller, "Frybread."

16. *Navajo Stories*, 32, 191, 242.

17. Thompson, *Army and the Navajo*, 18–19, 158.

18. Joint Special Committee on Indian Affairs, *Conditions of the Indian Tribes* (Washington DC: GPO, 1867), 379, 403, 405

19. Thompson, *Army and the Navajo*, 109; Joint Special Committee, *Conditions of the Indian Tribes*, appendix, 294.

20. Joint Special Committee, *Condition of the Indian Tribes*, 203–4, 404; *Navajo Stories*, 214, 224, 225–26.

21. Joint Special Committee, *Condition of the Indian Tribes*, 161, 179–80; Thompson, *Army and the Navajo*, 32.

22. *Navajo Stories*, 82, 149, 152.

23. *Navajo Stories*, 214, 233; Thompson, *Army and the Navajo*, 48.

24. Charlotte Frisbie and David McAllester, *Navajo Blessingway Singer* (Tucson: University of Arizona Press, 1978), 32.

25. Garrick Alan Bailey, *A History of the Navajos: The Reservation Years* (Santa Fe: School of American Research, 1986), 95.

26. Robb Redsteer, personal communication.

27. Northern Navajo Nation Fair, http://northernnavajonationfair.org/.

28. Peter Iverson, *Diné: A History of the Navajos* (Albuquerque: University of New Mexico Press, 2002), 126.

29. "Indians: Winter of Death?" *Time* 50, no. 18 (November 3, 1947): 23.

30. Sharlot Hall Museum Virtual Browsing Book, http://sharlot.org /img/detail_htmls/2295inn80lp.html.

31. "Report with respect to the House resolution authorizing the Committee on Interior and Insular Affairs to conduct an investigation of the Bureau of Indian Affairs," Pursuant to H. Res. 698, December 15, 1952, 82d Cong., vol. 11582; H. Rpt. 2503, p. 1221.

32. Robb Redsteer, personal communication; William Y. Adams, "Shonto: A Study of the Role of the Trader in a Modern Navaho Community," BAE, Bulletin 188: 12478 (January 10, 1962), H. Doc. 387, p. 81.

33. C. Ballew, Linda L. White, Karen F. Strauss, Lois J. Benson, James M. Mendlein, and Ali H. Mokdad, "Intake of Nutrients and Food Sources of Nutrients among the Navajo: Findings from the Navajo Health and Nutrition Survey," *Journal of Nutrition* (October 1997): 2085s–2093s.

34. Tristan Ahtone and Jolene Yazzie, "Navajo Nation's Nutrition Crisis," *Al Jazeera America*, January 14, 2015.

35. For example, *Canku Oka*, July 17, 2004, issue 117, http://www .turtletrack.org/IssueHistory/Issues04/Co07172004/CO _07172004_NavajoFieldTrip.htm.

36. James Hester, "Navajo Culture Change: From 1550 to 1960 and Beyond," in *Apachean Culture History and Ethnology*, ed. Keith Basso and Morris E. Opler, Anthropological Paper 21 (Tucson:

University of Arizona Press, 1971), 51–53. For discussion about the importance of corn in Hopi society, see Dennis Wall and Virgil Masayesva, "People of the Corn: Teachings in Hopi Traditional Agriculture, Spirituality, and Sustainability," *American Indian Quarterly* 28 (2004): 435–53.

37. Gordon Charles Davidson, *The North West Company* (Berkeley: University of California Press, 1918), 267; "Bannock Awareness," http://www.for.gov.bc.ca/rsi/fnb/fnb.htm.

38. Alexander Henry, *Travels and Adventures in Canada and the Indian Territories between the years 1760 and 1776* (New York: Riley, 1809), 52; Grace Lee Nute, *The Voyageurs* (New York: D. Appleton, 1931), 52; Hartwell Bowsfield, "The Buffalo," *Manitoba Pageant* 10 (Spring 1965).

39. ARCIA 1891, 393 for 52d Cong., H. Ex doc. 1, pt. 5, serial 2934.

40. James H. Howard, *The Ponca Tribe* (Lincoln: University of Nebraska Press, 2010), 46.

41. ARCIA 1893, 256, 398 for 53d Cong., H. Ex doc. 1, vol. 2, serial 3210; ARCIA 1895, 205 for 54th Cong., H. Doc. 5, vol. 2, serial 3382. The word *Siwash* is actually a derogatory term, probably meaning "no-good, drunken Indian."

42. ARCIA 1892, 669 for 52d Cong., H. Ex doc. 1, serial 3088.

43. ARCIA 1898, 171 for 55th Cong., H. Doc. 5, serial 3757.

44. *Boston Evening Transcript*, February 25, 1911.

45. Martin Reinhardt, personal communication.

46. For discussion about the foodways of the Five Tribes after their removal to Indian Territory, see Devon Mihesuah, "Sustenance and Health among the Five Tribes in Indian Territory, Post-Removal to Statehood," *Ethnohistory* 62 no. 2 (Spring 2015): 263–84.

47. Byrd, *IPH* 15:184–85; Baldwin, *IPH* 4:309.

48. Forney, *IPH*, 31:193–4.

49. Edwards, *IPH* 23:250; Cartarby, *IPH* 19:196; Miashintubbee, *IPH* 63:6; Culberson, *IPH* 21:292; Ward, *IPH* 11:191; Hampton, *IPH* 3:343.

50. Devon Mihesuah, "Medicine for the Rosebuds," in Mihesuah, *Cultivating the Rosebuds*, 85–94; *Cherokee Advocate*, August 26, 1893, 2; Frederick J. Simoons, "The Geographic Hypothesis and Lactose Malabsorption," *American Journal of Digestive Diseases* 23 (1978): 963.

51. "Springtime in the Ancestors' Gardens: Native Health and Finding Comfort," *Spezzatino Magazine* 4 (2008): www.Spezzatino.com.

52. Angela Cavender Wilson, "Grandmother to Granddaughter: Generations of Oral History in a Dakota Family," *American Indian Quarterly* 20 (1996): 7–13; Waziyatawin Wilson, "Introduction to 'Indigenous Knowledge Recovery Is Indigenous Empowerment," *American Indian Quarterly* 28 (2004): 359–72; L. R. Simpson, "'Traditional Ecological Knowledge: Issues, Insights and Implications," PhD diss., University of Manitoba, 1999; C. Higgins, "The Role of Traditional Ecological Knowledge in Managing for Biodiversity," *Forestry Chronicle* 74 (1998): 323–26.

53. Deborah Lupton, *Food, the Body and the Self* (London: Sage, 1996), 25.

54. W. W. Hill, *The Agricultural and Hunting Methods of the Navaho Indians* (New Haven: Yale University Press, 1938), 17, 52–166.

55. For discussions on culture change and identity, see Richard White, *The Roots of Dependency: Subsistence, Environment and Social Change among the Choctaws, Pawnees and Navajos* (Lincoln: University of Nebraska Press, 1983); Mihesuah, *Cultivating the Rosebuds*; Morris W. Foster, *Being and Becoming Comanche: A Social History of an American Indian Community* (Tucson: University of Arizona Press, 1991); Melissa Meyer, *The White Earth Tragedy: Ethnicity and Dispossession at a Minnesota Anishinaabe Reservation, 1889–1920* (Lincoln: University of Nebraska Press, 1999).

56. David V. Fazzino, "Traditional Food Security': Tohono O'odham Traditional Foods in Transition," PhD dissertation, University of Florida, 2007, 116–17.

57. Luci Tapahonso, *A Breeze Swept Through* (Albuquerque NM: West End Press, 1987). For discussions about tribal food changes, see Harriet V. Kuhnlein, "Dietary Change and Traditional Food Systems of Indigenous Peoples," *Annual Review of Nutrition* 16, no. 1 (1996): 417–42; Barry M. Popkin, "Nutritional Patterns and Transitions," *Population and Development Review* 19 (March 1993): 138–57.

58. Diné Policy Institute, "Diné Food Sovereignty," April 2014, 21, https://www.firstnations.org/publications/dine-food-sovereignty -a-report-on-the-navajo-nation-food-system-and-the-case-to -rebuild-a-self-sufficient-food-system-for-the-dine-people/.

59. Thomas Vennum Jr., *Wild Rice and the Ojibway People* (St. Paul: Minnesota Historical Society Press, 1988), 297.

60. Martin Reinhardt, Anishinaabe Ojibway, director of Native American studies at Northern Michigan University and founder of Decolonizing Diet Project, personal communication.

61. Jen Miller, "Frybread," Smithsonian.com, July 2008, http://www.smithsonianmag.com/arts-culture/frybread-79191/#VlRhPYy6FTWPeGZh.99.

62. Various studies discuss the addictive nature of such foods: Scripps Research Institute, "Scripps Research Study Shows Compulsive Eating Shares Same Addictive Biochemical Mechanism with Cocaine, Heroin Abuse," March 23, 2010, http://www.scripps.edu/news/press/2010/20100329.html; Diane Martindale, "Burgers on the Brain," *New Scientist* 177, no. 2380 (February 1, 2003): 21; *Navajo Stories*, 214, 233.

63. See, for example, Maria Yellow Horse Brave Heart, "The Historical Trauma Response among Natives and Its Relationship with Substance Abuse: A Lakota Illustration," *Journal of Psychoactive Drugs* 35, no. 1 (2003): 7–13; Maria Yellow Horse Brave Heart and Josephine A. Chase, "Historical Trauma among Indigenous Peoples of the Americas: Concepts, Research, and Clinical Considerations," *Journal of Psychoactive Drugs* 43, no. 4 (2011): 282–90; Jessica R. Goodkind, Julia Meredith Hess, Beverly Gorman, and Danielle P. Parker, "'We're Still in a Struggle': Diné Resilience, Survival, Historical Trauma, and Healing," *Qualitative Health Research* 22, no. 8 (2012): 1019–36.

64. Billi Gordon, "Symbolic Eating," *Psychology Today*, November 23, 2013.

65. Devon Mihesuah, "American Indian Identities: Comment on Issues of Individual Choices and Development," *American Indian Culture and Research Journal* 22 (1998): 193–226; Mihesuah, "Activism vs. Apathy: The Price We Pay for Both," *American Indian Quarterly* 27 (2003): 325–32. For information on American Indian boarding schools, see David Wallace Adams, *Education for Extinction: American Indians and the Boarding School Experience, 1875–1928* (Lawrence: University Press of Kansas, 1995); Michael C. Coleman, *American Indian Children at School, 1850–1930* (Jackson: University Press of Mississippi, 1993); Clyde Ellis, *To Change Them Forever: Indian Education at the Rainy Mountain Boarding School, 1893–1920* (Norman: University of Oklahoma Press, 1996); K. Tsianina Lomawaima, *They Called It Prairie Light: The Story of*

Chilocco Indian School (Lincoln: University of Nebraska Press, 1994); Sally J. McBeth, *Ethnic Identity and the Boarding School Experience of West-Central Oklahoma American Indians* (Lanham MD: University Press of America, 1983); Mihesuah, *Cultivating the Rosebuds*; Robert A. Trennert, *The Phoenix Indian School: Forced Assimilation in Arizona, 1891–1935* (Norman: University of Oklahoma Press, 1988); "In the White Man's Image," *American Experience*, PBS, February 1992.

66. Quoted in Miller, "Frybread"; *More than Frybread*, director Holt Hamilton (Holt Hamilton Films, 2012).

67. Judy Walker, "Frybread Is Demonstrated at New Orleans Jazz Fest," *Times Picayune*, April 30, 2013, https://www.nola.com /entertainment_life/festivals/article_7970ccc5-349d-5545-998e -a624e9f092a6.html. See also *Kenner (LA) Star*, November 17, 2008, 27; Naomi King, "New Chief to Lead American Indian Tribe," *Daily Comet*, May 14, 2010, https://www.dailycomet.com /article/DA/20100514/News/608082600/DC?template=ampart.

68. Carolyn Calvin, "The People's Flour," *Navajo Times*, September 30, 2010.

69. Liz F. Kay, "Frybread: Two Sides of a Powwow Staple," *Baltimore Sun*, August 23, 2006.

70. For example, the *Atlantic* notes that the site Native Recipes, http://nativerecipes.com/about/ is replete with dishes of nonindigenous ingredients.

71. Eric Hobsbawm and Terence Ranger, eds., *The Invention of Tradition* (Cambridge: Cambridge University Press, 1983), 1.

72. "Recipes," *Indian Country Today*, https://indiancountrytoday .com/archive/great-frybread-recipes-from-montana-to-argentina -5AcL3vHeGkmVRdh6RmN6lw.

73. Lauren Saria, "Arizona's Frybread Brings Native American Cooking into the Future," Dining section, *Phoenix New Times*, November 22, 2012.

74. Jeremy Hsieh, "Frybread: An Alaska Native Treat with a Mysterious Origin," KTOO (Juneau AK), June 23, 2014.

75. Melissa Elsmo, "Frybread Stacks to Honor—and Feed—Thy Father," *Evanston Review*, June 11, 2014.

76. Lee Allen, "Frybread House Honored among the Best of the Best," *Indian Country Today*, April 18, 2012.

77. Robert Bazell and Linda Carroll, "Indian Tribe Turns to Tradition to Fight Diabetes," NBC News, December 9, 2011, http://www.nbcnews.com/id/43257536/ns/health-diabetes/t/indian-tribe-turns-tradition-fight-diabetes/.

78. James Beard Foundation, "America's Classics: The Fry Bread House, Phoenix," May 7, 2012, https://www.jamesbeard.org/blog/americas-classics-fry-bread-house-phoenix; Chelsey Wesner, "Wellness in America," September 5, 2012, https://americanindianinstitute.wordpress.com/2012/09/05/toca/.

79. Vera Holding and Marijo Gibson, "Indians in Industry," *Oklahoma Today*, Spring 1974, 15–16; "Folks Can Feast on Indian Food at Red Corn's HA-PAH-SHU-TSE," *Oklahoma Today*, Spring 1981, 23–25.

80. Hsieh, "Frybread."

81. "'Necessity' Food Goes Gourmet," *Aberdeen Daily News*, October 20, 1987; Wooden Knife Company, "Campfire Talk," https://www.woodenknife.com/campfire_talk_9.html; Journals of the Lewis and Clark Expedition, http://lewisandclarkjournals.unl.edu/index.html. There is no mention of such a plant in the journals.

82. Katie Robbins, "Frybread Nation: The Birth of a 'Native' Cuisine," *Atlantic*, April 15, 2010, http://www.theatlantic.com/health/archive/2010/04/fry-bread-nation-the-birth-of-a-native-cuisine/38943/.

83. Kekuli Café, http://www.kekulicafe.com/.

84. Mitsitam Native Foods Café, http://www.mitsitamcafe.com/home/default.asp.

85. Divina and Divina, *Foods of the Americas*; Beverley Cox, *Spirit of the Harvest: North American Indian Cooking* (New York: Stewart, Tabori and Chang, 1991); Lois Ellen Frank, *Foods of the Southwest Indian Nations* (Berkeley CA: Ten Speed Press, 2002).

86. David Fazzino II, "Traditional Food Security: Tohono O'odham Traditional Foods in Transition," PhD diss., University of Florida, 2008, 116–17, http://etd.fcla.edu/UF/UFE0021669/fazzino_d.pdf.

87. "Choctaw Brothers Pioneer Aquaponic Farming System to Tackle Food Insecurity in Indian Country," *Indian Country Today*, December 20, 1013, https://indiancountrytoday.com/archive/choctaw-brothers-pioneer-aquaponic-farming-system-wGX8YTWdCkSAD14wkkR_rQ.

88. Martin Reinhardt, personal communication.

5. Calories, Exercise, and Fitness

1. Matthew Karsten, "Running with Mexico's Tarahumara Indians," *Expert Vagabond*, March 20, 2019, https://expertvagabond.com /tarahumara-runners.
2. See www.outsideonline.com.
3. Kelly D. Brownell and Katherine Battle Horgen, *Food Fight: The Inside Story of the Food Industry, America's Obesity Crisis, and What We Can Do About It* (New York: McGraw-Hill, 2004); Greg Critser, *Fat Land: How Americans Became the Fattest People in the World* (New York: Houghton Mifflin, 2003); Eric Schlosser, *Fast Food Nation: The Dark Side of the All-American Meal* (New York: Houghton Mifflin Company, 2001); Marion Nestle, *Food Politics: How the Food Industry Influences Nutrition and Health* (Berkeley: University of California Press, 2002); Gaylord Hauser, *Diet Does It* (New York: Coward-McCann, 1944).
4. George Catlin, Letter no. 13, *Letters and Notes*, https://user .xmission.com/~drudy/mtman/html/catlin/letter13.html.

6. Changing What We Eat

1. Decolonizing Diet Project, https://share.nmu.edu/moodle /course/view.php?id=33. See also April E. Lindala, Marty Reinhardt, and Leora Lancaster, *Decolonizing Diet Project Cookbook* (Marquette: Northern Michigan University, 2016) and Mihesuah and Hoover, *Indigenous Food Sovereignty*, 39–42. Another notable example of the benefits of Indigenous foods is non-Native Matt Graham, a long distance runner who lives outdoors under tarps, makes tools like spears and arrowheads from flint, runs only in sandals he made himself, and eats only foods he finds outdoors, such as raccoons and coyotes (from which he makes jerky); to fuel his body on long runs he depends on sunflower and chia seeds. This strategy of living off the land seems to work; he recently completed a fifty-five-mile race in less than seven hours, and the three racers who placed ahead of him were on horseback. Biana Dumas, "Back to Nature: Primitive Runner Discovered in Utah," *Trail Runner* 26 (March 2004): 18–19.
2. Sally Fallon and Mary G. Enig, "Guts and Grease: The Diet of Native Americans," http://www.westonaprice.org/traditional _diets/native_americans.html.

3. "Nutrition Content of Game Meat," http://www.wyoextension
.org/agpubs/pubs/B920R.pdf. See also Bonnie Brae
Farms' comparison of venison with other foods, http://www
.bonniebraefarms.com/venison.html.

4. "Activism vs. Apathy: The Price We Pay for Both," special issue
on "Problems in the Ivory Tower," *American Indian Quarterly* 27,
nos. 1–2 (2003): 325–32.

5. See Krista Scott-Dixon, "Springtime in the Ancestors' Gardens:
Native Health and Finding Comfort," *Spezzatino* 4 (2008): 34–41,
http://spezzatino.wpengine.com/wp-content/uploads/2009/03
/spezzatino-v4.pdf.

6. *Good Meat* (Native American Public Telecommunications, 2011).

7. Schlosser, *Fast Food Nation*; see also "The 59 Ingredients in a Fast
Food Strawberry Milkshake," *Guardian*, April 24, 2006, https://
www.theguardian.com/news/2006/apr/24/food.foodanddrink.

8. NIH/National Institute of Diabetes and Digestive and Kidney Diseases, https://www.niddk.nih.gov/health-information/diabetes
/overview/diet-eating-physical-activity/carbohydrate-counting;
Carb Counter, https://www.carb-counter.net/; Diabetes Wellness
Connection, http://www.laplaza.org/health/dwc/nadp.

9. Julie Beck, "More Than Half of What Americans Eat Is 'Ultra
Processed,'" *Atlantic*, March 10, 2016, https://www.theatlantic
.com/health/archive/2016/03/more-than-half-of-what
-americans-eat-is-ultra-processed/472791/.

10. Look at Bette Hagman, *The Gluten-Free Gourmet Cooks Comfort
Foods: Creating Old Favorites with the New Flours* (New York: Henry
Holt, 2004); Hagman, *The Gluten-Free Gourmet Bakes Bread: More
than 200 Wheat-Free Recipes* (New York: Owl Books, 2000); Hag-
man, *More from the Gluten-Free Gourmet: Delicious Dining without
Wheat* (New York: Owl Books; 2000); Hagman, *The Gluten-Free
Gourmet Cooks Fast and Healthy: Wheat-Free Recipes with Less Fuss
and Less Fat* (New York: Henry Holt, 1996); Jax Peters Lowell,
*Against the Grain: The Slightly Eccentric Guide to Living Well without
Gluten or Wheat* (New York: Henry Holt, 1995).

11. "How to Eat Smarter," *Time*, October 20, 2003, 55.

12. World Wildlife Federation, "Soy," https://www.worldwildlife.org
/industries/soy.

13. Charlotte Lillis, "What Are the Side Effects of Aspartame?" *Medical News Today*, January 14, 2019, https://www.medicalnewstoday.com/articles/322266.php.

14. Susan M. Kleiner, "The Devil's Candy," *Men's Health*, April 2000, 118, 120.

15. "The 'Dolly Parton' Diet," July 22, 2011, http://croninandhanrahan.blogspot.com/2011/07/dolly-parton-diet.html.

16. Nutritionix.com, https://www.nutritionix.com/brands/restaurant.

7. Importance of Backyard Gardens

1. Tamar Haspel, "Small vs. Large: Which Size Farm Is Better for the Planet?" *Washington Post*, September 2, 2014.

2. Rajeev Bhat, "Food Sustainability Challenges in the Developing World," in *Sustainability Challenges in the Agrofood Sector* (New York: Wiley, 2017), 2, 4.

3. There are hundreds of descriptions of historic agricultural and farming systems of the Natives of North America. Refer to the extensive references and bibliographical note in R. Douglas Hurt, *Indian Agriculture in America: Prehistory to the Present* (Lawrence: University of Kansas Press, 1987). See also Gayle J. Fritz, *Early Agriculture in the North American Heartland* (Tuscaloosa: University of Alabama Press, 2019) and the hundreds of articles, ethnographies, and books listed in GoogleScholar. The most thorough description of a postcontact garden is Gilbert L. Wilson, *Buffalo Bird Woman's Garden: Agriculture of the Hidatsa Indians* (St. Paul: Minnesota Historical Society Press, 1987). Buffalo Bird Woman was a Hidatsa and farmer born around 1839. She relayed information to anthropologist Wilson about how to cultivate the plant foods her tribe utilized as well as about the ceremonies needed for harvest.

4. National Family Farm Coalition and Grassroots International, *Food Sovereignty* (Washington DC: Grassroots International, 2010), 11.

5. William Bartram, "Observations on the Creek and Cherokee Indians" (1789; repr., New York: American Ethnological Society, 1853), 39–40. See also the series of "Mvskoke Country" articles authored by James Treat, https://mvskokecountry.wordpress.com/category/mvskoke-country/.

6. William Bartram, *Bartram: Travels and Other Writings* (New York: Literary Classics of the United States, 1996), 506–7.

7. Bartram, *Travels*, 506–7. See also Adair, *History of the American Indians*, 405–10.

8. Bartram, *Travels*, 56, 319, 557–60, 404–5.

9. Muriel H. Wright, "A Report to the General Council of the Indian Territory Meeting at Okmulgee in 1873," *Chronicles of Oklahoma* 34, no. 1 (1956): 9–10. This report also lists plants cultivated and animals raised by other Indian Territory tribes.

10. T. N. Campbell, "Choctaw Subsistence: Ethnographic Notes from the Lincecum Manuscript," *Florida Anthropologist* 12, no. 1 (1959): 9–24; H. B. Cushman, *History of the Choctaw, Chickasaw, and Natchez Indians* (Greenville TX: Headlight, 1899), 74, 168, 231–32, 250, 272, https://archive.org/details/histchoctaw00cushrich /page/n7/mode/2up.

11. Campbell, "Choctaw Subsistence," 10–11; John R. Swanton, "Aboriginal Culture of the Southeast," in *Forty-Second Annual Report of the Bureau of American Ethnology* (Washington DC: GPO, 1924–25), 695. There is no evidence that Choctaws planted corn, squash, and beans together in the manner of the "Three Sisters."

12. J. C. Moncrief interview, November 1, 1933, *IPP* 64:57.

13. Meton Ludlow interview, April 26, 1934, *IPP* 56:182.

14. Wright, "A Report to the General Council," 9.

15. Peter Alexander interview, April 18, 1933, *IPP* 71:150.

16. Devon Mihesuah, *First to Fight* (Lincoln: University of Nebraska Press, 2002), 20–21.

17. Northern Plains Reservation Aid, "Gardening to Get Through Winter," http://www.nativepartnership.org/site/PageServer ?pagename=airc_ziegler_garden. Note that there are many stories of families in Indian Territory and the early days of Oklahoma who depended on backyard gardens. See *Indian and Pioneer Papers*, Western History Collections, University of Oklahoma, Norman, https://digital.libraries.ou.edu/whc/pioneer/.

18. Devon Mihesuah, *The Roads of My Relations* (Tucson: University of Arizona Press, 2000).

19. I expound on this in Mihesuah and Hoover, *Indigenous Food Sovereignty*, 33–36.

20. "How to Start a Garden: 10 Steps to Gardening for Beginners," https://commonsensehome.com/start-a-garden/.

21. Jane Kirkland, *No Student Left Indoors: Creating a Field Guide to Your Schoolyard* (Lionville PA: Stillwater Publishing, 2009); USDA, *Start a School Garden: Here's How*, https://www.usda.gov/media /blog/2013/08/13/start-school-garden-heres-how; Eartheasy, *How to Start a School Garden: Your Complete Guide*, https:// learn.eartheasy.com/guides/how-to-start-a-school-garden-your -complete-guide/.

22. Gardeners Supply, http://www.vg.com/department.asp ?DeptPGID=18252.

23. NativeTech: Native American Technology and Art, "Planting a Three Sisters Garden," http://www.nativetech.org/cornhusk /threesisters.html.

Index

Achafa Chipota, 19–20
acorns, 11, 13, 15, 16, 17, 21, 22, 35, 41, 97, 157, 256–59
Adair, James, 24, 26
Afforable Care Act, 80
Africans, health of, 29
agriculture among tribes, 36
alcohol, 17
alcoholism, 48
Alexie, Sherman, 91
American Indian Exposition (Anadarko), 105
Anderson, Thomas F., 55
Anishinaabe, 14, 97, 100, 103, 138
antelope, 12, 13, 15, 16, 17, 26, 76, 92, 99, 234, 237, 290
Apaches, 16, 17, 21, 50, 69, 91, 92, 105
apples, 36, 68, 97, 119, 152, 277, 284
Arapahos, 50, 77, 97, 98
Arizona Native Frybread (business), 106
Armstrong, William, 24
Atlantic, 109, 143
Aztecs, 100

backyard gardens, 6–7, 39, 67, 103, 155–68; among Choctaws, 157–58; among the Five Tribes, 156; among Lower Brule Sioux, 159; among Mus-

cogees, 157; books about, 161–62; during Great Depression, 159; how to create, 161–65; of Mihesuah family, 159–61; as part of Promise Zone plan, 79
bamboo vine, 41
banaha, 111, 125
bannock, 96, 109, 235
Barker, E. O., 64
Barnard, Neal D., 42
Bartram, William, 156
basal metabolic rate, 126–27
beans: in bread, 269; cooking with, 40, 90, 242–43; in gardens, 36, 67, 155, 158, 160, 162; lima, 217–18; mescal, 12; mesquite, 13, 17, 67; in Mexico, 18, 128; Natives' use of, 9, 11, 13, 14, 22, 40, 70, 93, 95, 98, 99, 108, 119, 190; nutritional value of, 43, 76, 119, 122, 123, 151; as one of Three Sisters, 14, 39, 164–67; pinto, 251–52; screw, 14, 15, 17; storing, 38, 283; teaching about, 178–79, 183; tepary, 242–43; types of, 288; unhealthy, 108
beef, 93, 95
beefalo, 77
bees, 26, 86, 158, 204
Benson, John, 37

Berry, Wendell, 51
The Biggest Loser, 91
Big Timber Hill, 60
bioflavonoids, 121
BISHINIK, 45, 79
bison ranches, 77
Bitsui, Eddie, xiv
Blake, W. P., 40
Blue Bird flour, 106
Blue Corn Woman, 19
boarding schools, food served
    at, 74
boarding school syndrome, 105,
    139–40
body fat, 45
Bold Oklahoma, 84
Boomer Sooners, 82
Bosque Redondo, 91, 92
breads, 41, 97
Breiner (agent), 64
Brough, Carol, 91
Brown, Derek M., 42
Bureau of Indian Affairs, 84
Bureau of Land Management, 84

Café Press, 90
calcium, 121–22
calendars, tribal, 21–23, 100–101
California tribes, foodways of,
    15–16
calories, 117, 126, 135–37, 139
cancer, 42, 47, 48, 49, 84, 118,
    119, 140, 201, 208
carbohydrates, 117, 141–42
Carson, Kit, 92
Catlin, George, 24–25, 30–31,
    35, 131
cattle: at Bosque Redondo, 93;
    brought by colonists, 200;

damage to environment by, 83,
    86; at factory farms, 144; raised
    by Natives, 9, 36, 54, 55, 61, 62,
    63, 72, 77, 78, 88, 92, 158
celiac disease, 3, 43, 94, 142
Changing Woman, 19
Cherokees, 36, 55, 67–68, 77, 82,
    84, 314n32; cultural differ-
    ences among, 67–68; east-
    ern lands of, 34; food-related
    health issues of, 59, 98–99;
    Indian Territory lands of, 34–
    35; pre-removal diets of, 98;
    treaty rights of, 82
Cherokee seminaries, 57–58, 67,
    98, 314n32
Cherokee Temperance Society,
    56–57
Cheyenne River Agency, 96
Cheyennes, 12, 19, 50, 74, 77, 97, 98
Chickasaws, 35
chickens, 4, 15, 36, 144, 158, 200
chile peppers: cooking with, 140,
    144, 145, 147, 153, 216, 218,
    219, 220, 223, 230, 231, 232,
    234, 235, 239, 252, 281; dislike
    of, 140; in Latin America, 17,
    178; nutritional value of, 121,
    141; teaching about, 209; used
    by Natives, 11, 17, 70, 92
Chinooks, 97
Choctaw Nation Diabetes Well-
    ness Center, 46
Choctaw Nation Health Care
    Center, 45
Choctaws: and boarding schools,
    59; and corn, 19–21, 98; and
    Diabetes Multi-Resource Task
    Force, 80; festivals and foods

of, 111; food stories of, 19–21;
foodways of, in Southeast, 59;
gardens of, 157–58; hunting
and fishing rights of, 82–83;
Indian Territory lands of, 34–
35; Oklahoma lands of, 78;
physical activity of, 60–61; poor
counties of, 77–79; regional
clinic of, 81; and Senior Farmers' Market Nutrition Program, 80; treaty rights of, 82
Choctaw Small Business Development Services, 79
cholesterol, 118
Ciocco, "Chako" Anthony,
155–56
Civil War, 4, 5, 36, 41, 53, 55, 67,
70, 93, 158, 306n10
clams, 13, 14, 97, 119
coffee, 6, 36, 55, 56, 58, 59, 60,
69, 70, 93, 94, 95, 97, 110, 125,
152, 163
colonization, 51–52
Columbus, Christopher, 11, 25–26
Comanche Nation News, 50
Comanches, 12, 34, 50, 68–69,
74, 92, 190, 320n95
comfort foods, 104
commodities, 75, 76, 97, 98
container gardening, 167–68
cookbooks, 110
corn, 10–21, 39–41, 47, 92
Corntassel, Jeff, 31–32
Craig, Nephi, xiv
Creeks, 34. *See also* Muscogees
(Creeks)
Crisco, 103
Critser, Greg, 130
Crow Creek Agency, 93

Dardar, Noreen, 106
Declaration of Nyéléni, 72–73
Decolonizing Diet Project, 97
Department of Health and
Human Services, 81
depression, 104
diabetes, 43–44
diabetes programs (Choctaw
Nation), 45
diabetics, 43–44, 46, 53, 66–70
Diamond Pipeline, 85
diarrhea, 43, 58, 99
dietary changes of Indian Territory residents, 41, 53–54,
67–68
Diné Community Advocacy Alliance, 95
Diné Policy Institute, 102–3
diseases among Indian Territory
tribes, 54–55
Dodge, Richard Irving, 13
dogs, 15, 18, 37, 38
Dollar General, 103
Dow AgroSciences, 50
Downstream Casino Restaurant, 77
dumplings, 38, 40, 76; apple, 59;
grape, 8, 40, 60, 75, 107, 108,
274–75
DuPont/Pioneer, 50

Eaton, M. D., 27, 28
England, 96
environment: damage to, in
Indian Territory, 61–62, 70;
damage to, in Oklahoma, 83–
84; and fracking, 204, 316n53;
teaching about, 203–4
Euchee Butterfly Farm, 87

Fallin, Mary, 85
farming among tribes, 61, 68, 69, 79, 101, 107, 108, 112, 155, 156, 180, 194, 196
fast food, 6, 47, 126, 129
fat, 139, 146
Fazzino, David, 101–2, 111
fetal alcohol syndrome, 48
fiber, 118–19
fish, 12, 14, 15, 16, 17, 18, 86; contaminated, 84; in Indian Territory, 38, 86; nutritional value of, 119, 122, 124
Five Tribes, 3, 34, 98. *See also* Cherokees; Chickasaws; Choctaws; Muscogees (Creeks); Seminoles
food, personal views about, 188–89
food and agricultural foundations, 88
food deserts, 74
Food Distribution Program on Indian Reservations, 75
food initiatives, teaching about, 207–8
food security, 77–78
Foods of the Americas, 110
Foods of the Southwest Indian Nations, 110
foodways, school projects on, 210
foraging, 27–29, 199–200
Fort Defiance, 92
Fort Gibson, 54
Fort Sill, 64, 69, 159
Fort Smith, 57
Four Corners, 94
fracking, 83–84, 204
France, diets in, 47

Frank, Lois Ellen, xiv
frybread, 5, 90; myth of, 93–96; as nontraditional food, 108; nutritional aspects of, 104
Frybread House (Phoenix), 108

galettes, 96
game animals in Indian Territory, 36
games and sports, 29–32
gardening: backyard, 155–68; container, 167–68; and Three Sisters, 14, 39, 165–67
Garfield's Famous Frybread, 108
geographical areas, teaching about foodways in, 184–87
glucose, 43, 45, 46, 47
gluten, 43, 94, 99, 140, 142, 143, 238, 266
gluten sensitivity, 94
Good Meat, 99
Gordon, Billi, 104
gravy, 56, 59, 76, 98, 99, 104
Great Depression, 159
Great Plains tribes, 17
Green Corn dance, 19, 22, 32, 101
Guanahani (San Salvador), 25–26
gumbo, 41

Hadden, James M., 26
HA-PAH-SHU-TSE Indian Foods, 108
hard tack, 93
Harjo, Suzan Shown, 91
Haskell Indian Art Market, 106
health, teaching about decline of, 200–202
health care, teaching about, 208–9

health problems, 44–45, 53–54,
59–60, 98–99
Healthy Cooking on a Budget, 105
healthy eating, 8–10, 128–35, 141–
46, 150–54
Healthy O'odham People Promotion, 108
Heckewelder, John, 28
Hershey's chocolate syrup, 108
high blood pressure, 3, 44, 59,
72, 111, 112, 123, 141, 172
Hill, Wilburn, 53
historical trauma, 104
Hitchcock, Ethan Allen, 55
Hobsbawm, Eric, 107
hogs, 20, 35, 36, 40, 54, 59, 63,
67, 77, 86, 157, 158
Holt-Gimenez, Eric, 77–78
homeland, teaching about,
196–98
Hopis, 17, 23, 90, 92, 96, 101
Hopi tacos, 90
Horgen, Katherine, 130
Horineck, Mekasi, 84
Horse Capture, George P., 92
horses, 21, 24, 28, 30, 31, 32, 36,
54, 69, 92, 93, 157, 158, 336n1
Houma Nation, 106
House Bill 1123, 85
Hwéeldi ("place of suffering"), 91
hyperglycemia, 43

Illinois State University, 99
Indian and Pioneer Histories, 98
Indian Healthcare Improvement
Act, 80
Indian Health Service, 80
Indian Territory, 34–41, 53–91.
See also Oklahoma

Indigenous food sovereignty,
xiii, 2, 5, 50, 72, 99, 102, 103,
112, 156, 171, 172, 173, 188, 189,
193, 196, 200, 208, 210; attain-
ing, 87–89; challenges to
achieving, 72–89; definitions
of, 72–73; teaching about,
194–95
Indigenous peoples, problems
faced by, 51–52
Indigenous Seedkeepers Network, 49
indigestion, 99
insects, 13, 17, 64, 135, 176,
183–84
Intertribal Environmental Council, 84
invasive species, 86
Ireland, 96
ishtaboli (stickball), 111

Jackson, Andrew, 34
James Beard Foundation, 108
Jones, Wilson N., 62
junk food, 43, 94, 95, 104, 148
Justice, Daniel Heath, 9

Kalm, Peter, 24, 26
Karsten, Matthew, 128
Kekuli Café, 109
Kimber, Edward, 24
king's crib, 156–57
Kully Chaha, 83

LaBeau, Beau, 99, 140
Labor Day Festival (Choctaw), 45
lactase, 42–43
lactose intolerance, 42–43, 99

lamb's quarters (goosefoot): cooking with, 221, 223, 235; in gardens, 142; nutritional value of, 119, 122, 144; as a weed, 12

Leupp, Francis E., 97

Lewis, Dwayne, 106

Lewis and Clark journals, 109

liquor, 56–57

Long Walk, 91

Lowry, George, 55

Lupton, Deborah, 100

manoomin (rice), 103

McDonald's, 6, 47, 126, 129, 141

medicinal plants, 12

medicine: traditional, 61, 65–66; westernized, 61, 64–66

melons, 36, 38, 92, 95

Meriam Report, 64

mesquite, 13, 14, 17, 69, 92, 269, 288

Mexico, foodways of, 18–19

Michales, Jillian, 91, 105

Mihesuah, Joshaway, 159, 320n95

minerals, 113, 121–24

Mitsitam Espresso Coffee Bar, 110

Mitsitam Native Foods Café, 109–10

molasses, 36, 58, 59, 122, 146

Monsanto, 50

More than Frybread, 105–6

M'Robert, Patrick, 27

mules, 92, 93, 157, 158

Muscogees (Creeks), 3, 32, 34, 36, 39, 40, 55, 60, 64, 65, 87, 100, 156, 157, 160

Naataanii Alliance for Peace, 94

Nabakov, Peter, 32

Nance, R. Y., 107

National Fish and Wildlife Foundation, 87

National Indian Taco Championship (Pawhuska), 105

National Institute of Diabetes and Digestive and Kidney Diseases, 141

Native American Church, 101

Native American Diabetes Project, 142

Native diets, 55–56

Navajo BioEnergy Dome, 112

Navajos, 69, 91; dietary changes of, 70–71, 94–95; diet of, at Bosque Redondo, 92; health issues of, at Bosque Redondo, 94–95

Nestle, Marion, 130

New Orleans Jazz Festival, 106

"New World," 11, 190

nonindigenous foods (Western Hemisphere), 35, 36, 40, 50, 56, 59, 60, 68, 75, 76, 92, 93, 95, 97, 110, 118, 119, 120, 157, 250, 277, 284

Northeast tribes, foodways of, 14–15

Northwest Company, 96

Northwest tribes, foodways of, 15–16

nutrients, 113–24

Nvnih Chufvk (Sugar Loaf Mountain), 35, 83

Obama, Barrack, 46, 78

obesity, 3, 4, 29, 44–48, 50, 53, 69, 72, 78, 80, 95, 111, 112, 113, 141, 170, 172, 208

offal, 93, 99, 183–84

Oglethorpe expedition, 24
Ojibwas, 97. *See also* Anishinaabe
Oka Lawa Camp, 85
Oklahoma, 5, 31, 34, 45, 50, 108,
  233; challenges to achieving
  food sovereignty in, 73–89;
  changing diets in, 53–71;
  fracking in, 203–4
Oklahoma Department of Envi-
  ronmental Quality, 84
Oklahoma Department of
  Health, 44
okra, 56
okshash, 35
Old Salt Woman, 19
Osage purple dumplings, 108
"Other" (colonizer), 104
Outside (magazine), 47
Owen, Loretta Barrett, xiv
Oxendine, Clark "Little Bear," 107

Parker, Quanah, 97
Patel, Raj, 72
peanuts: as bread, 41, 97; in gardens, 36; nutritional value of,
  118, 120, 124, 146, 158; popularity of, 32–33; tribal use of,
  11, 17, 169
Pecos River, 94
pemmican, 13, 96, 282
physicality of tribespeople, 24–27
physicians, 63–64
piki bread, 96
piles (digestive disorder), 99
Pimas, 12, 16, 44, 48
piñons, 11, 15, 17, 92, 190, 218, 289
Pizza Hut, 47
*The Plains of North America and
  Their Inhabitants*, 13

Plains tribes, 12, 13, 34, 67, 74,
  101, 169, 186
Plateau tribes, 16, 176
plums, 13, 36, 68, 69, 157, 190, 277
poaching, 85–86
pollinators, 85–87, 202–4
potatoes: as comfort food, 104;
  cooking with, 145, 147, 222,
  229, 233, 244, 263–64; dried,
  38; in gardens, 36, 56, 68,
  158, 159, 160; Irish, 38, 157;
  nutritional value of, 119, 122,
  123, 142, 143, 147, 149; root or
  mud, 38; sweet, 33, 56, 119,
  120, 123, 153, 157, 246; teaching about, 182; tribal use of,
  14, 17, 18, 22, 58, 59, 128, 169;
  unhealthy, 76, 108, 152
potlatch, 97
poverty, 5, 45, 46, 64, 74, 77–78,
  100, 104, 170, 194
precontact foods, 2, 3, 11–19, 32–
  33, 76, 105, 138, 155, 171, 172,
  173, 193, 202, 210, 213, 287–92
preserving foods, 283–85
Promise Zone award, 46, 78–79, 160
protein, 29, 43, 95, 113, 117, 118, 119,
  142, 143, 153, 177, 217, 251, 264
Pruitt, Scott, 85
Pueblo tribes, 17, 19, 69, 96, 101
Puget Sound, 97
pumpkins: cooking with, 240–41;
  dried, 283–84; in gardens, 13,
  17, 36, 158; nutritional value
  of, 119, 123; tribal use of, 13,
  59, 60, 95, 155, 157

Quahadis (Comanche Band), 97
Quapaw Cattle Company, 77

Quapaw Mercantile, 77
Quapaws, 77–78

rabbits: in Choctaw stories, 20;
    cooking with, 67; in factory
    farms, 144; as garden pests,
    162, 165; hunting, 47, 62, 93;
    tribal use of, 12, 13, 15, 16, 17,
    38, 47, 92, 128, 157
racism, 10, 74, 81, 82, 84, 104,
    134, 139, 170, 194
ranching in Indian Territory, 74,
    79, 83, 88, 157, 158, 195
Ranger, Terence, 107
Raramuris, 129
Red Corn, Raymond, 108
Red Corn Native Foods, 108
Redford, Hope, 89
Redsteer, Robb, 94, 95
Reinhardt, Martin, 97, 103, 112, 138
religious significance of food,
    19–23
rematriation, 49, 50
resources, loss of, 62–63, 74–75,
    316n53
restaurant portions, 47
Rights of Nature, 84
rivers in Indian Territory, 35, 84, 85
Roads of My Relations, 159–60
roasting ear patches, 39, 156. See
    also backyard gardens
Romans, Bernard, 23, 41, 54, 60
Rozin, Paul, 47
Rush Springs, 86

salmon: as commodity, 77; cook-
    ing with, 99, 141, 232, 236;
    nutritional value of, 118, 119,
    120, 121, 122, 123; at potlatch,
97; in tribal calendars, 100;
    tribal use of, 10, 14, 15, 16, 17,
    68, 169
Scotland, 96
Schlosser, Eric, 130, 141
seed saving, 70, 73, 89, 158, 159,
    175, 196, 197, 205–7
Seminoles, 3, 34, 35, 36
Seneca-Cayuga Nation, 85
Sharlot Hall Museum, 94
sheep, 4, 19, 21, 36, 50, 54, 70,
    92, 138, 157, 158, 200
Shiprock Fair, 94
Siwash, 97
Smallwood brothers, 112
Smith, Sherry, 26
Smithsonian Magazine, 93
sodium, 113, 117, 120, 123, 144,
    147, 148, 149, 251, 256
sopapillas, 96
sour dock, 21, 36
sour stomach, 99
South America, foodways of,
    17–18
Southwest tribes, foodways of,
    16–17, 90, 176, 184–85, 242
"sovereignization," 89
Spanish, 32, 35, 67, 69, 92, 95,
    96, 110, 128
Spirit of the Harvest, 110
squash: cooking with, 153, 155,
    213, 224–25, 232, 240, 245, 249,
    259–60, 266–67; in gardens,
    70, 103, 159, 160, 161, 164, 165,
    166, 168; nutritional value of,
    76, 119, 124; teaching about,
    178, 179, 182; tribal use of, 9,
    11, 13, 14, 17, 22, 36, 39, 50, 67,
    69, 92, 99, 108, 157, 169, 190

stereotyping, 104
Subarctic tribes, foodways of, 16
sugar, 2, 3, 4, 6, 8, 9, 16, 29, 41,
    42, 50, 53, 55, 56, 57, 58, 59,
    60, 62, 68, 69, 70, 71, 74, 75,
    76, 77, 85, 90, 94, 95, 98, 99,
    103, 104, 108, 109, 113, 119,
    125, 129, 142, 145, 146, 147,
    148, 152, 158, 202, 213
Sugar Loaf Mountain. *See*
    Nvnih Chufvk (Sugar Loaf
    Mountain)
Sundance, 101
sweet potatoes, 33, 56, 119, 120,
    123, 153, 157, 246
Syngenta, 50

tanfula, 40, 111, 125, 151, 248–49, 264
Tanner, Trent, 106
teaching about foods, 169–211
terminology, 189–94
Texas tribes, 13–14
Thanksgiving, traditional dinner
    of, 11, 169
Three Sisters, 14, 39, 165–67, 189
timpsala (prairie turnip), 109
Tishomingo, 64
tobacco, 48–49
Tocabe American Indian Eat-
    ery, 109
Tohono O'odhams, 44, 102, 108
Tohono O'odham Community
    Action, 108
trading posts, 68, 94, 95, 158
"traditional," term of, 101
traditional foods: definition of,
    75–76; importance of promot-
    ing, 111–12
"tradition invention," 107, 111

treaty rights, 81–82
trees in Indian Territory, 35, 36,
    313n53
Tribal Environmental Action for
    Monarchs, 87
Tribal Grounds Coffee, 110
tribal princesses, 90
tribes, 99–102; cultural changes
    among, 51–70; cultural differ-
    ences among, 67
Trump, Donald, 80–81, 85
turkey: in bread, 269; cooking
    with, 223–24, 230–31, 232,
    248–49; hunting of, 37, 82,
    160; loss of, in Indian Terri-
    tory, 83, 85; in Mexico, 18,
    239; nutritional value of, 120,
    122, 123, 141, 143, 148, 154;
    taboo against, 17; in Thanks-
    giving dinner, 11, 91; on tribal
    farms, 36, 158; tribal use of, 9,
    13, 14, 15, 17, 36, 37, 62, 67, 76,
    97, 157, 160, 183, 290
Turner, Nancy, 83
"Turtle Island," 83

U.S. Dietary Guidelines, 42

venison: cooking with, 145, 160,
    226, 233–34, 235–37, 239,
    252, 282; hunting of, 160; not
    used, 99, 140; at potlatch, 97;
    tribal use of, 15, 36, 55, 60,
    157, 169, 250
Vennum, Thomas, 103
vitamins, 113, 119–21

Walk This Weigh campaign, 45
Walmart, 99

wannabes, 106

"weeds," 12

Weigle, Gayle, 91

Werewocomoco (restaurant), 190

West, Kelly M., 4, 53

wheat: and celiac disease, 43, 94, 142; dislike of, 56, 98; in frybread, 76, 97, 98; growing of, 7, 18, 50, 54, 77, 157; at Mitsitam, 110; Native health after introduction of, 4, 9, 53, 58, 60, 71, 90, 93, 99, 139, 158; Native health before introduction of, 3, 108; not used, 97, 98 109; nutritional value of, 118, 120, 121, 143, 154; in trading posts, 56, 71

Wheeler, Andrew, 85

White Corn Maiden, 19

white snakeroot, 38

Whitewater, Walter, xiv

wild onions, 21, 36, 157, 190, 213, 259

wind on the stomach, 99

wojape, 109

Wood, William, 25

Wooden Knife Company, 109

Works Progress Administration, 98

World Series of Stickball, 31

Wright, E. N., 65

Yankton Indian Agency, 93

Zergler, Alfred, 159

Zion National Monument, 134

In the At Table series

*Hoosh: Roast Penguin,
Scurvy Day, and Other Stories
of Antarctic Cuisine*
Jason C. Anthony

*Corkscrewed: Adventures in the
New French Wine Country*
Robert V. Camuto

Palmento: A Sicilian Wine Odyssey
Robert V. Camuto

Spiced: Recipes from Le Pré Verre
Philippe Delacourcelle
Translated and with a preface
by Adele King and Bruce King

Global Jewish Foodways: A History
Edited and with an
introduction by Hasia R.
Diner and Simone Cinotto
Foreword by Carlo Petrini

*A Sacred Feast: Reflections
on Sacred Harp Singing and
Dinner on the Ground*
Kathryn Eastburn

Barolo
Matthew Gavin Frank

*How to Cook a Tapir:
A Memoir of Belize*
Joan Fry

*Eating in Eden: Food and
American Utopias*
Edited by Etta M. Madden
and Martha L. Finch

*Recovering Our Ancestors'
Gardens: Indigenous Recipes
and Guide to Diet and
Fitness, Revised Edition*
Devon A. Mihesuah

*Dueling Chefs: A Vegetarian and
a Meat Lover Debate the Plate*
Maggie Pleskac and
Sean Carmichael

*A Taste of Heritage: Crow Indian
Recipes and Herbal Medicines*
Alma Hogan Snell
Edited by Lisa Castle

*Educated Tastes: Food, Drink,
and Connoisseur Culture*
Edited and with an introduction
by Jeremy Strong

*In Food We Trust: The
Politics of Purity in American
Food Regulation*
Courtney I. P. Thomas

*The Banana: Empires, Trade
Wars, and Globalization*
James Wiley

*Fried Walleye and Cherry Pie:
Midwestern Writers on Food*
Edited and with an
introduction by Peggy Wolff

*Predictable Pleasures: Food
and the Pursuit of Balance
in Rural Yucatán*
Lauren A. Wynne

Available in Bison Books Editions

The Food and Cooking of Eastern Europe
Lesley Chamberlain
With a new introduction
by the author

The Food and Cooking of Russia
Lesley Chamberlain
With a new introduction
by the author

The World on a Plate: A Tour through the History of America's Ethnic Cuisine
Joel Denker

Jewish American Food Culture
Jonathan Deutsch and
Rachel D. Saks

The Recipe Reader: Narratives, Contexts, Traditions
Edited by Janet Floyd
and Laurel Forster

A Chef's Tale: A Memoir of Food, France, and America
Pierre Franey
With Richard Flaste
and Bryan Miller
With a new introduction
by Eugenia Bone

Masters of American Cookery: M. F. K. Fisher, James Beard, Craig Claiborne, Julia Child
Betty Fussell
With a preface by the author

My Kitchen Wars: A Memoir
Betty Fussell
With a new introduction
by Laura Shapiro

Good Things
Jane Grigson

Jane Grigson's Fruit Book
Jane Grigson
With a new introduction
by Sara Dickerman

Jane Grigson's Vegetable Book
Jane Grigson
With a new introduction
by Amy Sherman

Dining with Marcel Proust: A Practical Guide to French Cuisine of the Belle Epoque
Shirley King
Foreword by James Beard

Pampille's Table: Recipes and Writings from the French Countryside from Marthe Daudet's
Les Bons Plats de France
Translated and adapted
by Shirley King

Moveable Feasts: The History, Science, and Lore of Food
Gregory McNamee

To order or obtain more
information on these or other
University of Nebraska Press titles,
visit nebraskapress.unl.edu.